COMPETENCY TO STAND TRIAL

COMPETENCY
TO STAND TRIAL

Ronald Roesch
and Stephen L. Golding

CALIFORNIA SCHOOL OF PROFESSIONAL PSYCHOLOGY
LOS ANGELES

UNIVERSITY OF ILLINOIS PRESS
Urbana · Chicago · London

Library of Congress Cataloging in Publication Data

Roesch, Ronald, 1947–
   Competency to stand trial.

   Bibliography: p.
   Includes index.
   1. Competency to stand trial—United States.
2. Insanity—Jurisprudence—United States.
3. Forensic psychiatry—United States. 4. Competency
to stand trial—North Carolina. 5. Insanity—
Jurisprudence—North Carolina. 6. Forensic psychiatry
—North Carolina. I. Golding, Stephen L., 1944–
joint author. II. Title.
KF9242.R63   345.73'04   80–12456
ISBN 0–252–00825–1

FOREWORD

In their seminal article on competency to stand trial, Robert Burt and Norval Morris (1972) recounted a telling colloquy between a trial judge and a psychiatrist.

Judge: Doctor, is he incompetent?

Psychiatrist: Your Honor, he is psychotic!

In this book, Ronald Roesch and Stephen L. Golding deftly demonstrate not only the inadequacy of the psychiatrist's answer, but the infelicity of the judge's question. To avoid dealing with complex and problematic questions of law, judges frequently solicit conclusory opinions from mental health professionals. Oblivious to the limits of their expertise, mental health professionals sink to the occasion.

Competency to Stand Trial is an extraordinary book, one that will shine as an exemplar in the fledgling field of psychology and law. I rest this assessment on three grounds.

The first is legal. While many psychologists of law fob off a few case citations to set the scene for their research questions, Roesch and Golding take the law seriously on its own terms. Their thorough analysis of case and statutory law on competence to stand trial is noteworthy for its sophistication as much as for its rarity. They address legal issues in their full and sometimes frustrating complexity, rather than adopt a common one-downsmanship strategy in defense of simplistic scholarship: "I'm only a social scientist, so too much legal knowledge should not be expected of me." They may be social scientists, but their treatment of the law of competency is as good as I have seen grace the pages of any law review.

Even more impressive is the *programmatic* manner with which the authors have approached their research tasks. From the conception of the research questions until its hard-cover birth, this book was five years in the making. Four separate studies are reported. How much more valuable this integrative approach is than the one-shot or at best disjointed research reports so often found in social science journals. While the authors published some of their major findings along the way—and thereby allowed other scholars an early look at the directions the research program was taking—they had the intellectual commitment and emotional perseverance to see their project as a unified whole, one that deserved the full exposition that only a book allows.

Finally, the explicit policy orientation of the latter part of this work adds to its distinction. Not content merely to "raise issues" for others to resolve, Roesch and Golding carefully lay out explicit procedures for competency evaluation that build upon both their legal analyses and their research findings. In the true spirit of experimental social innovators, however, they caution against the uncritical acceptance of even their own proposals, and the necessity for ongoing evaluation research to refine and modify them. In these proposals, the authors steer a steady course between the Scylla of mental health imperialism and the Charybdis of know-nothing anti-psychiatry. They are no less emphatic about the limits of the contribution psychiatrists and psychologists can make to the determination of competency than they are about the fact that a contribution *can* be made.

The depth of its legal scholarship, the incisiveness of its scientific analyses, and the wisdom of its policy recommendations make *Competency to Stand Trial* a major contribution to the psychology of law.

John Monahan
School of Law
University of Virginia

CONTENTS

ACKNOWLEDGMENTS

The research project which initiated our involvement in the issue of competency to stand trial was begun when the authors were associated with the National Clearinghouse for Criminal Justice Planning and Architecture (NCCJPA). We are grateful to several individuals at NCCJPA for their support in making the initial research possible. Joseph W. Maxey, who was then associate director, facilitated the project from its inception and provided continuous support and encouragement. Nancy Dutt and Jetta Watermann spent many hours completing the ratings of psychiatric reports and contributed to all stages of the research phase. Donald S. Dixon lent his expertise in analyzing data. Special appreciation is extended to many individuals in North Carolina, especially Franklin Freeman, Jr., and Michael Rieder. More recently, Polly Haddow, Mary LoPatriello, Bradford Lyerla, and Michael Mardus made important research and technical contributions. This book is an extensively revised and updated version of two earlier reports: *A Systems Analysis of Competency to Stand Trial Procedures*, published in 1977 by the National Clearinghouse for Criminal Justice Planning and Architecture (jointly authored), and a dissertation submitted by the first author to the University of Illinois.

We would like individually to thank those who made personal contributions to each of us:

I would particularly like to thank Edward Seidman, who served as chairman of my dissertation committee, for being both a teacher and a friend, and I am especially indebted to Julián Rappaport for his faith in my ability to do graduate work. The ideas of both Professors Seidman and Rappaport about community and social change are clearly reflected in this book and continue to have a major influence on my research. My wife, Kathy, has critically reviewed every draft of this manuscript and constantly prodded me to present my ideas with greater clarity and precision. More important, she has forced me to challenge my assumptions about creating change in systems like the one under review in this book. Finally, I wish to thank my mother, Irene Taylor, for continuing to have faith in me, even when I gave her more than enough reason to abandon it.—Ron Roesch.

I feel a particular intellectual debt to my uncle, Abraham Schwartz, M.D., whose early encouragement and stimulation were responsible in no small way for my professional development. I also want to thank my wife, Alison Sommers, for her moral support, critical advice, and faith.—Stephen Golding.

COMPETENCY TO STAND TRIAL

1

Introduction

Our interest in the issue of competency to stand trial[1] had its beginning in the summer of 1975. At that time the director of the forensic facility at Dorothea Dix Hospital in Raleigh, North Carolina, requested assistance from the National Clearinghouse for Criminal Justice Planning and Architecture (NCCJPA)[2] in preparing estimates on population trends and supplying architectural recommendations for a new forensic facility. The director intended to propose to the state legislature the construction of this new facility to replace the overcrowded, outmoded building that was then in use. A brief examination of the facility appeared to support this proposal. The hospital itself was initially constructed in 1856, following the reform efforts of Dorothea Lynde Dix. At that time it accommodated 40 patients but, like all state hospitals, it quickly grew. At the time of our study the hospital had a capacity of 1,200 patients and a staff of approximately 1,450. The forensic facility's original wing was built in the Depression and the last addition was constructed during the 1950s. The facility had a capacity of about 100, and patients lived in single-occupancy rooms. These rooms were quite small and, despite the fact that residents were locked in their rooms each night, contained no bathroom facilities.

The bulk of the patient population consisted of defendants referred from courts throughout the state so that their competency could be assessed. The other patients in the facility were defendants found incompetent to stand trial or not guilty by reason of insanity, or were problem patients transferred from other hospital wards. Since the facility was pri-

marily used for evaluating the competency of criminal defendants, we decided to concentrate our initial discussions (and ultimately the research
we conducted) on this group. Admissions for such evaluations had been
constantly increasing, with the total number of evaluations approaching
700 in 1975 (Figure 1.1). This figure represented one evaluation for every
44 felony cases filed in the state.

While we agreed with the hospital administration that the conditions
existing in the forensic facility were bad, the consultation and research
that resulted from the director's request led to the identification of solutions other than the construction of a new facility. In order to provide a
background to the research and model system described in this book, we
would like to briefly discuss the development of the research project as
well as the values and conceptions which guided our approach to it.

It has frequently been observed that strategies and tactics aimed at creating change depend heavily on the way in which the problem or issue is
initially defined (Caplan and Nelson, 1973; Goodstein and Sandler, 1978;
Rappaport, 1977; Ryan, 1971; Seidman, 1978). It seemed clear to us that
the forensic staff had defined their particular problem in a limited way but
had not fully considered other definitions and solutions. They viewed the
increasing numbers of referrals to the forensic facility as the source of the
problem, and the solution seemed to them to rest in increasing the capability of the facility in order to handle a larger flow of defendants.

The construction of a new building is perhaps the most obvious, and
simple, way of solving the problem of overcrowding. New jails, for instance, are being constructed throughout the country in response to ever-
increasing jail populations. Decisions to build are often based on projections which show that jail populations are likely to continue increasing.
The decision to build a larger facility, however, is based on the assumption
that the jails will continue to be used in the same way they are at present
or have been used in the past. In other words, the projection is based on
maintaining the status quo, which is accomplished by not considering
alternatives to detention in jail. For example, the introduction of changes
in the criminal justice system, such as diversion, reducing court delay, and
bail reform, can also reduce jail populations and thus lessen the need for
larger facilities (Roesch, 1976). Such changes are less likely to occur after
a new jail is built because there will be an obvious need to maintain the
population at close to capacity. To do otherwise would subject administra-

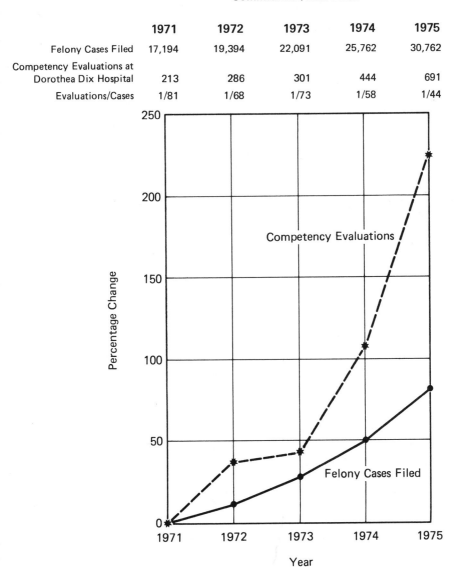

Commitment/Case Load

	1971	1972	1973	1974	1975
Felony Cases Filed	17,194	19,394	22,091	25,762	30,762
Competency Evaluations at Dorothea Dix Hospital	213	286	301	444	691
Evaluations/Cases	1/81	1/68	1/73	1/58	1/44

FIGURE 1.1   Competency Evaluation Rates Compared with Total Felony Cases by Year for North Carolina

tors to widespread political and community criticism. Furthermore, the costs of construction consume a substantial amount of limited resources, and obviously limit the exploration of other alternatives. Buildings often become an impediment to change, and for this reason alone we should be quite cautious in our decisions to construct new ones.[3] We obviously do not mean to suggest that we should entirely avoid construction of new facilities but, rather, that all alternatives which might reduce or eliminate the need should be fully considered before a decision about construction is made. If such alternatives are not considered, then we may adopt solutions that never really address the problem. In this regard, the work of Watzlawick, Weakland, and Fisch (1974) makes a significant contribution to understanding change. They suggest that some solutions will only serve to perpetuate the existing methods or system because they do not challenge the existing assumptions of a system or the way in which a problem has been defined. They refer to this as *first-order change*. They argue that true change, or *second-order change*, can only occur if we begin to challenge the rules and assumptions of a system, since the solution may require a change of some of the rules which govern the system. If we fail to examine the problem from this perspective, then the process of defining an issue or problem may result in the selection of the wrong problem and will, as a consequence, lead to an inadequate solution.

In summary, our early discussions with the forensic facility staff led us to the conclusion that we could not determine the need for, or size of, a new facility without first conducting a comprehensive study of the entire system that dealt with the issue of competency to stand trial. This necessitated involving and studying the legal system as well, since this was both the source of referrals and the system to which evaluated defendants were returned. The studies we designed as a result of this project are described in detail in Chapter 6, and they formed the primary basis for the series of changes we eventually proposed (see Chapter 7).

OVERVIEW

The process of determining competency requires substantial interaction between mental health and the law. The issue of competency raises a series of important theoretical and pragmatic questions regarding the nature of cognitive and emotional capacities required by a defendant in order to be tried fairly. As we have indicated, the project began when attention was shifted away from the construction of a new facility to a comprehensive study of legal and mental health procedures used to confront the issue of competency. As a consequence, we were able to collect data from multiple sources (including judges, attorneys, defendants, hospital reports, and court records) which formed the basis of our recommendations for a series of changes throughout the process.[4] We want to point out, however, that our major interest in conducting this research was not to simply find out what was wrong in this system (a relatively easy task) but to provide a better understanding of the theory underlying the construct of competency, the manner in which the current system operates, and changes in the system that would more effectively and equitably address the issue of competency.

Beginning in Chapter 2, we discuss current competency standards and definitions. Here we present a model for viewing competency as a construct, and discuss the implications that this view has for the definition and assessment of competency. Chapter 3 presents a general review of research on competency, including admission rates, base rates of incompetency determinations, types of diagnosis and criminal charges, and court outcome. In a final section two instruments designed to assess competency, from a legal as well as a mental health perspective, are reviewed.

In Chapter 4 we discuss issues centering on the use of expert witness testimony on competency, as well as problems in communication between the court and the evaluators. After discussing some major problems in the current evaluation methods, we present a model for evaluating competency from a "functional" perspective. This perspective suggests that evaluations should not focus primarily upon symptom description or diagnosis but, rather, must specify how a defendant's behavior relates to competency to stand trial in the particular case at hand. This functional approach implies that the basis of a decision about competency may vary from case to case and may necessitate the use of lawyers in the evaluation process to more directly assess the legal issues involved. In the last part of this chapter we briefly discuss the training issues for evaluators and research implications that follow from this model.

Chapter 5 provides an overview of legal issues surrounding competency procedures, including right to bail, right to a speedy trial, and the disposition of defendants found incompetent. In the last part of the chapter we discuss the practice in one state, North Carolina, to provide a clearer focus for these issues and to present a context for the research we describe in Chapter 6. This chapter presents the design and results of four studies in North Carolina which provided data on how competency was defined and evaluated, how evaluations were used by the courts, and what alternative evaluation methods might be feasible. The chapter also presents comparative data on competent and incompetent defendants, in terms of both evaluation and court outcome.

The studies described in Chapter 6, as well as our reviews of the legal and empirical literature, provided us with the basis for the model system we present in Chapter 7, in which we discuss how such a system would operate at each step in the process, beginning with methods for ensuring the accountability of lawyers requesting competency evaluations. A major feature of the model system is the use of a screening evaluation by a panel comprised of both legal and mental health professionals, in order to assure that both aspects of a competency assessment are adequately addressed. The concept of a provisional trial for incompetent defendants is discussed at length, including the continued involvement of the screening panel in evaluating competency in the actual legal proceedings. We conclude the chapter with recommendations for the disposition of defendants found incompetent, including treatment both before and, if necessary, at the conclusion of the provisional trial.

As anyone involved in institutional evaluation and program planning might suspect, we discovered, in the process of carrying out the research described in this book, a number of unanticipated and often unacknowledged problems and inequities in the procedures used to address the issue of competency. While a focus upon these problems was necessary, we also attempted to capitalize on the strengths of the two systems, legal and mental health, involved in the process. We hope that the fruits of our work will be a more effective system for the interaction of the legal and mental health professions vis-à-vis competency determinations, and an expanded use of evaluation research as a basis for policy.

Notes

1. Some jurisdictions use the term "fitness to stand trial" instead of "competency." We will use the latter throughout the book. We also use "competency to stand trial" in a broad sense to indicate competency to participate in the judicial proceedings, including plea bargaining as well as trial. Finally, while the issue of competency may be applicable to juveniles (*In re Causey*, 1978), this book will focus only on the process as it operates in the adult criminal courts.

2. At the time of the research project the authors were associated with the National Clearinghouse for Criminal Justice Planning and Architecture, an agency funded by the Law Enforcement Assistance Administration.

3. Seymour Sarason (1972) has summarized this issue: "The unexamined assumption that buildings are necessary is a bar to the recognition of the relationship between values, resources, and public policy. Put in another way: in the area of human service putting up new buildings tends to perpetuate the problem of limited resources, contributes to the inadequate services they ordinarily provide, and separates the setting from the larger society" (p. 160). With respect to the competency issue, for example, changes in the statutes or at the level of courtroom procedure could drastically reduce the number of evaluation referrals. Our early discussions with the forensic staff revealed, in fact, that many of them believed that defense attorneys were making inappropriate uses of the competency procedures for such reasons as delaying trial or obtaining treatment recommendations which could be used in subsequent plea bargaining. If this were true, and if the practice could be changed, the effect on the forensic unit would be obvious.

4. These changes are discussed in Chapters 5 and 7. With respect to the need for a new building, the results of our research suggested that other alternatives, including a shift from institutional to community-based evaluations, would minimize the need for a new building. If one was to be built at all, we recommended that it be approximately one-third that of the present capacity of the facility.

2

Competency Standards

The doctrine that the trial, conviction, or punishment of an incompetent defendant is not permissible, either as a matter of common or statutory law or as a matter of moral theory and practice, has long been a part of our legal system. According to Robertson (cited in Group for the Advancement of Psychiatry, 1974), the English courts as early as Edward I recognized that a defendant who did not plead could be either "mute by malice" or "mute by visitation of God." Since the Edwardian trial required a defendant to enter a plea in order to proceed, it is clear that such cases as Donald Lang's[1] have posed problems for the administration of justice over a considerable span of time. It is less clear that earlier courts considered or recognized subtler forms of mental and/or physical impairment that would disadvantage a defendant at other stages of trial as well. It is difficult to imagine that such issues did not arise before courts of the thirteenth century, but we can assume that, lacking a mental health profession, such cases were far less frequent than presently, and arose under fairly extreme circumstances. Furthermore, in view of the explanatory concepts of the time (Foucault, 1973; Rosen, 1969; Zilboorg and Henry, 1941), such cases were reviewed primarily in terms of demonic possession or divine visitation.

By the eighteenth century matters had progressed to the point where the arraignment, trial, judgment, or execution of an alleged capital offender could be stayed if he or she "becomes absolutely mad" (Hale, 1736, cited in Silten and Tullis, 1977, p. 1053). Hale's statements in this matter focus upon the defendant's memory abilities, but the language style (e.g., "phrenzy") implicates other forms of severe mental/physical impairment.

It is also important, from a historical perspective, to note that the right of the state to hold a person for trial while attempting to restore competency is also advocated by Hale: "(If) it appear that he is mad, the judge, in his discretion, may discharge the jury of him, and remit him to gaol, to be tried after the recovery of his understanding" (Hale, 1736, in Silten and Tullis, p. 1053). Blackstone, in his *Commentaries on the Laws of England*, reiterates the same points; indeed, the common law of the eighteenth and nineteenth centuries is replete with such examples.[2]

In modern times the constitutional standard for trial competency was set by the Supreme Court of the United States in *Dusky* v. *United States* (1960): "It is not enough for the district judge to find that 'the defendant is oriented to time and place and has some recollection of events,' but that the test must be whether he has sufficient present ability to consult with his lawyer with a reasonable degree of rational understanding—and whether he has a rational as well as factual understanding of the proceedings against him" (p. 402).

Most states have statutes with similar language,[3] and the federal statute, given in Section 4244 of Chapter 18 of U.S.C., defines incompetency as "presently insane or otherwise so mentally incompetent as to be unable to understand the proceedings against him or properly to assist in his . . . defense." As will become increasingly clear, the abstract, open-ended characteristic of these standards is a two-edged sword: broad and flexible applicability, but at the cost of considerable confusion and ambiguity.

Without apparent conscious recognition, the Supreme Court, in such matters as setting forth criteria for competency, has adopted an epistemology and a methodology known in the social sciences most commonly as construct validation (Cronbach and Meehl, 1955; Meehl, 1970b,c; and references cited immediately below). Readers trained in the philosophy of science will recognize this as the problem of "open-textured concepts" (Pap, 1953), but those whose training is in medicine or law may be unfamiliar with the concept, so we turn to a brief but important clarification.

COMPETENCY AS A CONSTRUCT

The basic principles of law are not unlike theories in the physical and social sciences. Their most essential similarities are (nonexhaustively) as follows:

a) They rely upon fundamental assumptions about the nature of the universe in general and human beings in particular. These fundamental assumptions, sometimes referred to as axioms, pretheoretical assumptions, or maxims, are *a priori* true. In law, these assumptions tend to originate in cultural tradition, religious teaching, and moral theory and involve such issues as the justifications for punishment, the moral nature of responsibility and capacity, the question of free will, and the nature of intent (Hart, 1968; Morris, 1961). Similar assumptions are part of the theories of science and mathematics and at times concern equivalent ideas—for example, determinism, the logic of inference, and the criteria for evidence (Meehl, 1970a,b,c; Popper, 1968; Suppe, 1974).

b) They have formal rules of evidence and procedure, such rules being relatively consistent over long periods of time, but subject to abrupt change as a function of new "discoveries" or "paradigm shifts" (Kuhn, 1970; Lakatos and Musgrave, 1972).

c) The content of their theories consists of at least two types of terms: observational and theoretical. Observational terms in the context of law would be, for example, that the defendant is mute, that the defendant said, "I'm going to shoot you, I have no choice," or that the witness's testimony was inconsistent with a prior statement. Usually such terms are "facts," but it is important to realize that even "observational terms" have a low-level inferential abstract quality. Theoretical terms in law would be constructs such as competency and *mens rea*. As a matter of commonly accepted assertion, the observational-theoretical dichotomy is a (sometimes) convenient, but inherently false, abstraction that labels the two extremes of a multifaceted continuum.

This third point of similarity is most crucial for our analysis of the construct of competency. Our assertion that competency should be viewed as a construct has important consequences, and leads to a method to clarify the confusion that surrounds this topic in the legal and psychological-psychiatric literature. Constructs have an interrelated and important set of characteristics, the most important of which is that the *meaning of a construct can never be fully reduced to a set of concrete operations and observational terms.* Constructs are frequently termed "open concepts" or "concepts with open texture" (Cronbach and Meehl, 1955; Meehl, 1970c; Pap, 1953) because of this open-ended characteristic. This open-textured quality of constructs means that they can never be completely reduced to a set of operational definitions. Thus *no absolute set of facts is ever dispositive of competency.*[4] Similarly, intelligence is not "nothing but" a score on an intelligence test. The inability to remember the facts of an alleged incident because of permanent amnesia is not necessarily to be equated with incompetency to stand trial (*Wilson v. United States*, 1968). As we shall see in our detailed examination of a set of leading competency cases, this open-textured quality of the competency construct has been well recognized, both implicitly and explicitly, by the majority of state supreme courts and by the federal courts at the appellate level and beyond. It is, however, poorly understood by the majority of psychiatrists, psychologists, lawyers, and trial judges. As our data from North Carolina demonstrate, and has been documented elsewhere (see Chapter 6 of this book, as well as Hess and Thomas, 1963; McGarry, 1965; Oliver, 1965), judges and lawyers frequently equate competency with mental illness and rely almost exclusively upon the conclusions of psychiatrists and psychologists who likewise misunderstand the legal construct of competency. The "rationally consult, assist, and comprehend" standard of *Dusky* (and the surrounding cases) is an attempt, albeit rather vague, to set forth the theoretical terms of the competency construct. It is implicit in this undertaking that competency is a theory that is evolving and changing; moreover, *to infer competency is to engage in a complex process of judgment that is situationally dependent upon the facts of the instant case, but is not completely reducible to a set of rules about those facts.*

We now turn to a set of empirical studies, legal opinions, and state and federal cases that collectively represents the theoretical and empirical particulars of the current construct of competency. For clarity of exposition, we discuss competency in five sections, each corresponding to a leading case and/or to a particular aspect of the competency construct. These are, respectively: competency to stand trial *per se* (*Dusky v. United States*); criteria for doubting a defendant's competency (*Pate v. Robinson*); competency to plead guilty (*Sieling v. Eyman*) or waive counsel (*Westbrook v. Arizona*); amnesia and competency; and drug-induced competency.

The Dusky Standard

The Supreme Court's *Dusky* decision is, asserts Federal Judge Oliver, somewhat unfortunate: "No one quarrels with what the Supreme Court actually held in *Dusky*; unhappiness with *Dusky* is produced by the fact that the Supreme Court said so little as to why it held what it did" (1965, p. 543). In fact, the Court's two-paragraph opinion relies heavily upon the government's brief and merely paraphrases some critical sentences. How is one to interpret the key phrases of *Dusky* in such a manner as to delineate its theory of competency more clearly?[5] Two interrelated strategies seem worthwhile to pursue:

a) Empirically examine the "normal" manner in which judges, lawyers, and mental health professionals make decisions about a defendant's competency. By examining the statistical relationship between the "facts" available to such individuals and the inferences (conclusions, decisions, recommendations) they draw about the defendant's competency, one can highlight the decisional rules used in actual practice. One can also compare the practice to theory and thereby gain important insights. This is one aspect of the research strategy we employed in our North Carolina study.

b) Abstract the critical issues that are "worried over" in leading cases and thereby clarify, expand, and revise as yet unelaborated implications of the original theory. (To carry the argument of the "construct" nature of competency further, such a generative view of theory construction and revision is currently the reigning view in the philosophy of science.)

We will concentrate on the second strategy below, summarizing, where appropriate, our research and that of others.

It is instructive to begin with *Youtsey v. United States* (1899). Youtsey was accused of embezzlement while a cashier in a Kentucky bank during 1894–95. He was indicted in September, 1897, but his trial was postponed until March, 1898, on grounds that he was mentally and physically unable to appear. In March Youtsey's lawyers petitioned the court for an additional continuance, alleging that Youtsey was an epileptic; that three physicians would testify to his having had two severe attacks of epilepsy that had resulted in severe impairment of memory, rendering him "unable by reason of said impairment of memory, to furnish counsel with any recollection of many of the vital transactions covered by said indictment which ought to be personally within his knowledge" (*Youtsey*, p. 939).

The judge overruled the motion. Youtsey was tried and convicted despite another epileptic seizure that required an adjournment of several days. The Sixth Circuit Court of Appeals reversed Youtsey's conviction and remanded it for retrial and a hearing on Youtsey's competency, arguing that "epilepsy is a progressive disease, and its effect upon the mind and memory is progressive. There was evidence strongly tending to show that the memory and mind of the accused shortly before and during the trial were impaired and rendering it doubtful whether the accused was capable of appreciating his situation, and of intelligently advising his counsel as to his defense, if any he had. This evidence indicated that the disease had progressed, and with it the impairment of mind and memory" (*Youtsey*, p. 947).

In addition to anticipating *Pate* by 67 years, Youtsey's case teaches us several things. To properly evaluate a defendant's competency, "some mode, in the discretion of the court, [must] be adopted for a thorough investigation of the sanity of the accused" (p. 947). By implication, the Court is saying that since sufficient evidence exists reasonably to doubt Youtsey's competency, an evidentiary hearing should have been held to explore and evaluate the facts. The judge would not have been required to empanel a jury on this matter, but "it was nevertheless his duty to consider the matter judicially" (p. 947). In reaching this conclusion, the Court relied heavily upon the sworn affidavits of Youtsey's lawyers that they could not defend him under the circumstances (their need to know certain facts and his alleged good-faith inability to supply them). Thus the "reasonableness" of the defendant's ability to understand the proceedings and assist defense counsel depends upon the circumstance. *Youtsey* implied that what is expected of a defendant's competency is context-dependent. In Youtsey's situation accurate memory for the circumstances was deemed necessary for a proper defense. In other cases more or less may be required.

Since *Youtsey* and the increased use of psychiatric testimony, the meaning of "reasonable ability" has been subject to an entirely different but extremely frequent interpretation: reasonable ability equals absence of severe forms of mental illness. Unfortunately, this particular rendering of incompetency is as erroneous as it is frequent, as we shall demonstrate. This problem is further compounded by the confusion of mental illness as a standard for both criminal responsibility and incompetency.

Competency and responsibility

The criteria for establishing competency and responsibility are frequently considered interchangeable by both the legal and psychiatric communities. The legal standard for competency to stand trial set forth in *Dusky* is entirely different than the standard for responsibility. The responsibility standard is derived from M'Naughten's case, decided in England in 1843, in which it was held that a defendant could not be held responsible for a crime if it were shown that at the time of the act "the party accused was labouring under such a defect of reason, from disease of the mind, as not to know the nature and quality of the act he was doing, or as not to know what he was doing was wrong" (cited in Bazelon, 1974, p. 19). Current responsibility standards differ from state to state and across federal jurisdictions as well. While the matter is inordinately complex, the subject of many texts, articles, and debates,[6] it should be apparent that the questions of competency and responsibility are two separate legal issues. The issue of responsibility refers to the defendant's mental state at the time of the alleged crime and is used as a trial defense. The issue of competency, on the other hand, primarily refers to the ability of the defendant to assist in the preparation of his defense.[7] Thus a defendant can be competent to stand trial (i.e., prepare his defense) but be found not responsible for the commission of a crime by reason of insanity. Conversely, a defendant could be found incompetent to stand trial but still be adjudged responsible for the crime when finally tried. Unfortunately, despite the important legal distinctions between competency and responsibility, both law and psychiatry continue to confuse the two standards and to apply indiscriminantly the mental health criteria for responsibility to competency standards. In both cases mental health professionals in general, and psychiatrists in particular, continue to exhibit a marked tendency to equate psychosis with responsibility and/or competency, in spite of the fact that this is not in accord with *either* legal standard.

The competency statutes of many states reflect this confusion and contribute to it (Rosenberg, 1970). The North Carolina statute (G.S. 15A-1001) is illustrative: "No person may be tried, convicted, sentenced, or punished for a crime when *by reason of mental illness or defect* he is unable to understand the nature and object of the proceedings against him, to comprehend his own situation in reference to the proceedings, or to assist in his own defense in a rational or reasonable manner" (p. 269, italics added). Note that despite the fact that the *Dusky* standard makes no specific mention of a relationship between mental illness and competency, the North Carolina statute, like those of many states,[8] requires that an evaluation of mental illness or defect be the basis for determining competency.

As we illustrate in Chapter 5, the orders for evaluation of competency issued by the courts also reflect a confusion between the competency and responsibility standards. Often a court order may in fact request *both* a competency and a responsibility evaluation simultaneously, even though the defendant is committed under a statute providing only for the evaluation of competency. Obviously, this practice does not clarify the task of the evaluators.

The psychiatrist as judge

All available empirical studies as well as critical commentaries agree that, in the average jurisdiction, judges rarely base their decisions on anything but the concluding statement in the psychiatric report to the court (Bazelon, 1975; Bennett, 1968; Hess and Thomas, 1963; Vann, 1965; Vann and Morganroth, 1965; and our own data, Chapter 6). It is extraordinarily uncommon in commitment hearings for the psychiatrist to testify in person, for the defense or the prosecution to cross-examine a witness, or for the whole procedural hearing to take more than five to ten minutes (Hiday, 1977; Kutner, 1962; Maisel, 1970; Scheff, 1964; Shah, 1974; Wexler and Scoville, 1971). We presume that similar results would hold for competency hearings. As McGarry (1965) notes, on the basis of his extensive study of the procedure in Massachusetts, "It would appear that the court usually accepts without question the medical judgment of the psychiatrist regarding the need for hospitalization and, in effect, the incompetency of the individual to stand trial" (p. 626).

This type of decision-making is not necessarily as pervasive as the preceding text suggests. Significant exceptions do exist, as is evident in the opinions of such cases as *United States* v. *Gundelfinger* (1951), *United States* v. *David* (1975), and *Wieter* v. *Settle* (1961). As a classic example, consider the following:

In many such cases this Court is confronted with a conclusion of the Neuropsychiatric Staff of the Medical Center, that the petitioner, considered from psychiatric discipline [sic], is unable to rationally understand the nature of the criminal proceedings pending against him and is unable to rationally cooperate with his counsel in defense thereto. However, when some such persons personally appear before this District Court in a habeas corpus proceeding it is evident from legal concepts that they, in all probability, are possessed of mental faculties that would sanction their right to stand trial on the charge made against them; and that this Court, in failing to recognize and so adjudicate that fact, would be on the threshold of cooperatively denying some such persons the right to a "speedy" trial as commanded by the Sixth Amendment to the Constitution of the United States. (*Wieter* v. *Settle*, p. 321)

Nevertheless, such examples are far from commonplace. In Chapters 4 and 7 not only will we consider various proposals for improving the quality of decision-making on the part of judges, but we will also consider the improvement of the quality of information available to them.

Severe mental illness and incompetency

The confusion of competency and responsibility standards, coupled with a long-standing abrogation of judicial authority to the "mental health expert," has led, rather uniformly, to a mental illness interpretation of competency to stand trial. Psychiatric professionals were intimately involved in determining competency even before *Youtsey*, but it has become patently clear that they have been overly involved in this process. We do not mean to denigrate the potential role of mental health testimony in such evaluations. However, the data on current procedures for determining competency and the empirical literature reviewed thus far (and below) clearly suggest that:

a) Psychiatric testimony heavily influences the outcome of judicial decision-making, thus undermining the court's authority.

b) Psychiatrists and psychologists typically testify in conclusory terms, often parroting the statutory language, thus depriving the court of the proper evidentiary base for its determination of the defendant's competency (Roesch and Golding, 1978).

c) Psychiatrists and psychologists often confuse the legal criteria for incompetency with criteria for the existence of mental dysfunction, criminal responsibility, and need for treatment.

d) Psychiatrists and psychologists, while competent to judge some aspects of behavioral and psychological processes, are (1) not able to predict future behavior at the level of accuracy often claimed, and (2) not sufficiently conversant with legal matters to be able to judge, *within the Dusky criteria*, whether or not *this* defendant, facing *these* charges, *in light of the existing evidence*, will be able to assist his attorney in a rational manner.

The lack of clear statutory direction for determining whether a defendant meets the *Dusky* criteria has contributed to the evaluation of competency primarily in terms of the presence or absence of psychosis. Our own empirical data (see Chapter 6), perhaps the most comprehensive yet collected on the processes underlying mental health professionals' decisional strategies, clearly support this point. The gross diagnostic categories of psychosis and mental retardation accounted for 83% of the determinations that the defendant was incompetent. It is important to note, however, that the equation of psychosis with trial incompetency has been uniformly rejected by the higher courts. Whether a defendant is mentally or physically diagnosable, the *test of competency should be, within the framework of Dusky, a functional one.*

An early case that illustrates functional impairment is *People v. Berling* (1953). Miss Violet Berling was accused of a particularly heinous child-murder involving torture and sexual abuse. She was convicted in spite of her having fainted or lost consciousness some 11 times during the trial, twice falling out of the witness box. She was reported "dizzy," "confused," or "dazed" on numerous other occasions and did not even know that her most important witness had not been called upon to testify. While the trial judge was obviously aware of her condition, he merely continued the trial with recesses ranging from minutes to a few days, once remarking, "I can't have the jury sitting here watching a defendant fall to the floor day after day in a fainting condition and in a condition that shows she gives every impression she is not able to look after her interests" (*Berling*, p. 266).

Berling was obviously unfit to be tried and her conviction was set aside on grounds of "the fundamental error of forcing the accused to stand trial while not in the full enjoyment of consciousness and mental power" (*Berling*, p. 270). Although we do not know if her condition was a product of physical disease (e.g., epilepsy, narcolepsy, cranial tumor) or some form of catatonic schizophrenia or dissociative reaction, in a very important sense her diagnosis does not matter. From any reasonable perspective her functional impairment relative to the circumstances of her case is the object of primary concern. Mental health testimony would have been appropriate only if addressed to the issue of whether or not her cognitive, memorial, and reflective abilities were sufficiently intact to allow her to understand her situation and assist in her defense, as appropriate under the circumstances.[9]

One of the earliest cases setting forth a reasoned argument that competency to stand trial is not to be equated with presence or absence of psychosis (or even delusions and hallucinations *per se*) is *Higgins* v. *McGrath* (1951). Higgins, accused of using the mail for obscene purposes, was examined by a number of psychiatrists, all of whom agreed, in essence, that he was a paranoid schizophrenic with delusions of a persecutory nature. His delusions also incorporated previous federal judges who had had contact with him. The psychiatrists concluded that Higgins was incompetent. He was committed as an incompetent defendant and filed a *habeas corpus*. The *Higgins* court granted relief and ordered him returned to the court of his commitment for a redetermination of his competency to stand trial. While on the surface this seems a routine *habeas* case, it is not. As noted below, the court clearly acknowledges that Higgins's delusions are not sufficient *per se* to bar his trial.

Petitioner has also filed with the court a typewritten document covering fifty-six (56) pages, which he entitles, "Evidence per Affidavit to Support Oral Testimony of Petitioner" given at hearing on writ of habeas corpus. This last-mentioned document presents a detailed statement of the personal life history of petitioner, including detailed background and facts concerning the commission of the offense with which he stands charged. We shall not begin to summarize the contents of either of said documents. Suffice it to say that the documents so filed may, from a medical standpoint, lend some support to the testimony of Dr. Glotfelty, that petitioner is suffering from specific delusions of persecution; on the other hand, they reveal that petitioner is fully cognizant of his present predicament, has a memory of all material details thereof, knows the nature of the charge made against him, and if the facts therein stated were revealed to counsel representing petitioner at the trial on said charges they would afford ample material to enable counsel to prepare a defense thereto, if petitioner has such a defense. We believe, from all the reports herein and the testimony considered as a whole . . . that any insane delusions or hallucinations with which petitioner is now afflicted, produce only partial insanity in petitioner; and, that the partial insanity under which he is laboring is not such as will probably prevent petitioner being tried on the charges now pending against him. (*Higgins*, pp. 677–78)

Clearly, a defendant may have a diagnosable severe mental disorder ("paranoid schizophrenia") or physical illness (cerebral arteriosclerosis) and *still* have sufficient capacity to understand and assist. In *United States v. Sermon* (1964) a district court held that Sermon, who was suffering from chronic brain syndrome secondary to cerebral arteriosclerosis, was sufficiently capable of assisting his attorney given the circumstances of the case and the nature of the defense, in spite of his difficulties with memory. A similar conclusion was reached in *United States v. Wilson* (1966). We cannot here fully elaborate upon the empirical facts that support this thesis, but it is sufficiently important to warrant some consideration.

The severest critics of psychiatry and psychology would argue that these disciplines are totally devoid of scientific substance. Such arguments are rejectable squarely on the basis of a century of increasingly sophisticated knowledge of the basis of human mental pathology and normal development. Less easy to deal with are the very genuine concerns that our knowledge base is subject to considerable bias, is much more tentative than is usually represented, and faces an uphill battle against powerful methodological problems (Ennis and Litwack, 1974; Meehl, 1970b,c, 1971, 1978; Poythress, 1977). These problems do exist and should be known in detail by the legal and judicial communities. But they do not imply that no expert knowledge base exists. Thus, to the present point, a considerable knowledge base indicates that (1) psychiatric diagnosis *can* be made more reliably and with far less bias than is alleged by critics (Beck et al., 1962; Feighner et al., 1972; Luria and McHugh, 1974; McLemore and Benjamin, 1979; Spitzer, 1976; Spitzer and Fleiss, 1974; Spitzer et al., 1970, 1978; Ward et al., 1962); and (2) in Sullivan's marvelous phrase, mental patients, even the most severely disturbed, are "much more simply human than otherwise" (1953, p. 32). Even the accurately diagnosed presence of a severe mental disorder does not imply that one is grossly impaired across the entire range of psychological cognitive functions in all situations and circumstances. A diagnosis of schizophrenia may be "accurately" made on the basis, say, of "delusions of control" and "formal thought disorder" (see Spitzer et al., 1974) without necessarily implying incompetence. Even such a phrase as "formal thought disorder," when properly understood as to its scientific meaning and method of assessment (and limitations thereto), does not necessarily imply functional impairment of a legally relevant nature, nor does it imply that such impairment is global, affecting the entire range of cognitive and rational abilities across a variety of situations.

The implications and suggestions of *Higgins* have been reinforced by a series of subsequent cases. In *Swisher* v. *United States* (1965) Judge John Oliver cites Judge Ridge's earlier *Higgins* and *Wieter* decisions with evident admiration. He then drives to the heart of the matter:

It must be understood at the outset that petitioner, like any other ac-cused, may well have been mentally ill at the time of the trial, but still could have been quite competent to stand trial. In other words, it must constantly be kept in focus that mere proof of the fact that petitioner may have been in fact mentally ill at the time of trial does not establish that he was then mentally incompetent to stand trial. Proof of such a fact would establish only one circumstance to which judicial attention must be directed; such proof does not establish anything more.

Most, if not all the legal and medical confusion that unfortunately characterizes many of the cases involving mental competency, as distin-guished from the entirely different question of criminal responsibility, is the result of efforts to sustain an absolute concept that a particular defend-ant is not competent to stand trial simply because he may be correctly diagnosed as being mentally ill at the time of his trial. . . . A medical judgment of mental illness *does not control* the determination of the essen-tially legal question of competency to stand trial. . . . If that were true, an insane defendant would never be given an opportunity to present a defense of insanity. (*Swisher*, pp. 931, 933, italics added)

Similarly well-argued conclusions are reached in *Lyles* v. *United States* (1957). Lyles was diagnosed as suffering from "sociopathic personality dis-turbance"; nevertheless, the *Lyles* court argued,

He may have a mental disease, and the mental disease may have been the cause of his criminal act, and he may be suffering from the same disease at the time of his trial; but it is a scientific fact that he nevertheless may be competent to stand trial under this definition of competency. A para-noiac or a pyromaniac may well understand the charges against him and be able to assist in his defense. "To assist in his defense" of course does not refer to legal questions involved but to such phases of a defense as a de-fendant usually assists in, such as accounts of the facts, names of wit-nesses, etc. The standard of measurement of competency to stand trial is different from the standard of measurement for responsibility for a crimi-nal act. (*Lyles*, pp. 729–30)

In a parallel fashion *United States* v. *Adams* (1969) and *Wieter* v. *Settle* (1961) held that defendants diagnosed as paranoid schizophrenics were competent to stand trial. *Feguer* v. *United States* (1962) states the conclusion most succinctly: "Presence of a mental illness [Feguer was diagnosed as a paranoid schizophrenic] does not equate with incompetency to stand trial. . . . And even expert testimony rises no higher than the reasons on which it is based; it is not binding upon the trier of the facts" (*Feguer*, p. 236, citations omitted).

While the *Dusky* standard itself is phrased in somewhat ambiguous language, the case law, federal holdings, and empirical data lead to the conclusion that competency to stand trial is an open-textured construct whose theoretical terms are agreed upon in a broad context. Testimony about mental and physical illnesses is relevant, but only insofar as it speaks to the functional ability of a defendant to *reasonably understand and assist in his/her own defense*. Defendants are not expected to be amateur lawyers, nor paragons of mental health, nor admirers of and true believers in the criminal justice system. [10] What is reasonable to expect of a defendant in these areas of comprehension, understanding, and assistance is related to the particular circumstances of the case as well as to his/her mental status. As Bennett observes:

In applying the functional test, the mental condition of the defendant must not be evaluated in a vacuum, but must be considered in relation to the circumstances of the case. The anticipated length and complexity of the trial is an important factor. A defendant who would be competent for a one day trial might well deteriorate under the stress of a long proceeding. Similarly, a defense against certain crimes might require a lesser degree of competency than against others. For example, it is easier for an accused to assist in a defense to the crime of rape than in a conspiracy charge involving many complicated transactions. Moreover, crimes for which specific intent is required, such as larceny, would require a greater degree of competence than a crime such as rape where the criminal intent is assumed from the act. In those offenses requiring specific intent, there are added defenses which often can only be presented by the defendant. (Bennett, 1968, p. 577)

We will return to some suggestions about mental health testimony and the *Dusky* standard in Chapter 4; we can, however, think of no more succinct a statement of the functional meaning of *Dusky* than Judge Ridge's in *Wieter* v. *Settle*, when he listed the following characteristics of a competent defendant:

1) that he has mental capacity to appreciate his presence in relation to
time, place and things; 2) that his elementary mental processes be such
that he apprehends (i.e., seizes and grasps with what mind he has) that
he is in a Court of Justice, charged with a criminal offense; 3) that there
is a Judge on the Bench; 4) a Prosecutor present who will try to convict
him of a criminal charge; 5) that he has a lawyer (self-employed or Court-
appointed) who will undertake to defend him against that charge; 6) that
he will be expected to tell his lawyer the circumstances, to the best of his
mental ability, (whether colored or not by mental aberration) the facts
surrounding him at the time and place where the law violation is alleged
to have been committed; 7) that there is, or will be, a jury present to pass
upon evidence adduced as to his guilt or innocence of such charge; and
8) he has memory sufficient to relate those things in his own personal
manner:—such a person from a consideration of legal standards, should
be considered mentally competent to stand trial under criminal procedure, lawfully enacted. (*Wieter*, pp. 321–22)

THE PATE STANDARD

The *Dusky* standard concerns the construct of competency to stand
trial. For procedural reasons there is a related, though often confused,
standard that concerns the level of doubt required to *force* the raising of
the competency question. In *Pate* v. *Robinson* (1966) the Supreme Court
held that a trial judge *must* raise the issue of competency if either the
court's own evidence or that presented by the defense or prosecution raises
a "*bona fide* doubt" of the defendant's competency.

Bona fide or substantial doubt

The confusion that most typically emerges in applying the *Pate* standard
of "*bona fide*" doubt has to do, not surprisingly, with the influence of psychiatric and psychological testimony. The federal and state rulings in this
matter have been considerably confused over the issue of the proper role
of such testimony. Consider some typical (and influential) cases. In *Drope*
v. *Missouri* (1975) the Supreme Court held:

The import of our decision in *Pate* v. *Robinson* is that evidence of a defendant's irrational behavior, his demeanor at trial, and any prior medical
opinion on competence to stand trial are all relevant in determining

whether further inquiry is required, but that even one of these factors standing alone may, in some circumstances, be sufficient. There are, of course, no fixed or immutable signs which invariably indicate the need for further inquiry to determine fitness to proceed; the question is often a difficult one in which a wide range of manifestations and subtle nuances are implicated. That they are difficult to evaluate is suggested by the varying opinions trained psychiatrists can entertain on the same facts. (*Drope*, p. 180)

Drope was accused, with others, of the rape of his wife. Before his trial he was examined by a psychiatrist for the defense who reported that Drope was suffering from "(1) Sociopathic personality disorder, sexual perversion. (2) Borderline mental deficiency. (3) Chronic anxiety reaction with a depression" (*Drope*, note 1, p. 165). The psychiatrist did not specifically address the issue of Drope's trial competency. Just prior to the trial Drope apparently assaulted his wife, trying to choke her. During his trial he tried to kill himself by gunshot. The Supreme Court found this evidence sufficient to reverse Drope's conviction on the grounds that his behavior raised a reasonable doubt as to his competency, and that the court erred by not evaluating and deciding upon this issue.

The *Pate* standard is problematical because if interpreted too liberally, it results in an overuse of competency hearings (and commitments, with their attendant deprivation of liberty), while if interpreted too conservatively, it results in the denial of a defendant's due-process rights (not to be subject to trial and conviction while incompetent) and a judicial quagmire (how to determine in retrospect if a defendant *was incompetent* at the time of trial). Caught between Scylla and Charybdis, the courts in general have quite naturally steered a crooked course.

The Court of Appeals for the Ninth Circuit and the California courts have steered what seems to be the truest course. Their decisions show a constant weighing of the evidence from a functional perspective. In *People v. Laudermilk* (1967) the California Court of Appeals observed that "more is required to raise a doubt than mere bizarre actions . . . or bizarre statements . . . a statement of defense counsel that defendant is incapable of cooperating in his defense . . . or psychiatric testimony that the defendant is immature, dangerous, psychopathic, or homicidal or such with little reference to defendant's ability to assist in his own defense" (*Laudermilk*, p. 285, numerous California citations for each phrase omitted).

We discovered the *Laudermilk* case after completing our empirical re-

search in North Carolina. It is nevertheless amazing to observe the extent
to which *Laudermilk* presciently lists the conclusions of our empirical
analysis of motions for competency hearings (Roesch and Golding, 1978,
and Chapter 6).

If no single act or diagnosis or psychiatric conclusion or description
alone is a necessary basis for raising a substantial or *bona fide* doubt, what
is? We again find that we are dealing with an open construct; one must
turn to representative cases to infer the proper scope of the theoretical
particulars. The issue of what constitutes *bona fide* doubt is clearly framed
in *People v. Pennington* (1967):

> *Pate v. Robinson* stands for the proposition that an accused has a consti-
> tutional right to a hearing on present sanity if he comes forward with
> substantial evidence that he is incapable, because of mental illness, of
> understanding the nature of the proceedings against him or of assisting in
> his defense. Once such substantial evidence appears, a doubt as to the
> sanity of the accused exists, no matter how persuasive other evidence—
> testimony of prosecution witnesses or the court's own observations of the
> accused—may be to the contrary. (*Pennington*, p. 949)

Pennington, accused of child-murder and sexual assault, had a long
history of psychiatric disturbance. In spite of Pennington's history, evidence that he was hallucinating, and his lewd and obscene conduct in the
courtroom, the trial judge denied repeated motions for competency hearings, stating, "This proceeding is not to try the sanity or insanity, but to
determine whether or not this Court has a doubt, and this Court does not
have a doubt and has not had a doubt" (*Pennington*, p. 946).

The California Supreme Court reversed Pennington's conviction, hold-
ing that, in spite of the trial judge having gathered some evidence on
Pennington's competency, he erred by not holding the proper hearing.
The court argued:

> At the oral argument of this case the People urged that the proceedings
> conducted by the judge when he took evidence to aid him in deciding if
> a doubt of defendant's sanity existed constitute the "hearing" on the issue
> of competency to stand trial which *Pate v. Robinson* requires. We disagree.
> In *Robinson*, where the United States Supreme Court found a violation of
> due process of law in failure to conduct a hearing on present sanity, the
> Illinois trial judge had also taken certain evidence the only purpose of
> which could have been to guide him in determining if a doubt of Robin-
> son's competence to stand trial existed. The distinction between a com-

plete hearing to decide if an accused is competent to stand trial and special proceedings conducted by a judge to determine whether he should
declare that a doubt of the accused's present sanity exists is well recognized
in this state. . . . The decision of the United States Supreme Court in
Pate v. Robinson demonstrates that the type of "hearing" which due process requires when the accused has come forward with substantial evidence of present insanity has not been accorded the accused when the
judge merely takes evidence to guide him in determining if he should
declare the existence of a "doubt." A "hearing" is generally understood to
be a proceeding where evidence is taken to the end of determining an
issue of fact and a decision made on the basis of that evidence. (*Pennington*, pp. 950–51, citations omitted)

The *Pennington* court caused a certain amount of confusion. A close
reading of the case reveals that considerable dispute was raised before the
judge by both defense and prosecution as to the meaning of the defendant's behavior in and out of the courtroom. While the evidence was not
part of a formal hearing, it was considerable. *Pennington* is most confusing,
however, because it sets the stage for higher courts to "play doctor," i.e.,
enter into (retrospective) disputes with lower courts as to the *proper conclusions* and *proper diagnoses* to be drawn on the basis of the available
evidence.

Consider, for example, the case of *Noble v. Black* (1976). Noble was
indicted and convicted of the "cold blooded murder" of his wife. Although Noble had three months prior to his trial to request a psychiatric
examination, his attorney waited until the day of the trial. On that day
he requested a continuance because Noble had headaches and his physician had told him to consult a psychiatrist. The motion was denied, and
Noble sought *habeas corpus* relief claiming he was denied due process and
was incompetent at the time of the trial. Evidently there was no compelling evidence that would raise a *bona fide* doubt as to Noble's competency
to stand trial; moreover, the government claimed, and the U.S. Court of
Appeals, Sixth Circuit, agreed, that

the only information with which the trial judge was confronted bearing
upon appellant's competence to stand trial was the affidavit of his counsel
to the effect that appellant's physician had suggested consultation with a
psychiatrist and the demeanor of Mr. Noble during the course of the hearing held upon his motion for a continuance *and throughout the remainder
of his trial.* The transcript of the continuance hearing at which appellant
was the only witness indicates that he was alert and lucid and that his

responses to questions propounded to him were relevant, coherent, and appropriate. . . . There was no evidence presented of a history of mental illness suffered by appellant. (*Noble*, pp. 588–89)

Nevertheless, the *Noble* court, after reviewing the sorts of indicia that led the *Pate* and *Drope* courts to find that reasonable doubt existed as to trial competency (thereby mandating a hearing on the issue), concluded that sufficient doubt existed:

Under the circumstances in the instant case, the abduction of the baby boy from the mother by appellant, his dangerous habit of carrying a loaded pistol with him at all times, even taking it to bed with him each night, although no one had ever threatened him, his demand on his separated wife to return to him and, upon her refusal, his killing her by shooting her twice in the back while she was sitting with her mother, his coolly walking away from the scene of the crime, with no effort to hide himself, or escape, his claim of suffering torturing headaches, his doctor's advice to see a psychiatrist—all of these circumstances created a sufficient doubt as to appellant's competence requiring further inquiry as to his mental responsibility for the killing of his wife, and these should have been inquired into, as hereinafter shown, at whatever stage of the proceedings such evidence was sought to be introduced and became available, even after verdict and judgment, as bearing upon appellant's competency and sanity. . . . The foregoing permits a collateral attack upon the conviction based upon mental incompetence at the time of trial. (*Noble*, pp. 591–92)

In both *Pate* and *Drope* the defendants presented considerable evidence to substantiate a doubt as to mental competency. Here the *Noble* court evidently felt that the mere commission of such a crime in such a way gives rise to doubts as to the defendant's mental state. We concur with Judge Bazelon in his comments on another case: "It cannot reasonably be supposed that Congress intended to require the accused to produce, in order to get a mental examination, enough evidence to prove that he is incompetent or irresponsible. That is what the examination itself may, or may not, produce. If the accused already had such evidence, there would be little need for the examination" (*Mitchell* v. *United States*, 1963, p. 360). Nevertheless, we do not think Noble's evidence can reasonably be seen as rising to the required level. Mitchell's case is quite unlike Noble's. While the evidence presented was not conclusive, it did raise substantial doubts in the mind of the reviewing court. Mitchell's attorney introduced evidence that he was an epileptic and had written some frankly peculiar letters to the President of the United States, for example: "Mr. President, if you recall, your last letter to me specifically stated that if I can be of any help to you don't hesitate to call on me. . . . These words are very powerful. The wisest man on earth once said, life and death are in the power of the tongue. . . . Mr. Moses advises us in both of his books to square our actions with the Ten Commandments, and Jesus said it by the Sermon on the Mount. Mr. President . . . you, yourself, gave me your honorable words that should I be in need, just call on you" (*Mitchell*, p. 358).

While neither of these facts might convince a judge *per se*, they do rise considerably higher than the facts in Noble's case. Nevertheless, the basic problem with *Pate* remains—the "evidence" offered in support of questioning the defendant's competency is frequently only in terms of psychiatric labels (at best) or jargon (at worst), and rarely do courts get involved in the "facts" and "reasons" upon which such conclusions are based.

While we have described numerous cases in which trial and appellate judges have gotten involved in the actual facts, this should not be taken as representative of actual trial practice. In our analysis of North Carolina procedures, 56% of the motions for competency hearings were routinely granted (of those, less than 10% were subsequently found incompetent). The "facts" presented rarely justify granting the motion or holding a hearing. *Pate* has frequently been misinterpreted to imply that once the issue of competency has been raised, the trial court must grant the motion and then obtain mental health evaluations and recommendations. The *Pate* decision only requires such a hearing given "reasonable doubt." Because trial court judges usually do not specialize in mental health issues, however, they are ill equipped to view the evidence offered from a *reasonable knowledge base*. This problem is compounded by the fact that the motions themselves are rarely anything other than a parroting of the statutory language, and contain little information about the basis of the request.[11]

The series of cases arising from the Ninth Circuit have attempted to further delineate the meaning of substantial doubt. An early attempt to delineate the procedural steps and to clarify the meaning of *Pate* is *Moore v. United States* (1972):

Under the rule of *Pate v. Robinson* . . . a due process evidentiary hearing is constitutionally compelled at any time that there is "substantial evidence" that the defendant may be mentally incompetent to stand trial. "Substantial evidence" is a term of art. "Evidence" encompasses all information properly before the court, whether it is in the form of testimony or exhibits formally admitted or it is in the form of medical reports or other kinds of reports that have been filed with the court. Evidence is "substantial" if it raises a reasonable doubt about the defendant's competency to stand trial. Once there is such evidence from any source, there is a doubt that cannot be dispelled by resort to conflicting evidence. The function of the trial court in applying Pate's substantial evidence test is not to determine the ultimate issue: Is the defendant competent to stand trial? It [sic] sole function is to decide whether there is any evidence which, assuming its truth, raises a reasonable doubt about the defendant's competency. At any time that such evidence appears, the trial court *sua sponte* must order an evidentiary hearing on the competency issue. It is only after the evidentiary hearing, applying the usual rules appropriate to trial, that the court, decides the issue of competency of the defendant to stand trial. (Moore, p. 666)

In Moore's case the Court of Appeals held that the trial court erred by not taking two psychiatric reports as "substantial evidence casting a reasonable doubt" and holding an evidentiary hearing on Moore's competency. Moore's case gives the reasonable proposition that the evidence contained (or alluded to) in two rather descriptive reports, *their conclusions notwithstanding*, constituted sufficient grounds for a Pate doubt. Both reports mention Moore's having visual hallucinations and having engaged in suicide attempts, self-mutilation, manic-depressive mood swings, and a series of other acutely disturbed behaviors. The Moore court was not arguing that these alleged behaviors would be sufficient grounds to find Moore incompetent; they were, however, "facts that compelled a Pate evidentiary hearing" (Moore, p. 666). By implication, the mere availability of the psychiatric reports, without the physical presence of the author, and without an opportunity for direct testimony and cross-examination, could not constitute the basis of a proper evidentiary hearing; but their contents (evidence of severe mental disorder) did compel a hearing. Thus the holding of the Moore court has direct implications for the usual practice of deciding the issue of a defendant's competency based upon unchallenged psychiatric reports whose author is frequently not present.

Another ruling from the Ninth Circuit expands upon Moore. Geza deKaplany was accused of killing his wife by pouring nitric acid over her (murder by torture). Prior to his trial deKaplany was examined by three court-appointed psychiatrists, two of whom reported to the court before jury selection began. The first report found him "sane"; the second "concluded that he was presently suffering from no mental illness and . . . able to cooperate with counsel and assist counsel in the preparation and presentation of a rational defense"; and the third report, filed after his guilty plea, stated that he showed evidence of "some suicidal thinking of the obsessional variety" but was "sane now and at the time of the commission of the alleged offense" (*deKaplany* v. *Enomoto*, 1977, pp. 977–78). After the start of the trial deKaplany changed his plea to guilty. He appealed on the grounds (*inter alia*) that the trial court erred by not conducting a hearing on his competency to stand trial and that his guilty plea was not knowingly, intelligently, and voluntarily made. During the "sanity phase" of his trial (subsequent to the "guilty phase" in California procedure), deKaplany's lawyer presented the testimony of three psychiatrists who testified to his insanity at the time of the crime, while the prosecution presented three psychiatrists who testified that deKaplany was sane.[12] No further evidence apropos his present capacity was presented. The majority opinion in *deKaplany* assessed the meaning of reasonable doubt in the following way:

> Genuine doubt, not a synthetic or constructive doubt, is the measuring rod. The emergence of genuine doubt in the mind of a trial judge necessarily is the consequence of his total experience and his evaluation of the testimony and events of the trial.
> Moreover, *Pate* and *Drope* teach that appellate review of a failure to provide a hearing on competence to stand trial is comprehensive and not limited by either the abuse of discretion or clearly erroneous standard. The question to be asked by the reviewing court is whether a reasonable judge, situated as was the trial court judge whose failure to conduct an evidentiary hearing is being reviewed, should have experienced doubt with respect to competency to stand trial. (*deKaplany*, pp. 982–83)

The court's distinction between genuine and synthetic doubt is meant to clarify an erroneous implication of *Moore* that "doubt necessarily exists, and thus a hearing is required, because certain evidence exists which would create a doubt were it not for other evidence which precludes doubt" (*deKaplany*, p. 982).

Thus the *deKaplany* court refuses to adopt any form of strict operational definition, such as the presence of at least one psychiatric conclusion of trial incompetency regardless of any number of contrary opinions. It preserves the open-textured quality of *Dusky* and *Pate*,[13] arguing:

We are not prepared to assert that in every trial in which the sanity of the defendant is contested there must be a good faith doubt which requires a hearing on competency. . . . It is clear from these cases that the California Supreme Court's "substantial evidence" test requires the evidentiary showing to be directed to the question of defendant's competency *at the time of trial*; a history of mental disorders, or evidence showing a present disorder which does not bear on defendant's competency to stand trial, is not enough. (*deKaplany*, p. 984 and note 9)

The logic and balance of *deKaplany* were further explained in one of the most recent cases in the Ninth Circuit's series, *United States* v. *Ives* (1978). Ives was indicted for first-degree murder in 1971, was found incompetent to stand trial, and was committed. Nine months later Ives was judged competent and his first trial began. One week later a mistrial was declared on account of Ives's incompetency and he was recommitted. Five months later he was found to have regained his competency, and he began his second trial. Nine days later Ives's attorney, claiming to have new evidence of Ives's incompetency supported by two psychiatrists and a deputy U.S. marshal, moved for another competency evaluation and hearing. The trial judge denied the motion. Ives appealed on the basis of *Pate*. The *Ives* court held that Ives's attorney's belief that Ives was incompetent, coupled with his offer to present "competent proof," constituted grounds for reasonable doubt, and hence the trial court erred. Since Ives's competency had been so variable, the trial judge should have allowed testimony as to Ives's competency. The court noted that "the refusal to accept this evidence under the particular circumstances of this case was clearly outside the standards set by *Drope* and *deKaplany*, which require evaluation of all available pertinent information as a basis for establishing whether doubt of the defendant's competency is sufficient to warrant a hearing" (*Ives*, pp. 1005–6).

It is worth noting, from a procedural viewpoint, that *Ives* distinguishes between grounds for denying a motion for an evaluation (or, equivalently, for putting on some testimony) and grounds for holding a full-blown evidentiary hearing. In federal courts a "proper motion" for a *competency evaluation* may not be denied: "if the motion for a psychiatric examination shows reasonable cause to believe that the accused may be incompetent, then the court is required to award an examination of the accused" (*Rose* v. *United States*, 1975, p. 1255). Unless the motion is made frivolously or without reasonable cause or good faith, the motion must be granted. Similar conclusions are reached in *United States* v. *Nichelson* (1977), where trial court erred in not granting motion despite defense counsel's personal difficulty in consulting with Nichelson; in *United States* v. *Bodey* (1977), where second motion was denied as showing no new evidence to doubt Bodey's competency; and in *United States* v. *Cook* (1964) and *Meador* v. *United States* (1969), where similar results may be found. Thus a trial judge has some latitude in denying a motion to evaluate a defendant's competency, but not much. The purpose of granting the motion is to generate more information for the court. When that information becomes available to the court, it must rise to the *Pate* "reasonable doubt" standard before denial of a hearing constitutes denial of due process (*People* v. *Hays*, 1976, and all *Pate* cases previously cited).

The screening panel procedure, as we propose it (Chapter 7), is designed to assist the trial judge at stages between the granting of a motion to evaluate a defendant and the time when a judicial determination of competency is made. Judges have some discretion in their decision to grant or deny a motion, but continued education of the judiciary is probably the only effective means of addressing the predominant tendency to "overgrant" motions (Roesch and Golding, 1978; *United States* v. *Taylor*, 1971). Screening panels would not have a great deal to contribute at this point; they are more helpful in assisting in the more complex balancing decisions that arise later in the process. The *Pate* standard, as a construct, is different from the *Dusky* standard, but both share important similarities. From an epistemological point of view, they are most similar in their reliance upon context-dependent decision-making. The extreme cases of "substantial doubt" and "capacity to understand and assist" are rather easy to spot; it is on the middle ground, where the signposts are less clear, that the lack of effective interaction between mental health and law takes its largest toll.

The Westbrook-Sieling "Standard"

The legal, psychiatric, and empirical literatures on competency have paid little attention to problem areas whose proportions are only now being realized: competency to plead guilty, to waive right to counsel and defend oneself, and to plea bargain. In a short *per curiam* opinion, *West-*

brook v. Arizona (1965), the Supreme Court ruled that a hearing on a defendant's competency to stand trial did not suffice in determining a defendant's competency to *"waive his constitutional right to the assistance of counsel and . . . to conduct his own defense"* (Westbrook, p. 150, italics added). In Sieling v. Eyman (1973) the Ninth Circuit extended the logic of Westbrook to competency to plead guilty; furthermore, the Sieling logic may be extendable to competency to plea bargain (Note, Duke Law Journal, 1974). The so-called "Sieling" standard, however, is not recognized in the majority of other circuits (see Allard v. Helgemoe, 1978). While the law in this area is considerably less settled or empirically researched, it has important implications for a multidisciplinary conceptualization of incompetency to stand trial, primarily because it begins to refocus the competency issue in terms of its wider manifestation in the criminal justice system. Competency as a construct now begins to subsume not only competency to defend oneself at trial but also competency to participate at a variety of levels of the criminal justice system.

The Westbrook-Sieling logic

In Westbrook the Supreme Court relied upon Johnson v. Zerbst (1938) to the effect that waiver of representation by counsel could be accepted if it was "intelligent and competent." Given the context that Westbrook's competency to stand trial had been evaluated, the Court found that such a waiver needed to be examined in terms of Pate. The Court specified no standard other than "intelligent and competent" and, by implication, Pate's "reasonable doubt." In Boykin v. Alabama (1969), the Supreme Court held that when defendants plead guilty, they waive their constitutional rights against "compulsory self-incrimination," "trial by jury," and "the right to confront one's accusers." Hence it must be "an intentional relinquishment or abandonment of a known right or privilege" (Johnson, p. 464).

In Sieling v. Eyman the Ninth Circuit Court held that "where defendant's lack of mental capacity lurks in the background" (Sieling, p. 214), the standard used to measure trial competency cannot be used to measure competency to waive constitutional rights. Sieling found that a higher standard, such as that suggested by Judge Hufstedler in her dissent in Schoeller v. Dunbar (1970), be adopted: "The standards measuring a defendant's competency to stand trial are not necessarily identical to those defining his competency to enter a plea of guilty. . . . To the extent that they differ, the standards of competency to plead guilty are higher than those of competency to stand trial. A defendant is not competent to plead guilty if mental illness has substantially impaired his ability to make a reasoned choice among the alternatives presented to him and to understand the nature of the consequences of his plea" (*Schoeller*, p. 1194, citation omitted).

It is not clear how this higher standard is to be interpreted functionally, but other courts of appeal have rejected the idea that there could be a class of defendants who are competent to stand trial but not competent to plead guilty. "The majority of the circuits examining the question of what degree of mental competence is necessary to plead guilty have concluded that the standard of incompetence to plead is the same as the standard of incompetence to stand trial" (*Allard* v. *Helgemoe*, 1978, and cases cited therein to the same effect, pp. 3–4). The *Allard* court agrees that the waiver of rights or the entering of a guilty plea needs to be closely examined. It believes, however, that the standard need not be different from *Dusky*, which is, after all, a *functional test*. Naturally, to comprehend the nature of a guilty plea, depending upon the charge, requires different functional knowledge and understanding than normally assisting a defense lawyer. But the standard need not be any different. To "understand and assist" during a trial involves many types of decisions, such as who shall be called to testify, whether or not to testify oneself, whether to accept a plea bargain, etc. Because the consequences of waiving counsel, pleading guilty, or plea bargaining are usually more dramatic (automatic conviction in the latter two cases), it makes all the sense in the world to examine the defendant's competency, but the logic of requiring a higher standard is not persuasive. As has been pointed out, "If *Sieling's* dual standard does have any practical effects, one may be to create a class of semi-competent defendants who are not protected from prosecution because they have been found competent to stand trial, but who are denied the leniency of the plea bargaining process because they are not competent to plead guilty." (Note, *Duke Law Journal*, 1974, p. 170).

The idea of dual standards for plea bargaining has, in fact, generated controversy:

If the prosecutor has some knowledge of the defendant's mental state or his intention to have his competency to plead determined at a hearing, there is no reason for him to spend any time bargaining until the hearing is completed. The individual found incompetent to plead would then be tried without benefit of plea bargaining. If found guilty, unless petitioner would postulate some sort of rule prohibiting judges from imposing the maximum sentence permitted by law on those incompetent to plead, such defendants would simply have their sentences determined by the discretion of the trial judge within the law—a far less reliable guarantee of leniency than a plea bargain would provide. (*Allard*, p. 4)

The hierarchical level of standards does not seem to be an idea that will prevail, nor is it clear that, empirically, one would be able to distinguish the two (or more) "levels of competency." Nevertheless, the *Sieling* controversy has a direct implication for our proposed reform in competency procedures (Chapter 7). We will propose there that defendants who have been found incompetent, and who have not benefited from reasonable treatment over a sufficient period of time, should be allowed a provisional trial. By implication, we would not want to deprive such a defendant of the opportunity to plea bargain, if he or she would also have an opportunity to stand trial in such a limited fashion. Procedurally, a defendant wishing to plea bargain is like a defendant (in our proposed system) who stands trial and is found guilty. The cases differ in that in the case of a trial, a judge's decision as to a defendant's competency is based upon a full set of data, including behavior in the courtroom, functional ability to assist defense counsel, as well as the testimony of mental health professionals. In the plea bargaining situation the data will ordinarily be more limited. We propose, in the spirit of *Sieling* (but not in terms of its standards), that in such a situation an intense evidentiary hearing, including close questioning of the defendant as well as professional (legal and mental health) testimony, be held, since a trial will not occur. Naturally a judge may choose to find a defendant incompetent to plea bargain (plead guilty, even if to a lesser offense); in a parallel fashion a judge may, under our proposal, set aside a defendant's conviction if he is found to have been functionally incompetent.

AMNESIA AND COMPETENCY

Can defendants who cannot recall the circumstances of their case, communicate facts or other information to their attorneys, or challenge witnesses and other evidence against them, be found competent to stand trial? In the past many courts have answered in the affirmative (*Commonwealth v. Price*, 1966; *United States v. Sermon*, 1964; Bennett, 1968; Note, *Yale Law Journal*, 1961), arguing that defendants who have amnesia may be required to stand trial, especially in cases of permanent amnesia in which the loss of memory is not crucial to the defense strategy. Halpern (1975) suggested that this practice reveals the absurdity of the competency laws, since it would appear that amnesia cases truly meet the criteria specified in *Dusky*. The decisions seem to be based on the notion that the circumscribed loss of memory, without an accompanying proof of its effect on the defense, is an insufficient basis for a ruling of incompetency (*Hansford v. United States*, 1966; *United States v. Sermon*, 1964). The *Sermon* court addressed the issue directly: "We think it must also be added that the primary assistance that must be rendered counsel is a full revelation of the defendant in areas which are in legitimate dispute. Inability to recall the ages of one's children or their grade in school, unless such facts are relevant and disputed, does not necessarily prevent a defendant from assisting in his own defense" (p. 978).

It has been suggested that a distinction should be made between permanent and temporary amnesia (Koson and Robey, 1973). A finding of temporary amnesia may justify a finding of incompetency and a limited treatment period. This would seem an appropriate action for temporary cases, but what of those who do not respond to treatment or who have permanent amnesia? Is there not a clear contradiction in allowing the trial of defendants who clearly do not meet the *Dusky* criteria? A recent Massachusetts case (*Massachusetts v. Lombardi*, 1979) held that permanent amnesia, in which a defendant was unable to recall circumstances surrounding the alleged offense, may prevent a fair trial. But rather than a finding of incompetency, the court concluded that such amnesia may merit the dropping of charges.

A 1968 U.S. Court of Appeals decision suggested a more functional approach to resolving this issue. In *Wilson v. United States* (1968) the court affirmed Wilson's conviction but required that the case be remanded for more extensive posttrial findings on the issue of whether Wilson's memory loss deprived him of a fair trial and effective assistance of counsel. Wilson had been tried and convicted of five counts of assault with a pistol and robbery. The testimony revealed that Wilson and another suspect

stole the victim's car after robbing him at gunpoint and were later involved in a high-speed chase by police. During the chase the suspects' car
ran off the road and struck a tree. Wilson fractured his skull, ruptured
several blood vessels in his brain, and remained unconscious for three
weeks. Testimony further revealed that he could not at present, and almost certainly never would, remember anything that happened from the
afternoon of the robberies until three weeks later. The lower court (*United
States* v. *Wilson*, 1966), in finding Wilson competent, said:

> This Court holds that amnesia per se in a case where recollection was
> present during the time of the alleged offenses and where defendant has
> the ability to construct a knowledge of what happened from other sources
> and where he has the present ability to follow the course of the proceed-
> ings against him and discuss them rationally with his attorney does not
> constitute incompetency per se, and that a loss of memory should bar
> prosecution only when its presence would in fact be crucial to the con-
> struction and presentation of a defense and hence essential to the fairness
> and accuracy of the proceedings.
>
> The rule to be applied in this case is whether insufficient information
> concerning the events at the time of the commission of the crime and
> evidence relating thereto is available to the defense so that it can be said
> that the presence of such an amnesia as we have here precipitates a situa-
> tion in which defendant's memory is indeed a faculty crucial to the con-
> struction and presentation of his defense. (Pp. 533–34)

The Court of Appeals essentially agreed with this ruling but added that
the trial judge must determine whether the defendant had been able to
perform the functions described in the above quote. Six factors were suggested to aid in this decision:

(1) The extent to which the amnesia affected the defendant's ability to
consult with and assist his lawyer.
(2) The extent to which the amnesia affected the defendant's ability to
testify in his own behalf.
(3) The extent to which the evidence in suit could be extrinsically recon-
structed in view of the defendant's amnesia. Such evidence would include
evidence relating to the crime itself as well as any reasonably possible
alibi.
(4) The extent to which the Government assisted the defendant and his
counsel in that reconstruction.
(5) The strength of the prosecution's case. Most important here will be
whether the Government's case is such as to negate all reasonable hypotheses of innocence. If there is any substantial possibility that the ac-

cused could, but for his amnesia, establish an alibi or other defense, it should be presumed that he would have been able to do so.
(6) Any other facts and circumstances which would indicate whether or not the defendant had a fair trial. (*Wilson* v. *United States*, 1968, pp. 463–64)

The Court of Appeals also held that the trial judge should, before imposing sentence, make detailed written findings concerning the effect of the amnesia on the fairness of the trial. If the trial court finds that the conviction should not stand because of unfairness of the trial caused by amnesia, the conviction should be vacated. The government would have an opportunity to retry the case, but if it could not overcome the unfairness that voided the first conviction, the indictment would be dismissed.

The *Wilson* case has implications which may well go beyond the narrow issue of amnesia. The decision calls for an approach that allows for a functional assessment of a defendant's abilities or lack thereof in an actual trial, as they relate to the effects of amnesia. At times this may involve the actual trial of a possibly incompetent defendant, followed by a post-trial assessment of whether the trial was "fair." We will argue later in the book that this functional approach makes a good deal of sense for *all* defendants who may be incompetent to stand trial.

DRUG-INDUCED COMPETENCY

The use of prescribed and nonprescribed drugs during the evaluation, treatment, and trial of defendants whose competency has been questioned has created a number of legal and ethical concerns. These concerns are perhaps best illustrated by the case of James Murphy (*State* v. *Murphy*, 1960). Murphy, who was charged with murder, was given tranquilizers by jail personnel shortly before he was to take the witness stand to testify in his own behalf. His behavior on the stand, in which he related the circumstances of the crime in what was described as a casual, cool, and lackadaisical manner, was in marked contrast to earlier behavior. His attorney described him as usually being very anxious and distraught while talking about the crime. The Supreme Court of Washington ruled that a new trial should be granted, based on the possibility that the jury might not have recommended the death penalty if Murphy had behaved differently on the witness stand. The court was careful to add that this decision does not call for a new trial in every case in which the defendant's demeanor might influence the jury but, rather, that each case should be decided on its own merits.

Murphy's case is an example of problems created by the presence of medications during a trial.[14] The most serious problem of drugs as they relate to competency is that some defendants may be competent only if they continue to take medication, and failure to maintain effective dosage levels may result in a rapid change in the defendant's state. During an evaluation for competency some defendants receive medication. Defendants being treated to restore competency also commonly take medication. Data from our own study of the North Carolina system showed that 75% of the incompetent defendants were taking medication during the last four months of hospitalization, all but six of whom were on some form of antipsychotic medication (see Chapter 6). Upon discharge and return to court as competent, 37% were instructed to continue taking medication. Medication was used less frequently for competent defendants. In fact, only 16% were taking medication while in the hospital, while only 11% were to continue taking medication after discharge.

When these defendants are returned to jail or are on bail while awaiting trial, there is often little supervision to ensure that the defendants continue taking the prescribed medication. If medication is not properly maintained, some defendants may not be competent when the trial begins. This potential problem is illustrated in *Whitehead* v. *Wainwright* (1978). Whitehead, who was incarcerated in a county jail during his trial, did not receive his usual prescribed medication on the evening of the first day of trial and the morning of the second day. At the trial he was described as being nervous, and the court granted a recess to allow him to be examined and treated. He was given several types of medications, including a tranquilizer and an antihistamine, at a county hospital and returned to jail, whereupon he also received his regular midday medication. He returned to court that afternoon and was described as appearing listless and drowsy and, in fact, fell asleep at the defense table at one point. The trial contined despite several requests by the defendant to be excused from the court. He reported that he remembered being found guilty but could not remember having made statements attributed to him in the transcript.

The district court held that the evidence demonstrated Whitehead was incompetent to stand trial during that particular afternoon, and ordered a new trial.

This possibility apparently led Smith (1966) to suggest the establishment of a policy for the trial of defendants whose competency is chemically induced: "These drugs are effective in improving the mental condition of many cases so that while receiving the drugs they may be regarded as competent. However, not infrequently such a patient will relapse if the medication is discontinued. Because of the problems involved in handling such cases in a trial proceeding, we believe that it is undesirable to return them for further hearing so long as they require tranquilizing drugs, a position which some courts have supported" (p. 27).

The Committee on Psychiatry and Law (1974) of the Group for the Advancement of Psychiatry was sharply critical of Smith's statement, arguing that "the position taken by Dr. Smith would certainly be unconscionable if it were the policy followed by psychiatrists in the disposition of other patients suffering from mental illness. If no patient could be returned to society unless free of medication, the major revolution in psychiatric treatment accomplished by psychoactive medication would be virtually worthless" (p. 902).

The committee's position that competency maintained by the use of drugs should be allowable is generally in agreement with court decisions (*People* v. *Dalfonso*, 1974; *State* v. *Hampton*, 1969; *State* v. *Plaisance*, 1968; *State* v. *Rand*, 1969), although it is by no means universally allowed. Winick (1977) found in a 1976 survey that the trial of a defendant while on medication is automatically barred by some courts in at least 13 states. Winick argued that the automatic-bar rule cannot be defended because of advances in psychopharmacology and a fair appraisal of the effects of drugs. He believes that the courts' objection may have been due to a misunderstanding that one of the effects of antipsychotic drugs, or major tranquilizers as they are often called, was a sedative-hypnotic state. Winick suggested that the courts may believe that this would result in a lower level of participation of the defendant.

Winick (1977) provides a compelling argument that the failure to provide potentially beneficial medication or the automatic bar of the trial of medicated defendants may be a violation of the equal-protection clause of

the Fourteenth Amendment and the right to a speedy trial as specified by
the Sixth Amendment. While many drugs do have negative side effects,
it should not be assumed that all drugs cause disabling side effects and
should automatically be barred. The courts should ensure that any effects
do not interfere with a defendant's competency. As Haddox, Gross, and
Pollack (1974) suggested, the courts should be concerned with the *effects*
of the use or nonuse of drugs, not simply with the mere *fact* of their use or
nonuse. The Committee on Psychiatry and Law (1974) recommended
that the court should be informed of the type and dosage of medication
and the possible effects on a defendant's behavior. At the discretion of the
defense and the judge, the jury could also be informed. The main concern
should be the effect that medication has on behavior, which, of course,
must be decided on an individual case basis.

In summary, the trend in most states, as well as the compelling arguments offered by such legal commentators as Winick (1977), clearly
points to the legal and pragmatic propriety of allowing trials of medicated
but competent defendants. This, of course, does not apply to defendants
who deliberately induce incompetency by taking or failing to take certain
medications, such as insulin (see *People* v. *Rogers*, 1957).

A particularly troublesome aspect of drug-induced competency has to
do with defendants who refuse to take psychiatric medication, even if
there is a reasonable assurance that they would be competent if medicated. Court decisions in this respect have been conflicting. In *State* v.
Maryott (1971) the court held that forced administration of medication
was a denial of due process. The Appeals Court cited expert testimony
which suggested that the dosages administered would have an effect on
the defendant's thoughts and behavior during the trial. The court ordered
a new trial because of the possible negative effect that his behavior may
have had on the original trial outcome. But the court was careful to add
that it found no error in the lower court's finding that defendant was
competent to stand trial, and thus the decision only applies to the issue of
medication without defendant's consent. Winick (1977) has cited some
cases which suggest that forced compliance would be appropriate. In fact,
he suggests that "the state has its own interests in the accuracy, dignity,
and apparent fairness of the criminal process—compelling state interests
that might be jeopardized by the trial of a defendant deprived of competence by his decision to discontinue drugs. Thus, should the state choose

to assert its own interests, the defendant's offer to waive his rights need not be accepted" (p. 814).

Thus the right of the state to force compliance is not clear, although a strong case can be made in favor of Winick's position, simply because it is in the state's interest to bring the matter to trial if at all possible. Winick offers a potential solution to the dilemma of state versus individual rights. He suggests that the court should allow a defendant who so requests to remain off drugs for a trial period, during which time less intrusive therapies could be provided. If this fails, then the court could authorize the use of medication.

Notes

1. The case of Lang, a deaf-mute accused of two separate murders, is discussed in detail in Chapter 7. Lang's case is particularly troublesome because it raises the problem of deciding upon a proper disposition for someone who is unlikely ever to regain competency.

2. See *Youtsey* v. *United States* (1899) for a scholarly review and a remarkably "modern" judgment in these matters.

3. While most states paraphrase the *Dusky* standard, other states (Maine, Massachusetts, and New Hampshire) give no definition of the standard for incompetency. Furthermore, state statutes differ in terms of their linkage of incompetency to mental illness. Fourteen states (Alaska, Connecticut, Delaware, Florida, Illinois, Indiana, Maryland, Mississippi, Pennsylvania, Rhode Island, South Dakota, Texas, Washington, and West Virginia) do not equate incompetency with mental illness, while the remaining use a form of "incompetent as a result of mental illness or defect."

4. This implies that not only future research in the competency area (see Chapter 7) but also the very assessment techniques employed by the courts and their agents must mirror the steps involved in the establishment of "construct validity." Briefly, this means that multiple sources of consistent and converging evidence must be sought to assert a defendant's incompetency. Thus incompetency could not be equated with amnesia *per se*, or a particular conclusory statement, or a low score on a particular test. Furthermore, given the *functional nature* of the construct of competency, the "facts to be sought" will be highly dependent upon the particular case.

5. The other Supreme Court cases in this area (*Drope* v. *Missouri*, 1975, and *Pate* v. *Robinson*, 1966) elaborate other aspects of competency but do not clarify or explain further any aspect of the *Dusky* standard itself. The *Drope* court concludes its relevant section thus: "we have approved a test of incompetence which

seeks to ascertain whether a criminal defendant 'has sufficient present ability to consult with his lawyer with a reasonable degree of rational understanding—and whether he has a rational as well as factual understanding of the proceedings against him' *Dusky* v. *United States*, 362 U.S. at 402" (*Drope*, p. 161). *Pate* is discussed subsequently in this chapter.

6. Two decisions from the District of Columbia Court of Appeals mirror the current developments in the standard for responsibility and the problem of expert dominance in decision-making (see also Chapter 4). In *Durham* v. *United States* (1954) Judge David Bazelon held that a defendant was not criminally responsible if the act was a *product* of mental disease or defect. Bazelon (1974) noted that the *Durham* decision was intended to allow psychiatrists to testify on clinical impressions and not be forced, as they were under the M'Naughten rule, to testify on their conclusions about a defendant's responsibility. The final determination of responsibility, it was argued, should be left to the court to decide. However, as Bazelon (1974) commented, psychiatrists continued to testify in conclusory terms. In response to this practice and after a series of attempts to save the *Durham* rule (Bazelon, 1975; Brooks, 1974), the District of Columbia Court of Appeals set aside the *Durham* decision in *United States* v. *Brawner* (1972), which held that a person was not responsible if the act was a *result* of a mental illness or defect. Thus the word "result" was substituted for "product." Bazelon (1974) acknowledged that this change in wording did not affect the problem of expert dominance. In a more recent statement Bazelon (1975) concludes, "I am just about convinced that no form of words will produce the information necessary for a proper consideration of the issue of responsibility" (p. 184).

7. See Goldstein (1967), Livermore and Meehl (1967), Monahan (1973), and Morris (1975), for more complete discussions of the insanity defense issues.

8. See note 3, this chapter.

9. One hastens to add that such testimony would be helpful only under the assumption that it is potentially rebuttable by contrary fact, and not based upon dogmatic assertion and conclusory jargon. See Chapter 4 for more on this aspect of testimony.

10. One conceptual reason why McGarry's Competency Screening Test and Competency Assessment Instrument are problematic is, as Brakel (1974) and we (Chapter 3) point out, that they partially equate competency with belief in the fairness and justice of the criminal system.

11. It is for this reason that we recommend, in Chapter 7, that such motions detail the behaviors that the defendant is alleged to have exhibited, and how these might relate to his/her inability to "understand and assist."

12. The "battle of the experts" as exemplified in the *deKaplany* case clearly points to the assessment and decision-making problems we elaborate upon in Chapter 4. The fact that experts can disagree so markedly about the same case suggests that the assessment and decision models are not sufficiently specified or uniform to allow reliable (and valid) decisions.

13. While some might argue, quite rightly, that there is an almost imperceptible line between "open texture" and "constitutional vagueness" when matters are pushed to an extreme, we feel that accusation would be unfair in this case. The precedent of an equation between a psychiatric conclusion and a *Pate*-level doubt would be disastrous.

14. See especially *Hansford* v. *United States* (1966), where Hansford's self-induced narcotic sedation rendered him incompetent; see also *Hayes* v. *United States* (1962).

3

Competency Research

There have been few empirical studies of the process of competency determination or of the characteristics of competent and/or incompetent defendants. Most have been purely descriptive (e.g., psychiatric diagnosis, the number of defendants found incompetent, or the type of offense), while a very few have attempted to provide comparative data by contrasting groups of evaluated and nonevaluated defendants. In this chapter we will review all studies providing any statistical information on defendants evaluated for competency. The following areas will be considered: admission rates for evaluation and/or treatment; base rates of incompetency determinations; relationship between psychiatric diagnosis, type of offense, and competency status; court agreement with evaluation recommendations; and court outcome. In the last part of the chapter we will review the available data on the reliability and validity of several measures which have been developed to assess competency.

ADMISSION RATES FOR EVALUATION AND/OR TREATMENT

Scheidemandel and Kanno (1969) published the results of a national survey of hospitals which treated criminal offenders. In 1967 50 primary hospitals (primary facility within a state for treating offenders) reported that, of 11,209 admissions, 38% were for competency evaluations; defendants committed following a determination of incompetency accounted for an additional 14%. Thus commitments for evaluation and/or treatment accounted for over one-half of the total admissions in the offender category. These 50 hospitals admitted over 5,800 of these defendants in 1967 alone.

A statistical note published by the Department of Health, Education, and Welfare (1974) provides more recent information. The results are based on a stratified random sample of state and county mental hospitals that provided data on the legal status of admissions during 1972. Projections from these data indicate that there were 403,924 admissions to state and county mental hospitals throughout the country. The incompetent-to-stand-trial category, which included evaluations for competency and commitment of incompetent defendants, accounted for a total of 9,261 admissions (2.3%). Only 5% of these admissions were female.

Goldstein (1973) presents data which show that in New York City the number of competency evaluations rose from 601 in 1967–68 to 1,085 in 1969–70. Joost and McGarry (1974) provide data on changes in the number of competency evaluation commitments in Massachusetts. In 1959 there were 1,054 such admissions, a figure which rose to 1,888 in 1971. However, this figure dropped to 944 in 1972, owing to some changes in the mental health laws which allowed for noninstitutional evaluations of competency. A similar change occurred in Tennessee, where Laben and her colleagues (1977) developed a community-based evaluation procedure as an alternative to institutional evaluations.

In summary, while available data are scarce, studies of admission rates suggest that the use of competency evaluations has been steadily increasing throughout the country, with few exceptions. In light of the results of our research (Chapter 6), this increase, representing a substantial cost in terms of hospital expenditures and professional time, may be unnecessary. As we will suggest subsequently, there are several procedural changes which could reduce both the number and the cost of competency evaluations.

BASE RATES OF INCOMPETENCY DETERMINATIONS

How many defendants referred for competency evaluations are actually found to be incompetent? A review of ten studies[1] reporting data on this issue revealed that the percentage found incompetent is usually quite small (Table 3.1), less than 50%; it averages 30% across all ten studies. That is, only one of three referred for competency evaluations is found incompetent.

TABLE 3.1

Percentage of Evaluated Defendants Found Incompetent

Source	Total Evaluated	Total Found Incompetent	Percent Found Incompetent
Bendt, Balcanoff, and Tragellis (1973)	1,888	76	4.0
Fitzgerald, Peszke, and Goodwin (1978)	174	66	38.0
Gold (1973)	455	350	77.0
Goldstein (1973)	1,085	276	25.4
Laczko, James, and Alltop (1970)	435	104	23.9
McGarry et al. (1973)	163[a]	36	22.2
	501[b]	6	1.2
Pfeiffer, Eisenstein, and Dabbs (1967)	85	30	35.0
Roesch and Golding (1977)	151	11	7.0
Sussman et al. (1975)	1,512	219	14.0
Vann (1965)	83	42	51.0

[a]Based on 1963 data.
[b]Based on 1971 data.

While the average percentage is quite low, there is considerable variation in the ten studies. There are several possible explanations for this variation. State laws regarding criteria for a determination of incompetency vary somewhat (see Chapter 5), as do the attitudes of both court and mental health personnel. Some courts and psychiatrists, for instance, are quite reluctant to find a defendant incompetent. Other courts or psychiatrists may view a determination of incompetency as an appropriate or satisfactory disposition of a case. For example, Gold (1973) has presented arguments heavily in favor of psychiatric intervention in legal dispositions. He states that "when a mentally disabled person, particularly one of the paranoid category, has committed a crime (and some have been horrendous), the paramount consideration is to recognize and treat his condition; and the best place to do this is in a hospital" (p. 127). Gold's (1973) study of competency evaluations conducted in Connecticut reflects this treatment-oriented view. Of 455 referrals, only 105 (23%) were returned to trial. Nearly one-half were committed as incompetent, and the rest were referred to psychiatric clinics or other social agencies.

The impact of changes in state laws is dramatically illustrated by data from McGarry *et al.* (1973). They reported that, of 163 evaluations conducted at Bridgewater Hospital in Massachusetts, 36 defendants (22.2%) were found incompetent. In fiscal year 1971 the number of evaluations had increased to 501, but, as a result of changes in both the evaluation and commitment procedures, only six (1.2%) were found to be incompetent.

Administrative changes in evaluation units may also have an effect. In a study conducted on the forensic unit at Dorothea Dix Hospital (Laczko, James, and Alltop, 1970), all admissions for evaluation between 1958 and 1964 were reviewed. Evaluations of 435 defendants resulted in incompetent determinations for 104 (23.9%) cases. But our own research (Chapter 6) showed that under a different director the percentage of defendants found incompetent was only 7% in 1976.

One reason for the overall low rate of defendants found incompetent is that many defendants are referred for competency evaluations for reasons not related to a concern about competency. Slovenko (1971, 1977) suggests that prosecutors or judges may use the evaluation commitment as a method for denying bail or providing preventive or long-term detention (Golten, 1972; Kaufman, 1972; McGarry, 1969; *Marcey v. Harris*, 1968; Stone, 1976), while defense attorneys may use the competency procedures in an attempt to avoid capital punishment or lengthy sentences, as a tactical maneuver to delay a trial, or to provide a basis for arguing for a reduction in charges or sentence (Chernoff and Schaffer, 1972; Cook, Johnston, and Pogany, 1973; Lewin, 1969). One of our studies (Roesch and Golding, 1978; see Chapter 6) provides additional support for the latter contention. We found that attorneys sometimes requested evaluations not because they were concerned about their defendants' competency but because they wanted to obtain recommendations for treatment and/or alternatives to prison. Obviously these recommendations could be extremely useful in plea bargaining or at sentencing, but it is improper to use the competency laws to obtain them.

Rosenberg and McGarry (1972) suggest that many attorneys simply do not know what competency means. Of the 28 attorneys they interviewed, ten had no knowledge at all of the legal criteria which should be the basis of requests for evaluations. We found support for this view in our study (see Study Four in Chapter 6) of 111 attorneys who had clients evaluated for competency. Reasons for requesting the evaluation often had little relationship to the legal criteria. For example, some attorneys referred their clients simply because of prior psychiatric treatment. Some admitted that they wanted an evaluation because of the seriousness of the charges, while others did so because the defendant's family requested it. Obviously these reasons should not be a basis for an evaluation but do help explain why most evaluated defendants are found competent to stand trial.

Differences between evaluators is another issue raised by these studies. This may be largely due to the lack of clear guidelines for evaluating competency. Many evaluators misunderstand the distinction between competency and responsibility. As we discussed in Chapter 2, the issue of responsibility refers to the defendant's mental state at the time of the alleged crime and is used as a trial defense, while competency refers primarily to the ability of the defendant to assist in the preparation of his defense. Unfortunately, these standards are sometimes confused and may lead to the evaluation of competency in terms of presence or absence of psychosis. For example, McGarry (1965), in his study of the Massachusetts procedure, found that, of the 106 defendants evaluated for competency, 31 received diagnoses of psychosis. Each of these were "declared to be in need of hospitalization, not criminally responsible and inferentially incompetent to stand trial" (p. 625). Conversely, the remaining defendants not receiving diagnoses of psychosis were found to be competent. McGarry (1965) concluded that the psychiatrists uniformly viewed psychotics as "incompetent to stand trial and criminally irresponsible, reflecting an exclusively medical frame of reference" (p. 629). Ennis (1972) also suggests that the prevailing psychiatric interpretation of incompetency is the presence of psychosis. In one case cited the examining psychiatrist concluded that the defendant was incompetent to stand trial and remarked that "all paranoid schizophrenics are not mentally competent to stand trial" (p. 24).

Since psychosis appears to be frequently thought of as nearly synonymous with incompetency, it is not surprising that studies which have looked at personality test differences between competent and incompetent defendants have found that incompetent defendants, on measures such as the Minnesota Multiphasic Personality Inventory (MMPI), receive scores indicating significantly more pathology (Cooke, 1969; Maxson and Neuringer, 1970). It has even been suggested (Maxson and Neuringer, 1970) that the MMPI could be used in place of more extensive evaluations. It is our view that this would be an unfortunate practice because it would perpetuate the incorrect conclusion that defendants who are psychotic are also incompetent to stand trial.

The orders for evaluation of competency issued by the courts also reflect a confusion between the competency and responsibility standards. Often a court order may in fact request *both* a competency and a responsibility evaluation simultaneously, even though the defendant is committed under a statute providing only for the evaluation of competency. For example, a North Carolina court order committing one defendant for evaluation under G.S. 15A-1001 contained the following statement: "It appears that it is necessary that an examination of the defendant be made to determine his capacity to proceed and to determine whether or not he was and is in condition to know the difference between right and wrong and to understand the probable consequences of his act."

It is not surprising, then, that psychiatrists frequently evaluate both issues simultaneously and interchangeably. Pfeiffer, Eisenstein, and Dabbs (1967) found in a study of 89 competency evaluations that in only 21 instances (24%) did the examining psychiatrist *not* offer an opinion about responsibility at the time of the alleged crime, regardless of whether this was requested by the court. Hess and Thomas (1963), in a study of competency evaluations at the Ionia (Michigan) State Hospital, found a consistent confusion of the two issues in diagnostic reports. They found that parts of the same report would refer to competency and other parts to standards of responsibility.[2]

In summary, most defendants referred for competency evaluations are found competent. There is considerable variation in the rate of incompetency determinations across studies. Two reasons for this overuse of incompetency evaluations are the facts that many defendants are inappropriately referred, and that confusion exists about the proper criteria necessary for a determination of incompetency.

PSYCHIATRIC DIAGNOSIS

Several studies, including our own (see Chapter 6), have found that not only are most referred defendants found competent but they also receive nonpsychotic labels (Cooke, 1969; Cooke, Pogany, and Johnston, 1974; Maxson and Neuringer, 1970). But it is the relationship between diagnosis and a finding of incompetency that is most interesting. As we have already noted, McGarry (1965) first reported data that showed a strong relationship between a diagnosis of psychosis and a determination of incompetency. This finding has been supported by Cooke (1969) and our own research. In our North Carolina study we found a highly significant difference in the diagnostic labels assigned to competent and incompetent defendants. The former usually received a label of "without psychosis" while the latter almost uniformly received labels of psychosis or, in a smaller number of cases, mental retardation.

As with a good deal of the research on competency, this relationship should be considered tentatively supported because very few studies have reported usable data. In fact, at least one study (Pfeiffer, Eisenstein, and Dabbs, 1967) reported that while the relationship between psychosis and incompetency was often found, there were also many cases in which a psychotic defendant was found competent. Nearly one-fourth of those given a diagnosis of a psychotic disorder were found competent. In our own research on diagnosis (Chapter 6) we found a much lower rate of psychotics being found competent, in that only about 10% of the competent group had a psychotic label.

TYPE OF OFFENSE

Several studies have looked at the relationship between type of offense and referral for competency evaluations. Steadman and Braff (1975) compared the distribution of 541 male felony defendants found incompetent with the distribution of all felony arrests in New York. They found that violent crimes against persons were highly overrepresented in the incompetent population. For example, the base rate for murder in New York in 1971 was eight out of every 1,000 arrests, compared with 144 of every 1,000 incompetent felony defendants accused of murder. Similar discrepancies were found for arson and rape. Such charges as burglary and grand larceny approximated the total arrest distribution. On the other hand, such crimes as forgery, drug offenses, and gambling were consistently underrepresented. Steadman and Braff (1975) suggest two explanations for this result. The first is that violent crime is linked to mental illness.[3] Based on a review of studies which demonstrate that the incidence of mental illness of convicted felons is not higher than the general population rates, Steadman and Braff reject this interpretation.[4] They believe their second interpretation is more consistent with the data. They suggest that the use of competency evaluations is frequently a defense or prosecution maneuver used for serious offenses and conclude that "the use of incompetency as a diversion from the criminal justice system greatly depends on nonmedical, dispositional, and procedural machinations" (p. 77).

Only one other study compared the offenses of evaluation referrals with the arrest rates for the state. Cooke, Johnston, and Pogany (1973) reported on 326 defendants referred for competency evaluations in Michigan. Most referrals were for homicide and assault. Robbery was fifth in terms of raw frequency. Comparison with the total arrest rates reveals a discrepancy similar to the one reported by Steadman and Braff (1975). Homicide accounted for only 1% of the total arrests, but almost 22% of the competency referrals were charged with homicide. Cooke, Johnston, and Pogany (1973) conclude that these data support the contention that competency evaluations are frequently misused as part of a defense strategy.

Balcanoff and McGarry's (1969) study using data collected in Massachusetts showed that most referrals for evaluation were charged with serious property crimes, with murder and armed robbery ranking second and third respectively. Laczko, James, and Alltop (1970) reported that the majority of their sample had been charged with larceny, with murder and assault being the next most frequent charges. Hess and Thomas (1963) found that "crimes associated with incompetency proceedings were most often those that were especially heinous or revolting such as bizarre murders and sexual offenses, or crimes which were clearly pointless such as repetitively minor offenses without hope of material gain" (p. 714).

In summary, the studies reviewed here suggest that a disproportionate number of defendants charged with extremely serious crimes are referred for competency evaluations. The conclusion of Steadman and Braff

(1975) that competency procedures are frequently used as tactical maneuvers, especially when the charges and consequences are severe, is in accord with our analyses of the legal profession's use of competency.

COURT AGREEMENT WITH EVALUATION RECOMMENDATIONS

The assumption that the court almost uniformly agrees with the evaluation recommendations has some support in the literature, but few empirical data exist. McGarry (1965) followed up 31 defendants who received recommendations for further hospitalization. It is interesting to note that these defendants never left the hospital; hearings were held without the defendants present. The court used only the hospital report to arrive at a decision. Two defendants escaped from the hospital before a disposition had been reached. Twenty-seven of the remaining 29 defendants were committed indefinitely, with charges pending. Thus the rate of agreement was 93%. Vann (1965) found unanimous court agreement when the recommendation was "competent to proceed." Unfortunately, the follow-up of incompetent defendants was incomplete. Data on many of these defendants were unavailable. Pfeiffer, Eisenstein, and Dabbs (1967) also reported unanimous court agreement for defendants who received recommendations of competent. Defendants who received incompetent recommendations from the evaluations were rarely tried. Thirty-four defendants received such recommendations, and only three were tried. This is a rate of agreement of approximately 88% for recommendations of incompetency. Most of the defendants not tried were committed to a psychiatric hospital or federal prison hospital.

Our experience in North Carolina supports the above studies. We found that when there was disagreement, it was usually because of a recommendation by forensic personnel that a defendant was competent. The courts sometimes rejected these recommendations because, forensic personnel believed, the judge or prosecutor did not want to try the case but also did not want the defendant released. The commitment of an incompetent defendant thus sometimes served as a convenient method for dealing with a particularly troublesome case. We do not know the validity of this assumption but suspect that there may be some truth to it. We also found that the forensic unit attempted to return some incompetent defendants to court following a period of treatment. The court sometimes rejected these defendants, despite protests by forensic staff that the defendants had been restored to competency. Again, this may suggest that other factors influenced the decision.

The above studies and our experience in North Carolina suggest that the courts typically follow the recommendations of the evaluators. This would not necessarily be a problem were it not for the evidence that suggests that evaluators may be making erroneous assumptions about the criteria for a determination of competency. Our work in this area clearly suggests the concern that the criteria for competency are unclear in the minds of mental health professionals and that competency is often confused with psychosis (or other severe mental disorders) or with responsibility. As we will discuss at more length later in the book, given the misunderstandings and confusion that exist, it is all the more important that the court assume a stronger role in ensuring that the recommendation is based on an appropriate definition of competency. This requires that reports to the court or testimony be communicated in such a way that the link between observed behaviors and inferences about competency or incompetency is valid. We will discuss this issue in considerably more detail later in the book.

COURT OUTCOME

One important aspect of the competency procedure is the effect that an evaluation of competency has on the legal disposition of the charges. Competent defendants are usually immediately returned to court, and presumably the fact that they have simply been evaluated for competency should not have a substantial effect on their court outcome. Defendants initially found incompetent are, of course, considered to be competent when they are returned for trial, but have spent varying lengths of time being treated. Again, having been found initially incompetent should not have an effect on the court outcome, although the length of treatment may have an effect on the type and length of sentence. There have been a few studies which have looked at this issue.

Four studies obtained data on the disposition of initially incompetent defendants, but unfortunately these studies do not provide any comparison groups or comparative data. Thus we do not know what would have happened to a similar group of defendants who were not evaluated or who were not found incompetent. Nevertheless, these studies provide data leading to some useful insights. McGarry (1971) obtained court follow-up data on 71 defendants previously found incompetent. These defendants had been hospitalized an average of 4.3 years (the median was about two years because of a few defendants with extraordinary commitment lengths). Charges were dismissed against 24 defendants; 14 were found not guilty by reason of insanity. Thirty-three defendants were found guilty, but only 14 defendants were sentenced to prison. A study conducted by the New York City Bar Association (1968) determined the disposition of 235 cases returned to court in 1964. Only 21 (8.9%) had their charges dismissed. Most entered a guilty plea (67% of the cases), usually to a reduced charge. Twelve defendants were recommitted as unfit to stand trial. The authors noted that many of those convicted were sentenced to time already spent in the hospital. Another New York study, summarized by Steadman and Braff (1974), followed up 19 incompetent felony defendants and found that 74% had their indictments dismissed. Vann (1965), following his review of 83 defendants evaluated for competency (approximately one-half had been found incompetent), concluded that "in a majority of cases the court has allowed confinement to a criminal mental hospital to serve as compensation for a prison sentence" (p. 31).

In a study similar to the ones described above, Geller and Lister (1978) followed up 83 cases which had been committed to Worcester State Hospital. Most of the cases had been immediately returned to court, with only ten remaining more than 60 days. Despite this quick return to the courts, Geller and Lister found that 72% of the cases were dismissed. Most of the defendants in the study were charged with misdemeanors. In fact, 30% of the defendants were charged with "disturbing the peace."

One issue raised by the Geller and Lister study is that the competency procedures are currently used to a greater extent than in the past because of changes in the civil commitment laws. As a number of states have made civil commitment more difficult, the legal system may be using the competency laws as a convenient method for getting treatment for persons whom the courts or other legal personnel consider to be in need. Stone (1978), in his comments on the Geller and Lister (1978) article, suggested that "when police learn that bizarre persons not imminently dangerous will not be involuntarily confined in the mental health system, they press criminal charges instead, which forces the judiciary to find still more dispositions like competency" (p. 62).

This use of competency procedures would at least partially explain why charges are ultimately dismissed against many such defendants. Stone (1978) holds that the misuse of the competency procedures by the judiciary accounts for the finding that 72% of the cases were dismissed. By using this procedure, the court can prevent bail and force a defendant to receive some treatment. When such defendants are finally returned to court, the charges are dismissed because the court's purpose has been served.

Two studies used comparison groups of nonevaluated defendants in order to more accurately determine the disposition effects. Vann (1965) compared a group of 14 defendants evaluated and found capable of standing trial with a group of 28 defendants adjudged guilty but never evaluated for competency. Defendants in each group were charged and convicted of either grand larceny or assault. Thus the only variable controlled for was type of offense. Vann (1965) acknowledges that the evaluation sample had a larger percentage of blacks. Also, data on age and type of counsel were not available. These three variables undoubtedly would have some influence on sentencing outcome. Prior record was available, but Vann (1965) does not indicate whether the two groups were comparable on this variable. Another problem with this design is that only defendants found guilty were included in both groups. Such a design does not permit an evaluation of the issue of a differential conviction rate. Vann (1965) concluded that evaluated defendants generally received harsher sentences.

The only other study which addresses this issue was done by Steadman and Braff (1974). They compared 88 felony defendants who were found incompetent and returned to the court after spending an unspecified period of time (up to one year) in a mental hospital, with a randomly selected group of 88 felony defendants not evaluated for competency. One major difference between the two groups was the type of charge. While 78% of the incompetent group were charged with crimes actually or potentially against persons (murder, manslaughter, assault, rape, robbery, burglary), only 49% of the comparison group were so charged. No information was available on age, race, prior record, or type of counsel. Thus it is not known whether this comparison group would be an appropriate one to use to look at differences between the two groups. Keeping this in mind, we will briefly summarize their results. In a recent book on these data, Steadman (1979) reported on the court outcome of 82 of the initially incompetent group and 70 defendants in the nonevaluated criminal group. He found that 73% of the incompetent group was found guilty, compared with 50% of the comparison group. Only six (7%) incompetent defendants were acquitted or had their charges dismissed, compared with 20% of the comparison group. The differences in conviction rates were significant, but this may well be attributed to the fact that the incompetent defendants were charged with more serious crimes, with the prosecution being less likely to dismiss charges and more likely to obtain convictions (Steadman, 1979). Steadman and Braff (1974) also compared the sentences received. Data on sentencing were available for 45 incompetent defendants and 50 in the comparison group. No significant differences were found between the two groups, although there was a trend for incompetent defendants to be sentenced to time served in the hospital.

In our own research (more fully described in Chapter 6), we compared the court outcome of 130 initially incompetent defendants with a comparison group of 140 competent defendants who were matched with the incompetent group by year and county of admission. Incompetent defendants charged with murder or assault were significantly more likely to have their charges dismissed. In an effort to determine whether the length of hospitalization had an effect on this outcome, we compared incompetent defendants found guilty with those found not guilty. Dismissed defendants originally charged with murder were hospitalized significantly longer than those found guilty, but this finding does not hold true for the assault cases. We found no other significant differences for the remaining offense categories.

In summary, very little is known about the effects of an evaluation or a determination of competency on court outcome. There have been very few studies in this area and our review indicates several conflicting findings. This clearly points to the need for additional research, particularly the type such as the one conducted by Steadman and Braff (1974), which compares evaluated defendants with those never evaluated.

COMPETENCY ASSESSMENT MEASURES

There have been few attempts to develop formal measures designed to assess directly a defendant's competency to stand trial. Apart from a checklist developed by Robey (1965), which focuses on court process–related issues (e.g., level of communication with attorney and understanding of the legal process), and a checklist and interview questions to assist psychiatrists in competency evaluations (Bukatman, Foy, and deGrazia, 1971), most of the work in this area has been done by A. Louis McGarry and his colleagues at the Harvard Medical School's Laboratory of Community Psychiatry. This group has developed two measures designed to aid in the assessment of competency: the Competency Screening Test and the Competency Assessment Instrument. In this section these two instruments as well as the checklist by Robey (1965) and the structured interview by Bukatman, Foy, and deGrazia (1971) will be reviewed.

Competency Screening Test

The Competency Screening Test (CST) was developed by Lipsitt, Lelos, and McGarry (1971) during a larger project studying the issue of competency to stand trial. The CST was designed for use as a screening measure to identify clearly competent defendants and thus avoid more lengthy and unnecessary evaluation. It was also intended to aid in distinguishing the competency issue from other legal and mental health issues. The CST is a 22-item measure in a sentence completion format. Typical items include "Jack felt that the judge——," "If the jury finds me guilty——," and "The way a court trial is decided——." Respondents are asked to complete each of these items. Each item is given a score of 2 (competent), 1 (questionable), or 0 (incompetent). Lipsitt, Lelos, and McGarry (1971) offer the following interpretation for low scores:

Responses that merit a score of one point are characterized by passive acquiescence, circularity, redundancy, or avoidance of the issue, or are impoverished, though not clearly inappropriate. Responses that receive a score of zero are characterized by substantial disorganization in grammatical structure and/or content, expressions of inability to relate or to trust, definition of the lawyer's role as punitive or rejecting, extreme concreteness, perseveration, or expressions of self-defeating behavior. A score of zero should reveal flattened affect or types of thought disorders that would substantially interfere with legal defense. (P. 106)

Thus the hypothesis is that lower total scores would suggest significant behavioral or cognitive deficits which might interfere with participation in the defense. They used a cutoff score of 20 to distinguish between low

scorers and high scorers, based on what they report as a qualitative difference in responses.[5]

McGarry et al. (1973) report an interrater reliability coefficient of .93
(with raters at a bachelor's degree level), using standard Z scores. While
McGarry et al. (1973) do not give the details of this procedure, it probably means that each rater's judgment was standardized relative to his or
her mean scale usage and variation. Such a procedure is highly questionable, since it would result in a spuriously high reliability coefficient by
eliminating rater differences in scale usage from the reliability analysis. In
the real world of its intended usage, such a removal of rater "biases" (tendency to be too hard or too lenient, to see more or less pathology) would
not be possible. The more accurate reliability figure (technically called a
"generalizability estimate" by Cronbach et al., 1972) would include the
sources of error owing to rater effects, and would probably be considerably
lower than reported by McGarry et al. (see Mariotto and Farrell, 1979).

The manual does not present any information about how this scoring
method was developed, but an analysis of the system reveals some interesting assumptions about competency as perceived by McGarry et al.
(1973). Some examples will be illustrative. On one item, "Jack felt that
the judge——," a response such as "was right" or "was fair" would receive
a score of 2, while responses such as "was unjust," "was too harsh," or "was
wrong" would receive a score of 0. This item is intended to tap the legal
criteria of understanding and awareness of court process and the psychological criteria of awareness of acceptance of court process. Another item,
"The way a court trial is decided——," also designed to tap awareness and
understanding of court process, is scored 2 if the respondent says "is by
the evidence" or "is the judge decides," but 0 if the respondent says "is
open for improvement" or "is on the majority of opinion."

There are several hypotheses one could make regarding scores in the
incompetent direction in addition to the assumption that a low-scoring
defendant might be incompetent. For example, past experience with the
criminal justice system may result in an increased feeling of powerlessness
to control one's outcome within that system. In the research we describe
in Chapter 6, we found a significant negative correlation between CST
scores and a measure of internal-external locus of control (Rotter, 1966).[6]
Thus, to the item "When Bob disagreed with his lawyer on his defense,
he——," the CST gives a score of 0 to a response like "figured there was

no sense arguing," implying evidence of incompetency. An alternative and equally plausible explanation is that the respondent is giving an accurate response based on his own past experiences with attorneys, or on a sense that the outcome is beyond one's control so that a response would be futile. It may also be that high scores reflect socially desirable responses. Scores of 2 on many items reflect a perception of a justice system which may be more ideal than real, especially for lower-class defendants. Brakel (1974) has termed this aspect of the CST a "game-playing theory": "Thus, ability or willingness to play the criminal justice game according to the rules is equated with competence, whereas resistance to orderly participation in this morality play is incompetence. . . . In a strictly logical sense, competence or at least one element of it, can be seen as the ability (competence) to play the game" (p. 1116).

A factor analysis of the CST (McGarry et al., 1973), involving a sample of 91 defendants, resulted in six factors accounting for 56.3% of the total variance. These factors (which may be thought of as relatively homogeneous clusters of items from the total set of 22 items) were labeled attorney relationship, understanding and awareness of legal process, reaction to accusation and guilt, participation in trial, trust and confidence in attorney, and future orientation in terms of consequences of legal proceedings.

When the CST was administered to a sample of 83 persons who had never been evaluated for competency, McGarry et al. (1973) reported that the factors did not produce any concepts related to competency and concluded that "the Competency Screening Test may thus be sample specific and may not measure competency in terms of the factors described above for populations differing from those in Bridgewater or populations not actively involved in the criminal justice systems" (p. 29). This lack of correspondence between factor structures in the two different populations that the CST is designed to discriminate implies that its items have different meanings to competent and incompetent defendants, and suggests that it may not discriminate the populations on the basis of competence to stand trial. The correlation between the CST and intelligence test scores reported below is a further hint of problems with the validity of the CST. Thus, according to McGarry, the CST may not be generalizable even to other samples of defendants being evaluated for competency.

Further evidence concerning the validity of the CST is based on one study conducted at Bridgewater State Hospital of a sample of 43 patients who were selected on the basis of some evidence of "serious mental pathology" (Lipsitt, Lelos, and McGarry, 1971). Competency Screening Test scores for these patients were rationally dichotomized into low (score of 20 or below) and high (score of greater than 20) and related to the court recommendations made by the Bridgewater staff. Table 3.2 is based on the data presented by Lipsitt, Lelos, and McGarry (1971) to illustrate the results of this predictive validity study.

TABLE 3.2

Relationship of Competency Screen Test
and Bridgewater Staff Recommendations

Competency Screening Test	Bridgewater Recommendations	
	Competent	Incompetent
Competent	17	3
Incompetent	7	16

Adapted from data provided by Lipsitt, Lelos, and McGarry (1971).

As can be seen, reliance upon the CST would lead to ten incorrect decisions out of the total of 43. That is, about 23% of the "decisions" would be in error. There are two types of error, each having different consequences for defendants. A false negative error occurs when the CST score indicates that a defendant is incompetent but, in fact, the defendant is competent. If decisions are based solely on the CST score, such persons might be incorrectly confined. The false negative rate was 34%. On the other hand, a false positive error occurs when the CST score indicates that a defendant is competent but, in fact, the defendant is incompetent. Again, if cutoff scores are solely used, such persons would be inappropriately brought to trial.[7]

Another serious problem with the validation study by Lipsitt, Lelos, and McGarry (1971) is that it seriously violates the context for which the CST was intended. The CST was intended for screening in a context where the base rate of incompetency is quite low (approximately 10 to 20%). To validate it in a sample where the base rate is 44% (19/43) is to risk serious misrepresentation of its validity (Meehl and Rosen, 1955; Wiggins, 1973).

In our research we used the CST with two samples of defendants (see Chapter 6 for details). Using the cutoff scores suggested by Lipsitt, Lelos, and McGarry (1971), we found that six of 11 competent defendants (55%) were misclassified as incompetent, while 60% of the defendants judged incompetent by the courts were misclassified. In another study we found that the prediction based on the CST was wrong for 22 of 123 competent (17%) and two of five (40%) incompetent defendants. Thus the use of the CST can result in misclassification of serious proportions. Additional concern was the highly significant correlation between the CST scores and intelligence, as measured by the Slosson Intelligence Test. Individuals with low scores tended also to score lower on the intelligence measure, and also had low arithmetic scores on the Wide Range Achievement Test. In this regard, it is not surprising that various student and other nonhospitalized groups would score higher on the CST (Lipsitt, Lelos, and McGarry, 1971).

One further problem in validational studies such as these is that one assumes that the recommendations of the hospital staff are the correct ones and that any potential instrument must measure up to this criterion. As noted previously, psychiatric recommendations do control the court outcome, but this is an unfortunate state of affairs. It may be that the staff recommendations are based on assumptions and methods not related to a defendant's ability to stand trial. Thus we only have a measure of the validity of the measure in relation to another unvalidated measure.

Schreiber (1978) recently completed an examination of the use of the CST in four states (Tennessee, Ohio, North Carolina, and West Virginia) that had some degree of contact with McGarry's work. He found that the CST was not adopted or was discontinued in three of the states, being used consistently only in West Virginia, where the number of evaluations is quite small. The other states had considered or employed it but had rejected it for several reasons. Schreiber (1978) reports that forensic staff in those states reported that it was cumbersome, biased toward those with a favorable attitude toward the criminal justice system, and was not easy to use with illiterate or semi-illiterate defendants. Some respondents also suggested that it was not an effective substitute for clinical judgment.

In summary, the Competency Screening Test represents an important attempt to develop a measure which assesses aspects of capacity to stand trial that are primarily based on a legal, rather than a mental health, perspective. However, its psychometric properties, as well as the underlying assumptions about the definition of competency, would suggest that the CST be viewed as an experimental measure not for use in actual decision-making. Perhaps further refinement of the scale, especially the scoring criteria, would result in a useful measure of competency. At present, it is apparent that the CST has not been sufficiently validated to justify its applied use.

Competency Assessment Instrument

McGarry et al. (1973) also developed a semistructured interview and rating scale known as the Competency Assessment Instrument (CAI). The CAI is based on a semistructured interview, usually conducted by a psychiatrist but potentially usable by other disciplines. The CAI contains 13 items "related to an accused's ability to cope with the trial process in an adequately self-protective fashion" (p. 99), and appears to be based upon the *Wieter* v. *Settle* (1961) criteria (see Chapter 2) as well as generally agreed-upon interpretations of *Dusky*. Some examples of items and their definitions are given below (adapted from McGarry et al., 1973, pp. 101–2):

Appraisal of available legal defenses: This item calls for an assessment of the accused's awareness of his possible legal defenses and how consistent these are with the reality of his particular circumstances.

Unmanageable behavior: This item calls for an assessment of the appropriateness of the current motor and verbal behavior of the defendant and the degree to which this behavior would disrupt the conduct of a trial. Inappropriate or disruptive behavior must arise from a substantial degree of mental illness or mental retardation.

Quality of relating to attorney: This item calls for an assessment of the interpersonal capacity of the accused to relate to the average attorney. Involved are the ability to trust and to communicate relevantly.

Planning of legal strategy including guilty pleas to lesser charges where pertinent: This item calls for an assessment of the degree to which the accused can understand, participate, and cooperate with his counsel in planning a strategy for the defense which is consistent with the reality of his circumstances.

Capacity to disclose to attorney available pertinent facts surrounding the offense including the defendant's movements, timing, mental state, and actions at the time of the offense: This item calls for an assessment of the accused's capacity to give a basically consistent, rational, and relevant account of the motivational and external facts. Complex factors can enter into this determination. These include intelligence, memory, and honesty. The difficult area of the validity of an amnesia may be involved and may prove unresolvable for the examining clinician. It is important to be aware that there may be a disparity between what an accused is willing to share with a clinician as opposed to what he will share with his attorney, the latter being the more important.

The scale was developed on the basis of courtroom and clinical experience and was designed to include all possible bases for a determination of incompetency. Each item is scaled from 1 to 5, ranging from "total incapacity" to "no incapacity." It is interesting to note that the CAI is primarily designed to assess legal, rather than mental health, dimensions of competency.

In addition to definitions of each item, the manual for the CAI contains clinical examples of levels of incapacity corresponding to the ratings. Unfortunately, little reliability and no validity data are currently available on the CAI. Reliability was determined in only two studies. Two raters independently rated 16 subjects on an earlier version of the CAI, with interrater correlations ranging from .09 to .895. A later version of the CAI, which included the use of the manual and structured interview described above, was used to rate 18 subjects. McGarry et al. (1973) do not report the complete results. The ratings of three experienced raters (undefined) were compared with three raters without previous experience in evaluating competency. Correlation coefficients for the experienced raters ranged from .84 to .97, with an average of .92. Correlation coefficients for the least experienced raters ranged from .43 to .96, with an average of .87. McGarry et al. (1973) argue that, with appropriate and sufficient training, the CAI can be reliably used. Again, no study was conducted exploring the relationship of these ratings to competency.

Despite McGarry et al.'s (1973) contention, the reliability of the CAI has not been adequately studied. Only one reliability study of the final version of the CAI was done, and this was based on a sample of only 18. More important, the lack of predictive validity support renders the CAI unusable in a decision-making sense. Obviously, more research evaluating both the reliability and validity of the CAI would have to be available demonstrating its effectiveness in reliably assessing competency.

The CAI fared somewhat better in the implementation review completed by Schreiber (1979). The CAI is used rather extensively in West Virginia and Tennessee (Laben et al., 1977) but primarily as an interview structuring device. It is important to note that McGarry originally intended the CST and the CAI to be used in a two-stage screening process. The CST would screen out clearly competent defendants, and the CAI would be used for a more in-depth examination of the remaining cases. However, none of the four states in the Schreiber review are currently using the two instruments in this manner.

Other Checklists and Structured Interviews

As noted earlier in this section, little research on instrument development has been completed. Robey (1965) proposed the use of a checklist by psychiatrists for communication with the court. The checklist included three primary areas: (1) comprehension of court proceedings, (2) ability to advise counsel, and (3) susceptibility to decompensation (undefined items such as violence, suicidal depression), which are rated either "O.K.," "mental illness," or "intellectual deficiency." This latter area was defined as a Wechsler Adult Intelligence Scale I.Q. score below 60. The Robey checklist, to our knowledge, was never systematically studied. The problems with this type of checklist, particularly the lack of definition of many items, should be obvious. The only other instrument development attempt was a series of interview questions developed by Bukatman, Foy, and deGrazia (1971). They outlined a series of questions designed to tap understanding of the current situation and cooperation and participation in the defense. The importance of this work is its attempt to promote a legal focus of the competency evaluations. However, neither the Robey nor the Bukatman measure has been used sufficiently to justify its adoption at this time, although they may be useful as a guide for interviewers.

Conclusion

The primary problem with any of the measures we have reviewed is that they are heavily based on expectations about ability to participate in a trial which may be both too high and unrealistic. What should be expected of a defendant? While the measures discussed have obviously moved away from a dominantly psychiatric perspective to one centering on legal issues, they still may not result in a proper functional analysis of the necessary participation of a defendant. Should there, for example, be a different standard if a defendant is going to plea bargain as opposed to participating in a trial? We have dealt with this issue at length (Chapter 2), but it is important to remember here that such definitional issues dramatically affect one's perception of the adequacy of legally based assessment measures.

Notes

1. Some studies (e.g., Ciccone and Barry, 1976; Geller and Lister, 1978; Piotrowski, Kosacco, and Guze, 1976) are not included here because their groups include both defendants being evaluated for competency and defendants whose responsibility was being questioned.

2. It is important to note that a number of court decisions have suggested that mental illness or psychosis *per se* is insufficient as a basis for a determination of unfitness. See *Higgins* v. *McGrath* (1951); *Lyles* v. *United States* (1957); *Feguer* v. *United States* (1962); *United States* v. *Adams* (1969); *United States* v. *Horowitz* (1973); see also Engelberg (1967); Hardisty (1973); Rosenberg (1970); and our extended discussion of these cases in Chapter 2. Sufficient ambiguity exists, however, which undoubtedly leads to a situation in which different criteria are used by decision-makers.

3. A recent study by Steadman, Cocozza, and Melick (1978) reports that the arrest rate on violent crimes for released mental patients in the state of New York has increased considerably during a two-period time sample (1968 and 1975) and is also considerably higher than the rate for the general population. The arrest rates were based on 19-month follow-up data after the patients were discharged from a mental hospital. The authors explain this result by pointing to the fact that the number of patients with arrest records prior to hospitalization has also increased, thus indicating that current patients are more likely than the general population to commit new crimes. See Rabkin (1979) for a general review of the research on the criminal behavior of discharged mental patients.

4. It might be added, as further support to their rejection of this interpretation, that a finding of mental illness does not necessarily mean that a defendant is not capable of standing trial (see Chapter 2).

5. As we note in the preceding discussion, a defendant's score on the CST is not intended to be a sole determinant of competency or incompetency. Rather, it is intended to suggest more in-depth evaluation, including the use of the Com-

petency Assessment Instrument. However, the use of cutoff scores may affect subsequent perceptions and evaluations of persons scoring below the cutoff, and will
mean that high scorers will not be further evaluated.

6. The Internal-External Locus of Control Scale was developed by Rotter
(1966) to measure the degree to which individuals perceive events in their lives
as largely controlled either by themselves or by forces outside their control. When
events in an individual's life are perceived as being the result of luck, chance,
fate, or under the control of other, more powerful individuals, the belief is labeled
external control. On the other hand, persons who view events as being largely
contingent on their own behavior and influence are considered to have a high
degree of *internal control*.

7. The interested reader is referred to Wiggins (1973) for a detailed discussion
of decision theory.

4

Diagnostic versus Competency-Oriented Testimony

The vast majority of mental health testimony confuses the *criteria for competency* with the *criteria for psychopathology*. Since the psychiatrists and psychologists who testify in court or who write evaluation reports typically have little legal training, and since, conversely, attorneys and judges are relatively uninformed about the domains of psychiatry and psychology, such a state of affairs is understandable. We can begin to address this problem by discussing critically the *kind* and *form* of testimony that would be of maximal utility for all parties concerned.

Since the criteria used by mental health evaluators in decisions about competency have been unclear (as we discussed in Chapters 2 and 3), it is not surprising that diagnostic testimony, delivered in conclusory form, has dominated competency hearings. But, as we have argued thus far, this is a misuse of mental health expertise as well as a source of continual confusion. Competency is an open-textured construct that is perhaps best evaluated in a multidisciplinary context. Mental health professionals can aid in this evaluation process by providing whatever expertise they have in describing, observing, and inferring various behavioral and mental processes. However, in terms of a decision about competency, it is surely irrelevant whether or not a defendant is, or is not, a properly labeled paranoid schizophrenic. *Bruce* v. *Estelle* (1976) is a good example of the absurd position that diagnostically oriented decision-making generates. In *Bruce* the Fifth Circuit Court of Appeals actually reversed a lower court's ruling on the basis that "the trial court's finding that petitioner was a sociopath and was not schizophrenic was clearly erroneous" and "the trial court's ultimate conclusion that the petitioner [Bruce] was competent to stand trial was in error" (p. 1051). Without quibbling over the details of the court's logic (which is, in our professional opinion, seriously questionable), one must note the sad state to which this court has sunk when it now enters the arena of the defendant's "proper" diagnosis. Nowhere in *Bruce* does the court address the functional issue; instead it argues, "Once Bruce's schizophrenia is acknowledged, the conclusion that the disease prevented him from rationally communicating with his attorney and understanding the proceedings is most compelling" (p. 1062). *We could not agree less.* There is no compelling or empirical basis for establishing such a relationship between formal psychiatric diagnosis and competency. A more reasonable assertion might be that Bruce's occasional visual hallucinations (which responded to medication) rendered him incompetent, but even here one cannot validly assert such a relationship. The domains of psychopathological behavior, experiences, and mental states are potentially relevant to competency, but one has to establish a functional relationship based upon the particulars of a given case. As we demonstrated in Chapter 2, the higher courts in general have rejected the idea that the presence of a pathological symptom *per se* is sufficient ground for a determination of incompetency.

There certainly are instances in which concepts from the domain of psychopathology (e.g., auditory hallucinations, grandiosity, paranoid state) are relevant to the determination of competency, though not dispositive of it. When such concepts are to be addressed, the court and the defendant have the right to expect that the issue will be dealt with at the highest level of professional standards. Ethical issues of the profession being assumed, we can also expect that, if diagnosis of the defendant is undertaken, it will be properly done. This implies that diagnosticians spend an adequate amount of time at the task and use the most valid and reliable diagnostic aids and instruments at their disposal.

We now turn our attention to these issues. First, we review the literature on the reliability of psychiatric diagnosis and symptom description, and then we review some of the more recent advances in the area of psychopathological description and evaluation, with an eye toward the necessary conditions that must hold for its proper use. We then turn to the broader, and more directly relevant, question of what it means to utilize functional criteria for the determination of competency, and the proper locus of authority in such decision-making. Finally, we briefly comment on the use of training materials for lawyers and mental health professionals, and conclude with some suggestions for important research directions in the development of criteria for competency and procedures for its evaluation.

DIAGNOSTIC RELIABILITY

Although diagnostic categorization may not be directly relevant to a defendant's competency, it is frequently used in psychiatric testimony, and therefore we need to examine its reliability. Moreover, more modern forms of "diagnostic" description that rely upon narrower categories or less inferential description also must be evaluated in terms of their validity. The issues surrounding the reliability and validity of diagnosis and psychopathological description are highly complex and are the subject of much controversy and debate. Basically, reliability refers to the precision with which a given statement, observation, or measurement can be made. Numerous sources of error lower reliability of psychiatric diagnosis: lack of agreement between diagnosticians (including differences in skill and sensitivity to certain cues), the effect of context or situation on the behaviors in which a patient might engage, confusion in the definition of terms, and confusion in the theoretical details of what symptoms are required for a given diagnosis. This area has generated considerable "heat" and ideological controversy, but little by way of substantive conclusions.[1] In what follows, we present a most cursory overview, and we caution the reader against accepting any conclusions (ours included) without careful examination of the sources upon which the conclusions are based.

Psychiatric diagnoses may be envisioned as judgments (a diagnosis, a determination of competency, a statement that the patient is delusional, a prediction of dangerousness) that are based upon information about an individual consisting of a set of cues or pieces of information. Each given bit of information about the individual in question (a test score, an observed inability to recall some date, a bizarre form of speech, low blood sugar level, a tendency to misperceive others as hostile or aggressive) is given a particular weight by the clinician in making a judgment; in a parallel fashion the cue has a proper weight in the sense of its relationship to the criterion.

Thus, for example, a clinician may have available the following cues:

(1) defendant has clear memory for the circumstances surrounding alleged crime; (2) defendant has a history of suicide attempts; and (3) defendant is accurately diagnosed as "schizo-affective disorder, depressed type," and, specifically, has delusions of thought broadcasting (i.e., that his thoughts are broadcast to the outside world). On the basis of this information a typical clinician (see Chapter 6) might weight the second and third cues heavily in deciding for incompetency, on the theory that the defendant is not emotionally capable of withstanding the pressures of trial and that his delusions of thought broadcasting prevent him from sufficiently trusting his attorney. Working entirely within the psychiatric frame of reference, this hypothetical clinician may not even be aware of a fourth cue that defendant can supply a competent attorney with sufficient detail to impeach the state's witness against him. Other cues may also be relevant; for example, the defendant, in spite of his delusional system, has an appreciation of the workings of the legal system and of the meaning of the crime for which he is accused, at a level equal to that of the average defendant in a court of law. Since competency is an open construct, we do not know, in any certain sense, what weights various cues ought to have. However, we do know that cues which serve to indicate severe mental disorder are not to be equated with incompetency (see Chapters 2 and 6).

We will return to the proper use of a variety of cues in evaluating competency later in this chapter. For the moment we would like to consider the relevance of the single cue which is used most heavily in arriving at a decision about competency, that of psychiatric diagnosis. Diagnosis may be unreliable for three primary reasons: *patients* are inconsistent between the time periods or the settings in which the diagnosis is made (they exhibit different cues at different times and/or in different settings); *diagnosticians* may use (weight) the cues differently in arriving at a particular judgment, may be differentially sensitive to certain cues, or may be differentially skilled in eliciting the needed information; and, finally, the *diagnostic system* itself may be unclear in describing a particular cue or may require inappropriate distinctions. Ward et al. (1962) argued, on the basis of their judgments about a set of diagnostic disagreements, that these reasons were responsible for 5.0%, 32.5%, and 62.5% of the disagreements in psychiatric diagnosis respectively. More recent data, collected in a somewhat different context, would lead one to believe that these estimates would now be questioned, particularly the probable underestimate of the influence of patient inconsistency and the influence of setting and situations (Bowers, 1973; Golding, 1975; Mischel, 1968, 1973). Until recently, diagnostician disagreement was the explanation most frequently studied. The early, "classical" studies (Beck et al., 1962; Cooper et al., 1972; Kreitman, 1961; Sandifer, Pettus, and Quade, 1964; Schmidt and Fonda, 1956) are commonly cited in attacks on psychiatric diagnosis as demonstrating that "there is a substantial body of scientific and professional literature to the effect that psychiatric diagnoses are not very reliable and not very accurate" (Ziskin, 1975, p. 307). As Helzer et al. (1977) pointed out, however, these early studies of diagnostician agreement cannot be trusted because the methods used to analyze agreement were fundamentally in error, and the research designs used to generate the data were inadequately conceived (see also Fleiss et al., 1972; Meehl, 1970c, 1973).

The problem of analyzing agreement can be understood by realizing that agreement between two (or more) psychiatrists or psychologists in terms of how they sort patients into diagnostic categories can be influenced by extraneous factors, such as how frequently each judge uses each category. A simple example is given in Table 4.1, adapted from Spitzer and Fleiss (1974). As can be clearly seen, diagnosticians A and B agree

TABLE 4.1

Hypothetical Data for Agreement on Defendant's Competency between Two Psychiatrists, Expressed in Proportions[1]

| | Psychiatrist A | | | |
Psychiatrist B	Incompetent	Unknown	Competent	Total
Incompetent	.75	.01	.04	.80
Unknown	.05	.04	.01	.10
Competent	.00	.00	.10	.10
Total	.80	.05	.15	1.00

[1]A particular row or column will not sum to 1.00 unless the diagnostician uses this category and no other. This "base rate for diagnosis" will be a function of the *true* frequency of occurrence of the category and the diagnostician's accuracy and sensitivity to that base rate, and tendency to use this category.

75% of the time with each other on their judgment of incompetency. Their agreement rate with respect to competency, on the other hand, appears to be quite poor. However, just the opposite is the case. Psychiatrists A and B both use the "incompetency" category 80% of the time. If A interviews 100 defendants, 80 will be called incompetent. Suppose those 80 are interviewed by B; he in turn will call 80% of these incompetent. Therefore, 64 defendants (80% of 80) will be called incompetent by both. Thus A and B will agree on the specific judgment of incompetency 64% of the time by chance alone *even if they make their judgments randomly*. Their actual 75% agreement thus needs to be evaluated relative to chance expectancies. When one uses the proper index, called weighted kappa (Cohen, 1968), the agreement, corrected for chance, is actually highest for the judgment "competent" (partly because the expected agreement by chance for judgment "competent" is only 1.5%).[2]

When one examines the issue of agreement, using the correct statistic as in Spitzer and Fleiss (1974), one observes, averaging over most of the classic studies, indices of diagnostic agreement of the sort depicted in Table 4.2. Close inspection of these data produces several important points.

When the diagnostic system used is clearer and more objective, agreement between diagnosticians tends to increase, sometimes dramatically. Thus the Research Diagnostic Criteria (RDC) of Spitzer, Endicott, and Robins (1978) and the criteria of Feighner et al. (1972) are quite different from the traditionally used DSM–II.[3] These newer systems are quite explicit in their diagnostic procedures and force the interviewer/diagnostician to use rather unambiguous criteria, with a uniform set of decision rules, and relatively uniform interview procedures. The Research Diagnostic Criteria, for example, are tied to a semistructured interview schedule, to minimize the effect of interviewer skill in eliciting the needed information. All of these factors contribute to the observed increase in diagnostic agreement. In this system diagnosticians no longer use their own idiosyncratic weights in combining cues to make a judgment, because the combination is done routinely and automatically by the criterial definitions of each diagnosis.[4] Perhaps more important, diagnosticians are given explicit guidance in what a particular cue means and are also given uniform procedures for eliciting the cues. One of the major sources of disagreement in diagnosis may be traceable to differences in the diagnostician's ability/knowledge to elicit the appropriate information upon

TABLE 4.2

Diagnostic Reliabilities as a Function of
Clarity of Diagnostic Category

Diagnostic Category	Mean of Six Classic Studies[1]	Recent DSM-II Study[2]	Study Using Feighner Criteria[3]	Study Using Revised Feighner Criteria (Research Diagnostic Criteria)[4]
Schizophrenic	.57	.48	.58	.84 (.80; .90)
Anxiety neurosis	.40	.42	.76	.52 (.—;[a] .74)
Major depressive disorder	.41	.25	.55	.66 (.88; .70)
Minor depressive disorder[e]	.26	.07	—[c]	.56 (.38; .64)
Alcoholism	.71	—[b]	.74	.66 (.86; .90)[d]
Drug abuse	—[c]	—[b]	.84	1.00 (.77; .90)[d]

All reliabilities are kappa coefficients of agreement, corrected for chance.

[1]Spitzer and Fleiss's (1974) mean of six studies.

[2]Spitzer and Endicott's (1975) analysis of 120 cases using the old Diagnostic and Statistical Manual of the American Psychiatric Association (DSM-II).

[3]Helzer et al.'s (1977) analysis of 101 cases using a modification of Feighner et al.'s (1972) research criteria for diagnosis.

[4]Spitzer and Endicott's (1975) analysis using an extensive modification of Feighner criteria, called the Research Diagnostic Criteria (Spitzer, Endicott, and Robins, 1978). Numbers in parentheses reflect studies reported by Spitzer, Endicott, and Robins (1975) and Spitzer, Forman, and Nee (1979) respectively.

[a]Not reported in Spitzer et al. (1975).

[b]No data on this category in Helzer et al.'s (1977) reported results.

[c]Not used as a category in Helzer et al.'s (1977) reported results.

[d]Reported as "Substance abuse disorder."

[e]Translates to neurotic depression in DSM-II.

which to base a judgment. A most embarrassing (and frequently commented upon) aspect of typical psychiatric testimony in the courts is the poorly and hastily collected interview data upon which much of that testimony is based (e.g., Golten, 1972; Wexler and Scoville, 1971). In contradistinction, these systems help to guarantee a more comprehensive psychiatric examination of defendants.

There are further complications in analyzing and understanding the re-

liability of psychiatric diagnosis that warrant some attention. The studies
cited all differ from each other methodologically. Some studies trained
their diagnosticians on a sample of cases with feedback and discussion
used to minimize disagreements (e.g., Luria and McHugh, 1974). Relatively few studies, however, control for the level of training of the diagnosticians or their skill at diagnosis. Lack of agreement among poorly
trained diagnosticians would hardly be surprising. Moreover, some of the
disagreement that exists, particularly between individuals espousing somewhat different theories of psychopathology, is not all "bad." Schizophrenia, for example, is a complex open construct (see Chapter 2), and it is
expected that legitimate differences will occur in its assessment (Cooper
et al., 1972). An exploration of the sources of such disagreement has a
heuristic value (Kendell et al., 1971; Luria and McHugh, 1974; Sandifer
et al., 1968; Spitzer, Endicott, and Robins, 1975) that helps to clarify and
refine that construct. Furthermore, while it is popular to attack psychiatric
diagnoses, one should realize that even medical diagnosis is only *moderately* reliable.[5] This is meant not to excuse diagnostic problems but only
to point out that, where relevant, diagnosis should be allowed, with a full
appreciation of its failings and of the basis upon which it is made.[6]

With the exception of our work and a few other small sample demon-
strations, there has not been a comprehensive study of the reliability of
competency decisions made under representative field conditions. Two
studies using the Competency Assessment Instrument developed by the
Laboratory of Community Psychiatry (McGarry et al., 1973) report reliabilities in the .70 and .80 range for raters making judgments about various aspects of competency, based on a brief interview. Stock and Poythress
(1979) reported 100% agreement between pairs of psychologist evaluators
who did competency evaluations by means of conjoint interviews, and
who were extensively trained together before the research project started.
Roesch (1979) reported similarly high agreement, and also demonstrated
that judgments made on the basis of a brief interview were highly related
to judgments based on more lengthy institutional evaluations. These data,
however, were based upon rather careful training of the decision-maker
and, in the cases of McGarry and Roesch, also used a semistructured interview to elicit information. The data presented in the more inadequate
diagnostic reliability studies may, in a paradoxical fashion, be a quite valid
reflection of the level of reliability expected from the (typically poorly

trained) diagnostic examiner (no matter what his/her credentials on paper or the number of examinations performed). It is doubtful that the kind of reliabilities reported in research studies would generalize to the more usual nonresearch-based situation. The fact that there is such a high degree of relationship between competency determinations and gross diagnostic categories (see Chapter 3) suggests that the reliability of competency decisions as currently practiced would not exceed that of gross psychiatric diagnostic categories. The studies of psychiatric diagnostic reliability cited previously generally report corrected reliabilities in the neighborhood of .70 for gross categories. We suspect that unless competency decisions are based on more well-collected and relevant data that are tied to more functional criteria and processed by screening panels trained explicitly in the problem of competency assessment, these marginally acceptable reliabilities will never be exceeded in nonresearch settings.

DIAGNOSTICALLY ORIENTED TESTIMONY

Diagnostic testimony, assuming that it is deemed relevant to the issue of competency, should be based upon the most sophisticated and psychometrically superior diagnostic system(s) available. We have already presented an extensive defense (Chapter 2) of the assertion that the presence or absence of many traditional psychiatric symptoms and/or diagnoses is tangential, at best, to the question of competency. We will shortly present some comments on *functional criteria* that ought to be more heavily weighted in the determination of competency. Thus, whether or not an individual has a delusional system is less important than the specific content and scope of that delusion, and the probability that it would interfere with standing trial (a judgment that is based on legal as well as mental health considerations). We focus now on the assertion that, if symptomatology is to be addressed in the report to the court, the procedures for its evaluation must be more standardized. Much of the unreliability in diagnosis and description procedures can be eliminated if standardized interview-rating formats, more objective assessment instruments, and behavioral observation schedules are used.

With respect to the assessment of competency, it is difficult to argue that one method of assessment (unstructured versus semistructured, standardized, psychiatric interview schedules, for example) is more valid than another because the notion of validity presumes that a "hard" criterion exists to be predicted.[7] Obviously, in the case of judgments of incompetency, no such criterion does or could exist.[8] However, existing research in the allied area of prediction of dangerousness (Meehl, 1970d, 1971; Monahan, 1973, 1977) enables us to infer the sorts of predictors which might be the most useful. As Meehl (1971) states, "Behavior science research itself shows that, by and large, the best way to predict anybody's behavior is his behavior in the past" (p. 88).[9] As this quote quite correctly implies, the majority of inferential judgments made in the behavioral sciences are on weak footing indeed. Twenty years of research in trying to predict such sundry criteria as suicide, treatment outcome, treatment responsiveness, and dangerousness, on the basis of the usual form of clinical judgment, support this statement (Ennis and Litwack, 1974; Matarazzo, 1978; Meehl, 1954, 1970d, 1971; Steadman and Cocozza, 1974; Wiggins, 1973). Often such criteria turn out to be simply not predictable (by anyone). When such criteria are predictable, one can often achieve only moderate success, and then usually on the basis of observational data that require only low-level inferences. Moreover, as Meehl points out in the above quote, the most useful data usually turn out to be quite closely related to the criterion in both time and function. For example, the fact that defendant X was diagnosed a paranoid schizophrenic ten years ago is potentially relevant to the probability that he will now be assaultive, but the fact that he is *currently* delusional and was observed stabbing an effigy of his mother just prior to a weekend visit is, on empirical grounds, more likely to be predictive, if anything will be, of assaultiveness. The information upon which a judgment or prediction is made should also come from multiple sources or perspectives that converge or "triangulate" on each other, in order to reduce the error inherent in any particular method.[10]

Currently there is a wide variety of structured, psychiatrically based interview procedures that produce symptom- and diagnostically referenced description at respectable levels of reliability. It is beyond the scope of this chapter to discuss all of these instruments, but the more prominent and currently available ones, designed for general-purpose use, ought to be mentioned. There are three major sets of instruments: (1) the instruments related to the so-called "St. Louis" criteria for research diagnosis (Feighner et al., 1972); (2) such instruments as the Psychiatric Status Schedule (PSS) (Spitzer et al., 1970), the Schedule for Affective Disorders and Schizophrenia (SADS) (Endicott and Spitzer, 1978), and the Research Diagnostic Criteria (RDC) (Spitzer, Endicott, and Robins, 1978), which form the basis of the third edition of the *Diagnostic and Statistical Manual for Mental Disorders*; and (3) the Wing et al. (1974) Present State Examination (PSE) that is more in the tradition of descriptive psychiatry and is adopted for cross-cultural research by the World Health Organization (Luria and McHugh, 1974; Wing, Birley, and Cooper, 1967). These systems are basically designed to describe patients' psychopathology in as reliable a fashion as possible. The domain of pathology described in these systems is moderately traditional but also includes (especially in the PSS) aspects of work adjustment, role functions, and social interactional behavior. Each system has generated its own advocates and research traditions. Nevertheless, an accurate impression of the nature of these systems can be gained from comparing, as suggested by Spitzer et al. (1975), the criteria for a DSM-II diagnosis of manic-depression with a RDC diagnosis of major depressive disorder (remember that more than just the criteria differ; RDC is tied to a semistructured interview whereas DSM-II leaves the extensiveness of the interview procedure up to the examiner—this is a major source of unreliability). The comparison appears in Table 4.3.

The other systems ("Feighner's criteria" and the "Wing criteria") differ in many technical details but share in common the most important characteristics. Most fundamentally, they try to operationalize the criteria and use explicit rules for inclusion and exclusion, as is evident in criteria E–1 through E–6. Furthermore, the systems encourage the examiner not to diagnose anything if the criteria aren't met, in contradistinction to the more traditional "over diagnosis bias." Finally, many traditional concepts, such as inappropriate affect, that figure so prominently in many psychiatrists' reports that a defendant isn't competent to stand trial, are missing from this system[11] because they were found to be too unreliable to be included.[12]

The development of more sophisticated diagnostic systems is critical because it leads to a respectable (but still quite improvable) level of reliability (Spitzer, Endicott, and Robins, 1978). It is all the more impressive because, for the first time, the psychiatric establishment is trying, seri-

TABLE 4.3

Comparison of Diagnostic and Statistical Manual (II) and Research
Diagnostic Criteria for "Major Depression"[1,2]

DSM-II

Manic-Depressive Illnesses

These disorders are marked by severe mood swings and a tendency to remission and
recurrence. Patients may be given this diagnosis in the absence of a previous history of
affective psychosis if there is no obvious precipitating event. This disorder is divided
into three major subtypes: manic type, depressed type, and circular type.

296.2 Manic-depressive illness, depressed type

This disorder consists exclusively of depressive episodes. These episodes are characterized by severely depressed mood and by mental and motor retardation progressing occasionally to stupor. Uneasiness, apprehension, perplexity, and agitation may also be
present. When illusions, hallucination, and delusions (usually of guilt or of hypochon-
driacal or paranoid ideas) occur, they are attributable to the dominant mood disorder.
Because it is a primary mood disorder, this psychosis differs from the *Psychotic-depressive
reaction*, which is more easily attributable to precipitating stress. Cases incompletely
labeled as "psychotic depression" should be classified here rather than under *Psychotic-
depressive reaction*.

Major Depressive Disorder

This category is for episodes of illness in which a major feature of the clinical picture is
dysphoric mood accompanied by the depressive syndrome. This category is distinguished
from less severe disturbances of mood which are not accompanied by the full syndrome
and which in this classification are called Minor Depressive Disorder. This category
should also be used for mixed states, in which manic and depressive features occur
together, or when a patient cycles from a period of mania to a period of depression, or
the reverse.

A. Dysphoric mood characterized by symptoms such as the following: depressed, sad,
   blue, hopeless, low, down in the dumps, "don't care any more," irritable, worried.
   The mood disturbance must be prominent and relatively persistent but not necessarily
   the most dominant symptom. It does not include momentary shifts from one dysphoric mood to another dysphoric mood, e.g., anxiety to depression to anger, such
   as are seen in states of acute psychotic turmoil.

B. At least five of the following symptoms are required to have appeared as part of the
   episode for definite and four for probable:

   1. Poor appetite or weight loss or increased appetite or weight gain (change of one
      lb. a week over several weeks or ten lbs. a year when not dieting).

2. Sleep difficulty or sleeping too much.

3. Loss of energy, fatigability, or tiredness.

4. Psychomotor agitation or retardation (but not mere subjective feeling of restlessness or being slowed down).

5. Loss of interest or pleasure in usual activities or decrease in sexual drive (do not include if limited to a period when delusional or hallucinating).

6. Feelings of self-reproach or excessive or inappropriate guilt (either may be delusional).

7. Complaints or evidence of diminished ability to think or concentrate, such as slow thinking or indecisiveness (do not include if associated with formal thought disorder).

8. Recurrent thought of death or suicide or any suicidal behavior.

C. Dysphoric features of illness lasting at least one week. Definite (sign) if lasted more than two weeks, probable if one to two weeks.

D. Sought or was referred for help from someone during the dysphoric period or had impaired functioning socially, with family, at home, or at work.

E. None of the following suggesting Schizophrenia is present:

1. Delusions of control or thought broadcasting, insertion, or withdrawal (as defined in this manual).

2. Hallucinations of any type throughout the day for several days or intermittently throughout a one-week period unless all of the content is clearly related to depression or elation.

3. Auditory hallucinations in which either a voice keeps up a running commentary on the patient's behaviors or thoughts as they occur, or two or more voices converse with each other.

4. At some time during the period of illness had delusions or hallucinations for more than one month in the absence of prominent affective (manic or depressive) symptoms (although typical depressive delusions, such as delusions of guilt, sin, poverty, nihilism, or self-deprecation or hallucinations of similar content are permitted).

5. Preoccupation with a delusion or hallucination to the relative exclusion of other symptoms or concern (other than delusions of guilt, sin, poverty, nihilism, or self-deprecation or hallucinations with similar content).

6. Definite instances of formal thought disorder (as defined in this manual).

---

[1]See text for references.

[2]RDC's category actually includes manic depression as a subset of major depressive disorder.

[3]Statements of cues are tied to the SADS interview; see Spitzer et al., 1978.

the past, theoretical distinctions, whether or not supported by data, and political considerations were the primary determinants of the diagnostic distinctions. The Research Diagnostic Criteria and the forthcoming DSM-III, currently undergoing field testing (Spitzer, Forman, and Nee, 1979; Spitzer and Forman, 1979), are not without their critics, and many of their objections (Schacht and Nathan, 1977) and alternative systems (McLemore and Benjamin, 1979) should be consulted by the reader wishing to understand the diagnostic controversy. Schacht and Nathan quite cogently argue that, while DSM-III is a vast improvement over DSM-II, it is still a political document because it seeks to disenfranchise psychology and other social and behavioral sciences by insisting that mental disorders are still medical diseases. This interdisciplinary rivalry is frequently based on nothing more than financial opportunism (seeking to exclude psychologists from the insurance reimbursement network or courtroom forensic testimony; or, conversely, to make psychologists eligible "just like" doctors).[13] We deplore this "down-in-the-mud level" of interchange, and view it as unfortunate that the more serious levels of interdisciplinary disagreement, as exemplified by McLemore and Benjamin's article, are not the rule instead of the exception.

FUNCTIONAL CRITERIA FOR COMPETENCY DETERMINATIONS

It would be inconsistent with the thrust of our arguments if we were to supply operational definitions of *the* criteria for competency. The determination of competency is context-dependent and needs to be decided on a case-by-case basis within the general framework of *Dusky* (Chapter 2, this volume; Comment, *Harvard Law Review*, 1967; Eizenstat, 1968; Oliver, 1965).

The crux of competent decision-making is the information upon which it is formulated. It is clearly recognized by all that expert testimony rises no higher than the quality of observation upon which it is based (*United States* v. *Horowitz*, 1973). This implies, given the current state of the art in psychological and psychiatric assessment (e.g., Wiggins, 1973), that testimony to the courts must have a firm evidentiary base. Testimony should be as concrete and behaviorally specific as possible; the person testifying should indicate the rules of inference that lead from observation to conclusion and should specify as well the empirical and/or theoretical justifications that exist for such inferences.[14]

As our work (Roesch and Golding, 1978; Chapter 6) indicates, however, current reports to courts are most frequently stereotyped in form, often containing only summary conclusions ("defendant is competent") or relatively abstract psychiatric phraseology ("defendant showed evidence of persecutory delusions"). The psychiatric community has a well-deserved reputation for testifying in conclusory, mystique-producing ways, clouding the real uncertainties of their conclusions. As Bazelon (1975) puts it, "Psychiatrists have never been able to understand that conclusory labels and opinions are no substitute for facts derived from disciplined investigation. . . . [An opinion] is only as good as the *investigation*, the *facts*, and the *reasoning* that underlie it" (p. 181).

If the quality of decision-making is to be improved, it is necessary that reports to the court contain as much particular information as possible, indicating not only what behaviors were observed but what their significance is. In general, these reports (one hopes the product of a screening panel as described in Chapter 7) should not focus primarily upon symptom description or diagnosis; rather, the more relevant issues are the *behaviors and mental processes observed*, and an evaluation of how these behaviors and mental processes relate to competency to stand trial in the particular case at hand. Reference to such unqualified psychopathology descriptors as "inappropriate affect," "incoherent," "irrelevant," or "confused," with no behavioral support given as the basis for these opinions, and, more significantly, no justification for the relationship of these terms to competence, should be avoided at all costs. Ideally, no conclusory phrases or jargon would be used at all, but, if present, the data upon which they are based should be included.

An analysis of a sample report (taken at random from the reports collected as part of our study) illustrates the nature of the problem quite well:

This 27 year old, white, single male was admitted the first time to this Hospital on 7 June 1969 from Gaston County by Court Order. It appears, that this patient is under the Indictment of Crime Against Nature and his hospitalization was ordered in accordance of G.S. 112–83, although the Order refers to an observation to determine his mental capacity to plead to the Bill of Indictment.

This patient was admitted on eight different occasions to the Broughton Hospital, Morgantown, North Carolina. His first hospitalization was on 28 March 1961 and he was discharged from the last, the eighth hospitalization, on 7 June 1969. His hospital records indicate that during the first few hospitalizations at Broughton it was felt that his main problem was a personality disorder, which was manifested primarily in anti-social behavior and excessive drinking. During the last few hospitalizations at Broughton, however, *it has become apparent that this patient is suffering of schizophrenia, he displayed bizarre behavior and ideations and obviously the patient was delusional.* [a] The patient received a variety of different psychiatric treatments, his hospital course was rather unpredictable and also he has escaped a number of different occasions.

The personal past history indicates that he was born in 1942 in Shelby, North Carolina. This patient was reared mostly by his grandparents and there is very little known about his birth and early development. *It should be noted that his grandmother and two maternal uncles have been in Broughton Hospital as patients.* [b] Apparently he developed properly and at the usual age began school. He stopped his education at age 18 and was in the eleventh grade. It is stated that he has stopped his education on account of earning some money. Shortly after his school he entered the United States Air Force and remained in service for approximately six months. The reason for the separation was his emotional inability to adjust to service life. This patient is described while he was in high school as a fairly well adjusted individual who showed considerable interest in reading. From the age of 16 he began to drink, at times excessively. He has shown very little interest in the opposite sex and never married. Following his short service in the United States Air Force in 1960 this patient began to show disinterest in his environment and was reluctant to assume responsibilities. In 1961 he was hospitalized the first time at Broughton. From here on until the present date this patient has been in and out of the hospital and obviously has shown evidence of a mental disturbance.

On admission the patient appeared to be alert but his affect was rather fixed and at times inappropriate. [c] He was well oriented in time, place and person. He became somewhat confused and tense when he was asked about the circumstances under which he entered this Hospital. He freely admitted to *paranoid ideations and pedophilia.* [d] Obviously the patient was very preoccupied and there was evidence of dissociation of his thoughts. His hospital course was rather uneventful. On the ward the patient has presented no particular difficulties in his management. It is noted, that he is somewhat neglecting in his appearance and shows little interest in his environment. Generally speaking this patient appears to be tense and the psychomotor activity is somewhat increased.

During the consequent interviews the patient has expressed a great deal of his delusional system. It appears, that this patient firmly believes about his abilities

to determine some individuals' future by looking in the sun. With an inappropriate affect the patient stated, that 'you wouldn't understand' just what those
signs mean, nevertheless he does and therefore he is a different individual from
us. [e]

He gave a rather coherent and detailed account of the incidence [sic] leading
to his present charges. [f] The patient stated, that he cannot resist to these
impulses although he realizes the wrongness of such. During the interview
the patient has become several times confused and irrelevant. He appears
to be of above average intelligence and from that standpoint he is fully
aware of his present legal situation.

The physical examination on admission revealed a well developed and
nourished white male with a scar on the left knee, and otherwise the
findings were essentially within normal limits. The laboratory findings
were within normal, including a nonreactive VDRL. The skull x-ray revealed a little irregularity at the outer side of the left antral sinus and this
might possibly be the result of an old fracture. Otherwise the bony structure was normal and all other findings of the skull x-ray were normal. The
chest x-ray was normal. The electroencephalogram was normal.

The psychological testing revealed a full-scale I.Q. of 98, which places
this patient in the average intellectual functioning level.

Diagnosis: Schizophrenic Reaction, Chronic, Undifferentiated Type.
APA Code: 295.90.

Recommendations: The examination and observations reveals that this patient is subject to a mental disturbance constituting insanity. This condition is
manifested primarily in delusional thinking and inability to reason or to exercise
proper judgment. This patient is fully aware of the wrongness of his alleged act,
however, due to his mental disturbance he was unable to adhere to right and
because of his disorganized thinking he is unable to assist in his own defense. He
should continue hospitalization for a minimum necessary period of time as provided in G.S. 122–91 and 122–65 as being incompetent to stand trial at this
time. [g] [Italics added to certain key sentences and phrases]

In order to understand the problem inherent in this form of communication to the court, let us look at several sections in detail. (We needn't
concern ourselves with its obvious "dictated" quality or its lack of coher-
ence; such is all too typical of the products presented to the court.)

Consider first italicized phrase a. What use does this information have
for the court? It is nothing more than a vague diagnostic label, unelaborated at that. It can be of little use to the court unless the judge happens
to believe that presence of a delusion is sufficient grounds for a finding of
incompetency.[15] Moreover, the phraseology ("dissociation of his thoughts")
communicates little, and such unelaborated and undefended jargon is a

good example of what is wrong with the typical diagnostically oriented report. If this statement about thought disorder was made on the basis of a careful examination of a known nature (e.g., SADS), then one might have some faith in it. As it stands, however, one has good reason not to believe it, considering the well-known tendency of average diagnosticians to overlabel. Moreover, even if the description is accurate, it must be related, functionally, to the defendant's ability to "understand and assist." The same problem exists with the phrase "bizarre behavior and ideation." Upon what instances is this description based, and *how might these interfere with the defendant's competency?*[16]

Phrase *b* has no place in such a report. Why should this information be noted? The only conceivable explanation is to convince the court that this defendant comes from "crazy stock" and hence is unlikely ever to change. This simply prejudices the case and reinforces the inappropriate "insane-incompetent" assumption.

In phrase *c* we begin to get possibly relevant details, but they are communicated in an incomplete fashion. In what way was the defendant alert? If his affect was inappropriate, how so?[17] In what situations? More important, how would this affect his demeanor at trial or in consultation with his attorney?

In phrase *d* we do not know the extent of his paranoid ideation, nor do we know how or why it might affect his competency. The report that he admits to pedophilia is inappropriate, since it prejudices the court and violates the defendant's right to avoid self-incrimination (the defendant is, after all, accused of pedophilia).[18]

In phrase *e* we get details of his "delusional" system, but this seems to be a case of overlabeling. Many individuals believe in divination by the sun, or astrology, or Tarot cards. It isn't a consensual belief system, but it is somewhat overplaying the matter to label it delusional. More important, how would this affect his ability to stand trial? It seems unlikely that it would, at least as presented.

Phrase *f* comes to the heart of the matter and, as far as it goes, clearly indicates that the defendant has quite adequate ability to assist his counsel. How then is the recommendation (*g*) reached that he is unable to assist in his own defense? Not only is this a logical *non sequitur* but, insofar as any behaviorally specific evidence is given, the report *supports* a finding of competency.

This report is not atypical. One should not be too quick to find fault with psychiatry and psychology, however, since such reports reflect a long-accepted (but, one hopes, changeable) practice. Typically the courts have been all too willing to shift the burden of decisional responsibility to mental health professionals. To quote Bazelon (1975), "Make no mistake, on predicting dangerousness, society was glad to throw this particular hot potato into the collective psychiatric lap. But, it is also distressing to think that many psychiatrists so readily accepted the delegation of such power without first determining whether their knowledge and skills were up to it. Now they are trapped into pretending the potato isn't very hot" (p. 188). The same problem exists in this respect to competency testimony.

In the case of *United States v. Gundelfinger* (1951) the court clearly addressed the issue of the relevance of testimony and provided an example of the type of leadership role an informed judge can take, as the following excerpt makes clear:

It was apparent to the Court that the psychiatrists who examined the defendant did not understand the purpose of the examination and the narrow issue to be determined by the Court. Both doctors obviously made extensive psychiatric examinations of the defendant and both agreed that he was insane. However, *neither doctor testified regarding the ability of the defendant to understand the nature of the charges against him or to assist in his defense until specifically questioned in this regard by the Court.* It seems apparent that when the examinations were made, the doctors did not have in mind this specific issue. At the close of his direct testimony, the Court asked Dr. Mayer the following question:

Q. What would you say, Doctor, as to the ability of the defendant to understand the nature of the proceedings against him and as to whether he would be able to assist his attorneys in defending the charges against him?

A. In my opinion he does not understand the nature and consequences of what he proposes, and therefore, is unable to assist his attorneys. He is pathologically delusional and, therefore, cannot be changed into any other attitude.

This answer, while, we feel, not intentionally evasive, was none the less not wholly responsive to the question. Dr. Mayer did not say that the defendant was unable to understand the nature of the charges against him and only inferentially states that he is unable to assist his attorneys. In response to a question as to whether the defendant was able to understand the nature of the charges against him and to assist in his defense, Dr.

Wholey testified: '*The very nature of his psychosis prevents him from being able to have a sound interpretation of the questions involved with his convictions.* The only thing he can do is to defend these delusional ideas, if that may be of any help. That would be the extent to which he would be able to exercise it.'

This answer does not indicate that the defendant is unable to understand the nature of the charges against him, but deals rather with the defendant's appreciation of the consequences of his particular beliefs. It does not discuss at all the defendant's ability to assist in his own defense. The testimony of the physicians, therefore, does not establish with any certainty that the defendant lacks the capacity to be present mentally at his own trial. (*Gundelfinger*, p. 631, italics added)

This judicial sentiment, that mental health experts ought to testify in concrete terms relevant to the issue at hand, is a recurring theme in the findings of many (e.g., Oliver, 1965). Of course, adopting functional criteria for trial competency means that, of necessity, the decision is a joint one, ultimately made by a judge but in the context of recommendations from a multidisciplinary screening/evaluation panel that has the ability to evaluate the defendant's behavior and mental processes in the context of specific legal and judicial knowledge of what will be required in the case at hand (see Chapter 7).

We believe that the general form of the report ought to concern itself with the following areas and issues, adapted from Judge Ridge's criteria cited previously in Chapter 2 and from suggestions by Ausness (1978) and McGarry et al. (1973).

Functional memory. It is obvious that a defendant must remember the events that happened to him/her before, during, and after the time period during which the alleged crime occurred. It is less obvious that complete unbiased memory is necessary or possible (Loftus and Loftus, 1976; Loftus and Palmer, 1974; *United States* v. *Wilson*, 1966; Chapter 2, this book). Defendants must surely have access to some details of their behavior at the time of the alleged crime, but what is required depends upon the defenses potentially available. The degree and quality of memory necessary thus are context-dependent and cannot be evaluated without expert legal advice and knowledge (which, needless to say, the average forensic psychiatrist or psychologist does not have). Under some circumstances it may be critical that the defendant be able to remember intentions, motives, and other feeling states as well as physical details, sequences, and the like. The defendant must also, perhaps, need to know what happened during arrest and arraignment, whether "Miranda warnings" were given, be able to recognize a distortion in the testimony of police officers or other witnesses, etc. In another sense of memory the defendant must be able to remember the defense strategy and adhere to it (Ausness, 1978).

Appropriate relationship with attorney. The defendant must be able to assist a competent attorney effectively. Obviously, difficulty eliciting cooperation from a defendant may be a problem of the attorney, not of the defendant. Assuming modal interpersonal skills, a defendant must trust his/her attorney sufficiently to make effective defense possible. This is not to say that a young ghetto black, for example, would be incompetent if he refused to cooperate with an insensitive, court-appointed, white lawyer who didn't have much of a conception of the defendant's life position. However, if the young man's suspiciousness were so great that he suspected collusion even by the most obviously sympathetic source (a young black lawyer with a reputation in the youth's own community), one might realistically suspect that competency would be an issue. In a related fashion the defendant must be able to comprehend rationally what is expected of the lawyer-client relationship, including knowing enough to dismiss an incompetent or poor lawyer! One must demonstrate, in short, that the defendant has the realistic ability to cooperate effectively, given a proper chance. A somewhat delicate issue is raised in the case of a defendant who wants to plead guilty. An evaluation panel and a judge in that case would be faced with the rather tricky question of whether or not a desire for punishment is a moral manifestation of guilt or a masochistic manifestation of some rather more severe disturbance that led one to want to be punished according to an excessive standard of responsibility (a problem dealt with in exquisite detail by Dostoevsky in *Crime and Punishment*).

Appreciating the legal situation. Most of the functional aspects of competency fall in this area. Can defendants appreciate what is expected of them if they "take the stand"? Do they know what will happen if they waive the right to counsel or to a jury trial? If they plead guilty, what will happen (see Chapter 2)? Do they appreciate the adversary nature of the prosecutor's role? Are they sufficiently able to trust the judge to a realistic degree? One could, of course, go on and on. The general principle seems quite clear.

A sample report. Given the above discussion, the following report is offered, not as an ideal (it was purposely drawn up as realistic) but as what ought to be expected as an average report:

The defendant, Allen, is firmly committed to a delusional system in which he believes that his current attorney is receiving commands from God to make sure that he is punished. Upon questioning, Allen also stated that "no other attorney could defend me either because all lawyers are born of God's seed." Allen's attorney, Lehman, is of the opinion that Allen, who refuses to talk with him, cannot be defended in the present case because eyewitness testimony can be challenged successfully only if Allen can tell his attorney where he was on the night of June 12, 1975 and who also might have placed him somewhere other than the scene of the crime. The attorney members of this panel concur that Allen is not properly defendable under these circumstances. Each of the panel members has sought to communicate to the defendant that either he will be found guilty as charged if he does not cooperate, or he will not be permitted to stand trial because of his incompetency. The defendant is able to literally understand what we say (he can repeat back to us our statements), but he does not have a rational comprehension of his position. He insists that God will not be able to carry out his imminent punishment as long as he (the defendant) refrains from speaking to God's agent (the attorney) and twirls his body to the left three times a day to indicate his allegiance to the "dark spirit." Based upon these facts, it is our opinion that the defendant cannot now stand trial. Dr. Bond, our medical consultant, is of the opinion that Allen's delusional system is not organically based. Dr. Corso and Professor Delacourt are of the opinion that Allen's delusional system may respond to active one-to-one psychotherapy and perhaps chemotherapy. They further believe that if the defendant's delusional system does not change after six months of intensive treatment, it becomes increasingly unlikely, given the present state of knowledge, that it can be changed at all.

Under the circumstances described in this hypothetical case, the defendant might reasonably be found incompetent because he lacked appropriate capacity to understand the role of defense counsel in the adversary proceedings. Note, however, that the mere existence of the delusion is not a sufficient condition for a finding of incompetency. The evaluators must demonstrate the manner in which a delusional system would interfere with the defense.

We have purposely left undiscussed the suggestion that defendants should have an undifferentiated "capacity" to assist in the trial. The defendant must possess some minimal "capacity," depending upon the nature of the charge, to aid counsel in his defense, but it is not clear what that can possibly mean. In some cases, depending on the evidence available, even a profoundly retarded individual could be tried, if his assistance was not fundamental. Thus the screening panel described in Chapter 7 would need to determine the minimal capacity dictated by the case at hand, and determine whether or not the defendant measured up to this. We stress that this determination should take place on *functional*, not abstract, criteria. Scores on intelligence tests, for example, are less important than functional ability, which needs to be assessed in context.

THE PROPER LOCUS OF AUTHORITY IN DECISION-MAKING

We have discussed in previous chapters the empirical evidence that points to the degree of control that psychiatrists and psychologists have had in decision-making about competency. In this section we qualify and expand upon that evidence by reviewing some typical court and mental health opinions on the proper locus of decisional authority.

To our knowledge our North Carolina survey of judges (Roesch and Golding, 1978; see Chapter 6) is the only attempt to ascertain the scope of reasons behind most judges' (sometimes grudging) demurral to the mental health professions. In contradistinction to this usual state of affairs at the lower court level, most federal and Supreme Court decisions are far more protective of judicial authority. The matter is perhaps best stated by the *Harvard Law Review*:

Like criminal responsibility, incompetency is a legal question; the ultimate responsibility for its determination must rest in a judicial rather than a medical authority. In relying on conclusory psychiatric testimony, often expressed in the same terms as the ultimate incompetency question, courts shift responsibility for the determination to psychiatrists who have no special ability to decide the legal issue. Indeed, there is repeated evidence that psychiatrists often misunderstand the test of incompetency and confuse it with the test of criminal responsibility. Medical opinion about the defendant's condition should be only one of the factors relevant to the determination. A defendant's abilities must be measured against the specific demands trial will make upon him and psychiatrists have little familiarity with either trial procedure or the complexities of a particular indictment. In addition, psychiatrists may tend to give disproportionate weight to defendant's need for therapy, or to draw inferences from the refusal of a defendant who wishes to be tried to cooperate in a court-ordered examination. (Comment, Harvard Law Review, 1967, p. 470)

The sort of evidence typically available to a judge, and the inadequacy of "bottom line" conclusions without explicit logic connecting the observations (no matter how reliable) and the conclusions, are frequent sources of comment at the level of the Court of Appeals, as the following illustrates:

The examining psychiatrist was not called to testify; there is no indication that he was even present. No testimony of any kind was offered. The court forthwith found that Moore was competent to stand trial. Moore thereafter entered a not guilty plea.

The psychiatrist's report reveals an extensive history of mental illness, including hospitalizations for psychiatric disorders and repeated suicide attempts. During his stay at the Federal Medical Center, he was "kept in isolation and developed visual hallucinations." In describing Moore's mental condition at the time of the examination, the psychiatrist said: "Abnormal mental trends were manifested by self-destruction, mutilating behavior which occurs under stressful conditions. . . . He panics and has engaged in dangerous behavior to himself such as running before gunfire and swallowing razor blades in an attempt to get into a more protective situation. His mood swings are wide and rapid from deep depression to euphoria in a brief period. . . . His main problem is in sexual identity with fear of both men and women and this leads to panic. He will continue to act out both in custodial and psychiatric hospital placements. He feels that he has nothing to lose and therefore engages in impulsive acting out and controls the environment through his self-destructive acts."

The psychiatrist's diagnosis was that Moore's "competency will be subject to periods of impaired judgment during his panic reactions," that he has "deep-seated emotional problems of long duration," and "the prognosis is poor." He nevertheless concluded that "Moore is presently sane and presently able to understand the proceedings taken against him and to properly assist in his own defense." The psychiatrist did not undertake to offer any explanation for his ultimate conclusion. (Moore v. United States, 1972, p. 665)

The opinion in Moore restates Judge Ridge's frank and blunt statement that "any such psychiatric conclusion, if arrived at, is and cannot be legally binding. At most, it is merely opinion testimony, to be resolved by the legal finder of fact, in the same manner as is the testimony of all expert expressed opinions" (Wieter v. Settle, 1961, p. 322; see also Higgins v. McGrath, 1951).

The courts have gone further than simply objecting to the conclusory nature of most testimony offered,[19] and they have begun to question the authority of mental health professionals to observe and report elementary facts in a reliable and valid fashion. As noted in *Rollerson*, "The value of a psychiatrist's testimony depends largely upon his opportunities for observation and the facts he observes. The testimony of an expert, like that of any other witness, may be excluded if it reports mere opinion, unsupported by 'underlying facts'" (*Rollerson v. United States*, 1964, p. 270). In *Horowitz* the court held that "the testimony of medical experts on the issue is only one factor . . . and rises no higher than the reasons on which it is based and is not binding on the court" (*United States v. Horowitz*, 1973, p. 777). In *Horowitz* the court's challenge to psychiatric testimony was based upon its disbelief that Horowitz's tendency to "fall apart" when under stress, to lose his composure, and to cry, was a sufficient degree of impairment to create a state of incompetency. In *Rollerson*, however, the court (Judge Bazelon) directly attacked the quality of the report, the facts upon which it was based, and the logical and empirical justification of its inferences:

As far as the psychiatric testimony was concerned, Rollerson might as well have been tried *in absentia*. [He was] not present in the conclusionary labels of the psychiatrists or in the perfunctory leading questions of counsel.

We do not intend to imply that the breakdown of meaningful presentation of evidence is the fault alone of the psychiatrists. Lawyers seem not to ask questions which would elicit meaningful responses. They should approach psychiatric witnesses with the same probing skill with which they question doctors about whiplash injuries or with the attention to detail which they apply to "the chain of possession" when some piece of physical evidence is introduced. (*Rollerson*, p. 275, material deleted)

Bazelon is, of course, well known for his attempts to get mental health professionals to testify more relevantly and usefully in the courts, as is clear in the following: "The chief value of an expert's testimony in this field, as in all other fields, rests upon the material from which his opinion is fashioned and the reasoning by which he progresses from his material to his conclusion; in the explanation of the disease and its dynamics, that is, how it occurred, developed, and affected the mental and emotional processes of the defendant; it does not lie in his mere expression of conclusion. The ultimate inferences *vel non* of relationship, of cause and effect, are for the trier of the facts" (*Carter v. United States*, 1957, p. 617).

In his more recent statements to a legal as well as psychiatric audience, Bazelon (1975) reviews his multiple attempts to increase the usefulness of such testimony (*Durham, Brawner, Washington, Carter*) and concludes that little headway has been made, because "many psychiatrists are not convinced that any jurist has the knowledge or the right to criticize the operation of behavior scientists" (p. 175). Furthermore, their unwillingness to demystify their testimony, and their unwillingness to understand the legitimate adversary aspects of courtroom testimony, lead to the current unhealthy state of affairs.

There is little doubt that the psychiatric community casts a jaundiced eye upon the attempts of civil libertarians, jurists, and empirically oriented behavioral scientists to limit the exercise of psychiatric authority. Many psychiatrists see these attempts as ultimately harming patients by denying them proper and efficiently administered treatment (Hoffman, 1977; Treffert, 1977); others see the attempt as a more sinister manifestation of a pathologically motivated antipsychiatry bias. The most sensible (but perhaps not the most consensually believed) views on the locus of decision-making are to be found in the statements of respected and well-trained members of the psychiatric establishment such as Stone (1976) and Robitscher (1977, 1978) who acknowledge the natural limits of psychiatric authority and admit to the legitimacy of many of the challenges:

The mental health bar has labored hard to halt the reign of coercive and warehouse psychiatry. It now faces the equally disheartening prospect of benevolent abandonment. Its challenge is to place itself squarely in the vacuum and to help the mental health profession fashion a mediated flexible system of care for the mentally ill. The new system must use law, but it ought not succumb to a purely legal model just when it has broken with a purely medical model. The personal-caring model must remain a vital albeit distant ideal. Thus, the emerging mental health system may need the law, but it will need enlightened lawyers even more. (Stone, 1976, pp. 247–48)

This view of the mental health–law interface stands in contrast to the more typical view that sees psychiatry as having a great deal to contribute to the more humane treatment of mentally disturbed defendants, and views attempts to limit or challenge psychiatric authority with varying degrees of discomfort (see Bazelon, 1975, for one end of the spectrum; Blinder, 1974, and Bromberg, 1969, for the other). Psychiatrists and other mental health professionals may argue, for example, that such attempts interfere with the delivery of needed mental health intervention. Psychiatrists who espouse this view obviously do not appreciate the "how to attack psychiatric testimony" monographs (e.g., Ennis and Litwack, 1974; *Mental Disabilities Law Reporter*, 1976; Poythress, 1978; Ziskin, 1975, 1977) which are discussed in a subsequent section. Nor are they enamored of more modulated criticism from other behavioral scientists (e.g., Monahan, 1973, 1977). They certainly do not like the shared-responsibility rationale that lies behind screening panels (Balcanoff and McGarry, 1969; Lipsitt, Lelos, and McGarry, 1971; Rosenberg and Mc-Garry, 1972; Chapter 7, this volume). Nevertheless, we believe that such judicially and empirically based reforms are appropriate, and represent the *proper* utilization of mental health testimony. We argue (Chapter 7) that mental health professionals[20] can play a crucial and valuable role in competency evaluations when they participate in screening panels that give at least as equal representation to legal as to mental health opinion. Any recommendation to the court from this panel should address itself specifically to the observable or behavioral facts and should not be conclusory in form.[21] The court has the final responsibility for the determination of competency. If members of the screening panel cannot reach agreement, separate reports should be submitted to the court.

TRAINING MATERIAL FOR LAWYERS AND MENTAL HEALTH PROFESSIONALS

To assure defendants whose competency is questioned the most competent and valid decision-making, one could reasonably argue that they ought to be tried by judges who specialize in mental health law, be represented by lawyers who specialize in mental health law (or who have perhaps gone so far as to have joint degrees in jurisprudence as well as clinical psychology and/or psychiatry), and be evaluated by mental health professionals who are trained in the highest state of their art (regardless of how many "hundreds of evaluations" they've performed!). This is unlikely to happen. Most defendants will face a judicial and mental health system that is often not fully prepared to deal with the issue of competency to stand trial—a sad state of affairs, but one that must be recognized.

Within the past few years, there have been several source books designed to give lawyers "ammunition" to use in the courtroom against mental health professionals. We turn our attention now to a brief evaluation of these source books, leaving our summary recommendations for an optimum training philosophy to the last. Because Ziskin's (1975) book and the closely associated *Mental Disabilities Law Reporter Practice Manual* (Anonymous, 1976) have become so popular, it is useful to examine some aspects of these works that are illustrative of manuals of this sort.

Ziskin and the *Mental Disabilities Law Reporter Practice Manual* begin their suggested cross-examination strategies with such general questions as the following:

Q. Doctor, isn't it true that psychiatry consists mostly of a number of theories about human behavior, none of which have been scientifically proven?

Q. Doctor, isn't it true that there is a substantial body of scientific and professional literature to the effect that the psychiatric interview is influenced by many factors which affect the conclusions that are drawn but have little to do with the actual mental condition of the person being examined?

Q. Doctor, isn't it true that there is a substantial body of scientific and professional literature to the effect that psychiatric diagnoses are not very reliable and not very accurate?

Q. Doctor, isn't there a substantial body of scientific and professional literature to the effect that psychiatrists with considerable experience are no more accurate in their diagnoses than those with little, or even no, experience?

Q. Doctor, are you aware of any substantial body of scientific evidence that supports the assumption that psychiatrists are better able to diagnose or evaluate psychological conditions than are laymen?

Q. Doctor, isn't it true that many of your fellow psychiatrists are of the opinion that psychiatric testimony generally tends to confuse and mislead rather than assist judges and jurors to come to valid conclusions?

Q. Doctor, isn't it true that a substantial number of your fellow psychiatrists believe that the subject matter of psychiatry is not organic disease, but rather involves problems of psycho-social adjustment and learning deficiencies that are more psychological and sociological than medical? (Anonymous, 1976, p. 170)

Ziskin (1975) himself then goes on to say, "If the psychiatrist gives negative answers to any of the foregoing your rebuttal expert will be able to show him up as either ignorant or dishonest by recitation of the scientific and professional literature. However, as indicated, I think that more impact can be made on a jury by cross-examining the expert in more detail as described below" (p. 307). The remainder of Ziskin's book, like Ennis and Litwack (1974), is an attempt to marshal the evidence in the scientific literature that can be used to support these attacks on mental health testimony. A similar approach is followed by Poythress's (1976) manual for training lawyers to defend in civil commitment proceedings.[22]

These manuals and the literature they cite are beginning to have a significant impact on courtroom practice and judicial holdings.[23] In *Smith v. Schlesinger* (1975) the District Court of the District of Columbia found that the literature concerning the impact of social value judgments on psychiatric diagnoses is immense; further, "psychiatric judgments may disguise, wittingly or unwittingly, political or social biases of the psychiatrist; and excessive reliance on diagnoses will pre-empt the primary role of legal decision-makers" (pp. 475, 477).

In reaching this conclusion, the court relied heavily upon the Ennis and Litwack monograph as well as upon work by Szasz (1963). While we do not question the validity of the findings in *Smith*, given the details of his case, we are disturbed at the type of precedent it might set. Courts are increasingly relying upon the results of social science research to help them in the formulation of opinions, although unfortunately not always in the most effective fashion (e.g., Rosen, 1972; Saks, 1978). We obviously support the proper use of empirical data, but we must go on record as cautioning the courts to evaluate the degree of validity that various studies may possess. Research conclusions are, unfortunately, sometimes based upon fatally flawed research design and analysis procedures.

We obviously cannot approach a detailed evaluation of these critical books and monographs and the articles they cite, although such an analysis is clearly worthwhile to pursue. It is, as Meehl (1970d) states, "not easy for a lawyer, no matter how fair minded and intelligent he may be, to separate the gold from the garbage in fields like psychology, psychiatry and sociology" (p. 2). However, we believe that, as one of us cautioned the Illinois legislature, "much winnowing can take place if one can keep two cardinal principles in mind: a) expert opinion that is not supportable by, or is directly contradictory to, *well established empirical fact* should not weigh too heavily upon one's mind; and b) one ought not to be misled by the research evidence that is offered. If one presses one's witnesses as to why the 'data' they cite (if they cite any!) should be believed over someone else's 'data,' one will soon learn to spot the 'gold' from the 'garbage'" (Golding, 1978, p. 1).

The reader of Ziskin, in particular, faces a similar problem. Lawyers who read Ziskin and buy the research cited too cavalierly will find themselves in plenty of trouble if they go up against someone who has the real expertise necessary to separate the gold from the garbage. One could write a book on "Coping with behavioral science research" instead of "Coping with psychiatric and psychological testimony" (the title of Ziskin's book) in exactly the same rhetorical tone.[24]

The reader who wishes to sample the complexity of argument regarding issues in this area should consult the entire issue of the *Journal of Abnormal Psychology* (1975, vol. 84) devoted to an analysis and critique of Rosenhan's (1973) famous demonstration of misdiagnosis, "On being sane in insane places." It takes considerable expertise to evaluate the quality of the pro and con arguments presented, and the one-sided presentation in Ziskin (1977), *whether right or wrong in this case*, will lead the uninitiated into a potential hornet's nest.[25] A little knowledge can indeed be a dangerous thing in the courtroom. Poythress (1979) reaches the same conclusion when he observes that Rosenhan's research "is potentially devastating in the hands of a skillful attorney unless the expert is in a position to point out the flaws in that research, which he or she could quite capably do if familiar with Spitzer's (1976) excellent critique" (p. 617). These monographs are valuable collections of relevant research literature, but are unfortunately written as polemics.

We are not unsympathetic with some of Ziskin's goals; we too would like to see unsupported and generally erroneous psychiatric testimony roundly attacked. But we think that Ziskin in particular has let his legal training in adversarial tactics get the best of him. The purpose of the adversarial system is to bring out the truth by subjecting each side to the most strenuous questioning and cross-examination possible. That is expected. But the system becomes perverted when studies whose methodology is questionable are thrown together with otherwise sound studies under a *caveat emptor* philosophy. Ziskin's book leads one astray, not because one can ignore the data presented but because it is an unscholarly treatment of the data. It amounts to an almost unedited collection of everything nasty or derogatory anyone ever said or "discovered" about psychology and psychiatry. The aim of such books ought to be to educate lawyers and mental health professionals, not to provide them with ammunition of unknown quality.[26]

Poythress (1976, 1977, 1978) constructed a manual, as part of a doctoral dissertation, with the laudable goal of improving the quality of legal defense to defendants represented by guardians *ad litem* in civil commitment proceedings.[27] Quite unlike Ziskin, it attempts to provide a digest of important scientific studies whose data and conclusions could be used to challenge or support various sorts of testimony. Poythress's comments are more reasoned and scholarly, and hence the reader will come away educated to a certain extent. Nevertheless, the same pedagogical flaw is present: the empirical data dangle in a vacuum unless the reader knows how to interpret them. Lawyers especially seem to be distrusting of conclusions thrust upon them without an opportunity to cross-examine the logic that led to them. This is precisely the danger (or the ineffectiveness) of these manuals. As Poythress (1978) discovered, the lawyers he trained indicated that the training manual (and the workshop at which it was presented) was helpful and informative; nevertheless, they were not willing to change their behavior in the courtroom (e.g., aggressively challenge expert testimony). Poythress (1978) cogently argues that "failure of the training intervention appears to be with the failure of the role induction component. Simply put, the majority of attorneys, even when shown how to be potentially more effective advocates for their clients, were not persuaded to take that stance. The clear thrust of the workshop toward the *ad litem* attorney as advocate and the judge's letter of endorsement of that position did not deter the attorneys from taking a more traditional, passive, paternal stance toward the proposed patients" (p. 15).

We believe that other factors were also operating in Poythress's research, namely, that attorneys cannot use such information without more extensive training. A "fact" as a "critique" of the expert's opinion does one little good without the capability to follow through. The situation is analogous to the traveler who learns a phrase of French. Even if uttered with perfect pronunciation, he is lost as soon as a reply is given. None of the "facts" in these manuals work very well if the expert doesn't immediately "cave in." There is simply no shortcut to understanding in the field of mental health law.

Training implications

No list of articles, no matter how comprehensive, will serve a training purpose. This book, no matter how scholarly or authoritative, will not change legal and psychiatric practices without the active involvement of the "student." We have tried, by example, to provide useful references and sources on a variety of points, but generalized and comprehensive reference lists are practically impossible. Professor Golding's course on psychological and clinical assessment, for example, uses a bibliography of *basic articles* that runs to 60 pages and over 1,200 references. No lawyer can be expected to read all of that, but he or she must expect to invest considerable time consulting with experts who know that literature. There can be no shortcut to better handling of mental health issues. We believe that such manuals as Ziskin's miss the forest for the trees by supplying polemically based data without any attempt to genuinely educate the reader, to the detriment of us all. More balanced collections of data that bear on a particular issue, such as Poythress's manual, are worthwhile, but they do not seem to have a great impact, for reasons already discussed. We find ourselves in sympathetic agreement with Poythress's (1979) most recent statements: "It is clear that the courts are willing to act on incorrect 'expert' testimony" (p. 616) and, further, "Evidence of the gap between the presumed and the attained expertise of psychologists (and other mental health 'experts') lies in the expanding use of psychologists in the courts at a time when the legal and mental health journals abound with articles expressing skepticism about the quality of expertise provided" (p. 613). Poythress concludes that rigorous interdisciplinary training with no shortcuts is the only reasonable response. We could not agree more.

RESEARCH DIRECTIONS

It seems clear that considerable work must be done in order to develop a more efficient, reliable, and valid set of procedures for the evaluation of competency to stand trial. Development of assessment methodologies in this area is made particularly difficult because the final court decisions themselves, under normal circumstances, must be viewed as "soft" as opposed to "hard" criteria. As one can ascertain by examining court decisions in detail (e.g., *Bruce v. Estelle*, 1976), the final court outcome may in and of itself be "questionably valid." Our data and those of others (Chapter 3) indicate that court decisions routinely concur with professional mental health recommendations, and we have painstakingly shown that those recommendations are frequently irrelevant to competency properly understood as a construct (Chapter 2).

If competency is viewed as a construct, and if it cannot be reduced to a particular operational definition, and if even court decisions themselves are (more or less) fallible, then how can one proceed to improve the reliability and validity of assessment procedures used (or to be developed) in its determination? We cannot gaze too deeply into a crystal ball, but we do think it appropriate to discuss briefly the most basic considerations that should guide future work in this area.

While there are numerous assessment instruments designed to measure competency at the screening or determination stage (see Chapter 3), it is clear that only one, the semistructured interview format of the CAI (Competency Assessment Instrument), comes close to being a realistically useful device. As we have discussed elsewhere (Chapter 3), even this instrument has serious psychometric problems. More fundamentally, however, instrument validation and development cannot take place in the absence of a believable or defensible criterion. Therefore, it is crucial that future research use some form of "blue ribbon" panel to serve as an ultimate criterion against which to validate both various assessment procedures and courtroom decisions. Any number of theoretically and pragmatically useful studies can be done in this context. The crucial ingredient is the use of a "harder than usual" criterion, established by an in-depth study panel. Such blue-ribbon panels should be made up of judges, lawyers, and mental health specialists drawn from their respective professions on the basis of their peer reputation with respect to mental health law issues. In future studies such panels would be charged with examining the entire normal evaluation procedure used for each defendant, and reaching their own decision as well as commenting on the sources of adequacy and inadequacy with the decision as reached normally. This may seem to be an unnecessarily complex way of establishing an "ultimate criterion," but we believe that the history of the development of assessment techniques (Wiggins, 1973) supports such a procedure. Save for the scrutiny applied by higher courts in the case of appeal, no effort has ever been made to examine directly the "reasonableness" (one really can't say "validity") of a naturally occurring set of decisions or to provide a defensible rationale for choosing a research-based criterion. This criterion is the "hardest available" and can serve as an interim working criterion by which we can "pull ourselves up by our bootstraps" (Cronbach and Meehl, 1955; Meehl, 1973; Wiggins, 1973). Using this blue-ribbon panel, we would now be in a position to examine a number of important issues. How does gross psychiatric diagnosis actually relate to competency? Are there any stronger relationships at the level of psychopathological description (à la the items from the SADS or the PSS)? Are panels of more "ordinary" professionals (a lawyer, a psychologist, or a psychiatrist) as we describe in Chapter 7 able to reach more valid and cost-effective recommendations based upon functional criteria? What courtroom procedures produce the form of testimony (Bazelon, 1975) that leads to the best evidence upon which to make such decisions?

It is clear, even from this brief discussion, that many unsettled issues exist with respect to the assessment of competency as a construct. While some ultimate answer or procedure will never be attainable (because of the open-textured characteristic of constructs), the path toward such a goal is clear. When one reaches the understanding that the criteria for psychopathology and the criteria for competency are not interchangeable, a significant degree of progress has already been made.

Notes

1. For example, Ziskin's (1975) book and its supplement (1977) are quite comprehensive in their coverage of the issue of diagnostic reliability, but the material is presented in a highly rhetorical fashion. Moreover, the conclusions are overdrawn and could be forcefully attacked on empirical, methodological, and logical grounds. For even more extreme examples one should consult Roth, Dayley, and Lerner (1973). We try, in this section, to present a balanced summary of the most salient issues; we examine the basis of Ziskin's work in a subsequent section.

2. The reader who wishes to explore this complex issue in detail is referred to Cohen (1968), Fleiss and Cohen (1973), Fleiss et al. (1972), and Spitzer and Fleiss (1974). See Garfield (1978) and Meehl and Rosen (1955) for discussion of the issue of base rates and diagnosis.

3. The Research Diagnostic Criteria are currently undergoing revision into the "new" Diagnostic and Statistical Manual (III); see Spitzer, Endicott, and Robins (1978).

4. See Sawyer (1966) and Wiggins (1973) for a review of this area of the clinical judgment literature.

5. Garland (1960) and Koran (1975a,b) provide general reviews; see also Acheson (1960; a kappa of 0.70 for electrocardiograms); Felson et al. (1973; a kappa of 0.47 for chest X-ray); Markush, Schaaf, and Siegel (1967; causes of death); Norden et al. (1970; a kappa of 0.28 for intravenous pylography).

6. See *Addington v. Texas* (1979) for an application of such a balanced view by the Supreme Court to the problem of prediction of dangerousness in civil commitment. In *Addington* the Supreme Court rejected the idea that dangerousness need be beyond a reasonable doubt: "The subtleties and nuances of psychiatric diagnosis render certainties virtually beyond reach in most situations. The reasonable doubt standard of criminal law functions in its realm because there the standard is addressed to specific, knowable facts. Psychiatric diagnosis, in contrast, is to a large extent based upon medical 'impressions' drawn from subjective analysis and filtered through the experience of the diagnostician" (*Addington*, p. 1811). We hasten to add that more cannot be expected in the area of competency testimony until the focus begins to change to "facts," especially when those facts are observable on the basis of courtroom behavior and functionally related to competency.

7. The type of validity being considered here is *predictive validity*. For a general introduction to this and other types of validity see Cronbach (1964) and Wiggins (1973).

8. See Chapter 2; as we argue in the last section of this chapter, even court decisions may be "questionably valid" and "soft" in a number of respects.

9. See also Meehl (1970d) and Livermore, Malmquist, and Meehl (1968).

10. See Campbell and Fiske (1959); Cronbach and Meehl (1955); Golding (1977); and Wiggins (1973) for a general discussion of this point.

11. Luria and McHugh (1974), for example, also found this to be the weakest part of the Wing Present State Examination.

12. An extensive and current review of these various interview and diagnostic systems may be found in Matarazzo (1978).

13. The issue of psychologists testifying in court is treated in Smith (1976).

14. The necessity to tie observations to theory, and to elaborate on the connections so that the logic is available for scrutiny by the court, is clearly set forth by Judge Bazelon in *Washington v. United States* (1967):

"Dr. ——, this instruction is being given to you in advance of your testimony as an expert witness, in order to avoid confusion or misunderstanding. The instruction is not only for your guidance, but also for the guidance of counsel and the jury.

"Because you have qualified as an expert witness your testimony is governed by special rules. Under ordinary rules, witnesses are allowed to testify about what they have seen and heard, but are not always allowed to express opinions and conclusions based on these observations. Due to your training and experience, you are allowed to draw conclusions and give opinions in the area of your special qualifications. However, you may not state conclusions or opinions as an expert witness unless you also tell the jury what investigations, observations, reasoning and medical theory led to your opinion. . . .

"It must be emphasized that you are to give your expert diagnosis of the defendant's mental condition. This word of caution is especially important if you give an opinion as to whether or not the defendant suffered from a 'mental disease or defect' because the clinical diagnostic meaning of this term may be different from its legal meaning. You should not be concerned with its legal meaning. Neither should you consider whether you think this defendant should be found guilty or responsible for the alleged crime. These are questions for the court and jury. Further, there are considerations which may be relevant in other proceedings or in other contexts which are not relevant here; for example, how the defendant's condition might change, or whether he needs treatment, or is treatable, or dangerous, or whether there are adequate hospital facilities, or whether commitment would be best for him, or best for society. What is desired in this case is the kind of opinion you would give to a family which brought one of its members to your clinic and asked for your diagnosis of his mental condition and a description of how his condition would be likely to influence his conduct. Insofar as counsel's questions permit, you should testify in this manner.

"When you are asked questions which fall within the scope of your special training and experience, you may answer them if you feel competent to do so; otherwise you should not answer them. If the answer depends upon knowledge and experience generally possessed by ordinary citizens, for example questions of morality as distinguished from medical knowledge, you should not answer. You should try to separate expert medical judgments from what we may call 'lay judgments.' If you cannot make a separation and if you do answer the questions nonetheless, you should state clearly that your answer is not based solely upon your special knowledge.

"It would be misleading for the jury to think that your testimony is based on your special knowledge concerning the nature and diagnosis of mental conditions if in fact it is not.

"In order that the jury may understand exactly what you mean, you should try to explain things in simple language. Avoid technical terms whenever possible. Where medical terms are useful or unavoidable, make sure you explain these terms clearly. If possible, the explanation should not be merely general or abstract, but should be related to this defendant, his behavior and his condition. Where words or phrases used by counsel are unclear, or may have more than one meaning, you should ask for clarification before answering. You should then explain your answer so that your understanding of the question is clear. You need not give 'yes or no' answers. In this way any confusion may be cleared up before the questioning goes on.

"Some final words of caution. Because we have an adversary system, counsel may deem it is his duty to attack your testimony. You should not construe this as an attack upon your integrity. More specifically, counsel may try to undermine your opinions as lacking certainty or adequate basis. We recognize that an opinion may be merely a balance of probabilities and that we cannot demand absolute certainty. Thus you may testify to opinions that are within the zone of reasonable medical certainty. The crucial point is that the jury should know how your opinion may be affected by limitations of time or facilities in the examination of this defendant or by limitations in present psychiatric knowledge. The underlying facts you have obtained may be so scanty or the state of professional knowledge so unsure that you cannot fairly venture any opinion. If so, you should not hesitate to say so. And, again, if you do give an opinion, you should explain what you did to obtain the underlying facts, what these facts are, how they led to the opinion, and what, if any, are the uncertainties in the opinion" (*Washington*, pp. 457–58).

15. This would be improper. Mental illness *per se*, even if present, in no way implies incompetency. See our discussion of this in Chapter 2.

16. As indicated in Chapters 3 and 6, such statements in the psychiatric reports as "defendant is delusional" are quite predictive of a judgment that the defendant is, in the mind of the examiner, psychotic. Hence they also predict the final recommendation of competency or incompetency (because of the assumed psychotic-incompetent link). This further demonstrates the degree of influence inappropriately held by the single author of a report.

17. The prevalence of "inappropriate affect" in most reports deserves some note, especially because this description has consistently emerged as the *least reliable* within the domain of descriptors (Helzer et al., 1977; Luria and McHugh, 1974). This finding is particularly important because we suspect the courts rely heavily upon this phrase and phrases related to "thought disorder," another rather difficult observation to make reliably, in judging defendants to be incompetent.

18. See Chapter 5 for a discussion of this issue.

19. An extensive discussion may be found in the following cases: *Bruce v. Estelle* (1976); *Holloway v. United States* (1964); *Rollerson v. United States* (1964); *United States v. Brawner* (1972); *United States v. Taylor* (1971); *Washington v. United States* (1967).

20. The term "mental health professionals" is used to indicate that both psychiatrists and psychologists may be properly called upon to assess competency (see *Jenkins v. United States*, 1962; Pacht et al., 1973; Perlin, 1977; Report of the Task Force on the Role of Psychology in the Criminal Justice System, 1978; Silverman, 1969; and Smith, 1976, for discussions of the role of the psychologist). However, both professions require specific training in the area of forensic law (see Fenster, Litwack, and Symonds, 1975; S. Pollack, 1973; Poythress, 1979) and would benefit from an increased involvement of the legal profession in the evaluation of competency, as we propose in the screening panel process.

21. Diamond and Louisell (1965) present a quite balanced view: "We suggest that in all instances the psychiatric expert be allowed to relate to the court exactly how he reached his opinion and what were the sources of his information. He should be required to describe in fairly precise terms his own process of evaluating his source material; what information did he accept, and what did he reject; what sources did he place great weight upon, and what sources did he minimize; and why did he evaluate the clinical material in these ways. But always, the psychiatrist (as with all physicians) must be trusted to determine in his own way what are the relevant clinical facts upon which a professional opinion can be based. For this, the psychiatrist is accountable to the standards of his professional colleagues and their accumulated body of professional skill and knowledge. He is also subject to cross examination which may gain in incisiveness and pertinency proportion-

ally to the freedom accorded him to tell the whole story" (p. 1354). Other senior spokespersons for the psychiatric establishment present similar views (Guttmacher, 1955; Modlin, 1976; S. Pollack, 1973), acknowledging the legitimacy of adversarial confrontation that aims at better understanding.

22. Poythress's manual has much to commend it and is not written in the same strident, uncritical tone as Ziskin's manual, but it is included in the list because of functional similarity.

23. Poythress (1978), however, found that lawyers were generally unwilling to use the material he gathered for them in his training manual.

24. The literature on the adequacy of research designs is immense, a specialty of its own in the social sciences (e.g., Cook and Campbell, 1979; Meehl, 1970c). Judges, lawyers, and others who try to use social science data without some working acquaintance with the basics of research design can easily be misled.

25. One need not agree completely with all of Spitzer's (1976) comments about Rosenhan's study to realize that at many points he has Rosenhan cold, but none of this appears in Ziskin's (1977) comments. For example, Rosenhan's discussion of reliability in psychiatric diagnosis commits a serious and classically well-known error in psychometric theory that would be apparent only to an expert.

26. A counterpoint could be made to this argument. One could argue that all that counts is "winning the case," regardless of the known truth. As social scientists and as human beings, we reject such a moral philosophy. One of us (Golding) has had the opportunity to testify in federal court and before state committees, and knows that certain points could be made more forcefully by ignoring contradictory data. Such overt partisanship has, as an ideal, no place in the behavioral sciences, and we doubt it does in the courtroom either. The "best defense possible" may be an applicable standard for some purposes, but it perverts the involvement of mental health professionals.

27. Unfortunately Poythress's (1978) data indicate that lawyers did not use the manual, to the potential detriment of their clients.

5

Legal Issues and Procedures

As we discussed in Chapter 2, competency laws have evolved in order to protect the rights of a defendant to a fair trial. The assumption is that defendants will be denied due process if they do not make the expected contribution to their own defense. If they are not able to communicate properly with their attorney, for example, then they may not be able to relate certain facts which might lead to an acquittal. Ironically, however, it has been suggested that the procedures that the courts follow in affording defendants this protection may in practice produce substantial infringements on their rights. Bail is often denied during the period of evaluation (Golten, 1972; Kaufman, 1972; *Marcey v. Harris*, 1968; Slovenko, 1977; Stone, 1976); the court-ordered evaluation usually takes place in an unnecessarily restrictive environment (Golten, 1972; Kaufman, 1972; Wexler, 1976); commitment criteria for evaluation are less stringent than the criteria for civil commitment (a finding of dangerousness is not required for evaluation commitment); rights against self-incrimination in a compulsory psychiatric evaluation may be jeopardized (Berry, 1973; Golten, 1972);[1] and rights to a speedy trial may be jeopardized (Gobert, 1973; Kaufman, 1972; *United States v. Geelan*, 1975; *Williams v. United States*, 1957). In addition, once a defendant has been found incompetent, treatment usually takes place in an unnecessarily restrictive environment, thus violating the "least restrictive alternative" principle (*Covington v. Harris*, 1969; Golten, 1972; *Lake v. Cameron*, 1966; M. K. Pollack, 1973; *United States v. Klein*, 1963); also, incompetent defendants are frequently held in hospital longer than they would have been if convicted and sentenced to prison (Hess and Thomas, 1963; Janis, 1974; Kaufman, 1972; McGarry, 1971). These issues thus cast considerable doubt on the protection of rights afforded defendants whose competency is questioned.

In this chapter we will consider these issues at length by reviewing the constitutional and procedural issues that have arisen as the courts and mental health professionals attempt to confront the issue of competency. We also present a detailed analysis of the practice in one state, North Carolina, both to provide a clearer focus for these issues and to present a context for the research project that we conducted in North Carolina and discuss in the next chapter.

Right to Bail

Only one state (South Dakota) specifically denies bail during an evaluation of competency. All other states have some statutory provision for noninstitutional evaluations. If a defendant meets the conditions for release on bail, then the evaluation could presumably be held while free on bail. In practice, however, this may not be the case. The routine practice in many states is to commit defendants for evaluations in mental hospitals. North Carolina, for example, offers noninstitutional alternatives, but virtually all defendants whose competency has been questioned are sent to Dorothea Dix Hospital. Golten (1972) lists three reasons why this has also been the practice in the District of Columbia: "(1) more time is needed for a thorough study than is available with an outpatient; (2) the examining facility cannot handle the burden of performing outpatient examinations in addition to its regular functions; and (3) patients must be readily accessible when and if the doctors are available to examine them" (p. 391).

Our own data from North Carolina (see Chapter 6, Study One and Study Three) suggest that the observation time within a hospital setting does not add significantly to a decision about competency. Our observation of the evaluation process clearly showed that much of the time spent by defendants in an institution is unoccupied or is taken up by activities completely unrelated to the evaluation (such as recreational activities). Interviews with psychiatrists, psychologists, or social workers or completing psychological tests consume comparatively little time. As Golten suggests, these reasons do not seem sufficient to require institutional evaluations. In fact, at least one court decision (*Marcey v. Harris*, 1968) has held that pretrial commitment for evaluation does not constitute a valid reason for denial of bail if the defendant is eligible. We would agree with Kaufman (1972), who suggests that due process requires a hearing be held before commitment for evaluation and that the principle of the least restrictive alternative be applied.

SELF-INCRIMINATION

It is generally agreed that a defendant may be compelled to submit to a psychiatric evaluation without jeopardizing rights against self-incrimination, as long as the evidence obtained is limited to the question of competency and is not used at trial (see Pizzi, 1977). Nevertheless, some concerns have been raised related to the potential incriminating effects of information obtained in an evaluation on any subsequent trial. Berry (1973) discusses four areas in which information obtained in an evaluation might violate this constitutional right:

First, the most dramatic adverse use of a defendant's statements occurs when the examiner takes the stand at trial and repeats confessions or admissions of fact which directly implicate the defendant in the charged offense. Second, statements which are not directly incriminating might still be used to impeach the defendant should he take the stand. Third, even statements which are not directly useful as evidence can provide the prosecution with sources of additional material—impeaching character witnesses, for example. Finally, the defendant in discussing his autobiography could implicate himself in other unrelated crimes. (P. 929)

Berry reviews each of these areas at length and demonstrates a variety of ways in which information obtained in an evaluation can be used at trial, since the prosecution and sometimes the jury has been made aware of information obtained in the evaluation report or from testimony given by an expert witness in a competency hearing. As Berry points out, "The statement 'I killed X because he was plotting against me' may equally be evidence to a jury of the defendant's guilt and to a psychiatrist of a paranoid psychosis" (p. 932). In this sense, evidence about the crime or prior criminal activity may provide important evidence to the evaluator, but it may also have a significant impact on the outcome of the trial.[2] But how is the potential misuse to be reconciled? Berry cites an Arizona statute that allows for immunity for the defendant against all harmful use of statements but does not completely bar their use at trial (since a defendant may consent to the introduction at the trial of any statements made in a psychiatric evaluation) as a possible solution. This would seem to be important, especially in situations where a defendant has been found competent and then raises the insanity defense at trial. This dual use of a competency evaluation may be problematic, however, because it would add to the already blurred and confused distinction between competency and responsibility. The Arizona statute also does not seem to protect a defendant against the four areas of potentially incriminating evidence resulting from an evaluation. Golten (1972) argues that these possibilities call for more procedural safeguards, including having the defense attorney or a defense psychiatrist present at the examination, and allowing the attorney to limit the scope of the examination so that no evidence is obtained by the evaluator on the commission of the offense.[3]

RIGHT TO A SPEEDY TRIAL

In *Barker* v. *Wingo* (1972) the Supreme Court held that four factors should be considered in determining whether a delay was violative of the right to a speedy trial: (1) the length of delay; (2) the reason for the delay; (3) the defendant's assertion of the right; and (4) prejudice to the defendant caused by the delay. These factors would also be the basis for determining whether a defendant who had remained incompetent for a given period should have charges dismissed on speedy-trial grounds. Reflecting a functional approach to speedy-trial decisions, the courts have sometimes denied and sometimes affirmed incompetent defendants' motions to dismiss for lack of a speedy trial. A review of several cases will highlight the issues surrounding the right to a speedy trial as it may affect incompetent defendants.

In *United States* v. *Geelan* (1975) a U.S. Court of Appeals held that a six-year delay between indictment and arraignment was presumptively prejudicial. Commenting on Geelan's failure to assert his right to a speedy trial during this period, the court held that an incompetent defendant could not knowingly and intelligently waive any right. The court also cited the failure of the U.S. attorney to continually monitor Geelan's progress, apparently forgetting about him until he was about to be released from a state mental hospital. The court concluded that the lapse of time had resulted in a prejudiced defense. An important factor in this case may have been that Geelan was institutionalized during this period. In fact, the court commented that nearly five years in a mental hospital is too long a period of time to await the regaining of competency, and that under the circumstances the charges should have been dismissed. In *United States v. Lancaster* (1976), however, a different decision was reached, in part because the defendant was not in an institution. Lancaster, charged with murder, was found incompetent but spent less than two years in a mental hospital because he did not meet the civil commitment criteria. Lancaster later motioned the court for dismissal of the charges, arguing that maintaining the indictment would be in violation of his right to equal protection, due process, and a speedy trial. The court denied the motion, holding that no prejudice occurred because witnesses were still available, that the defendant was not psychologically sound since he was not anxious about the pending charges (based on expert witness testimony that Lancaster was not aware of the charges), and that the defendant was not incarcerated.

The functional approach is further illustrated in *State v. Freeman* (1975). Freeman was hospitalized for several years, first under an incompetency commitment and later under a civil commitment. The Supreme Court of Arizona held that the delay was not prejudicial to the defendant. He had been evaluated at regular intervals and had apparently received continuing medical treatment. Moreover, no prejudice to the defense was evident, as witnesses were still available. Thus the court held that the delay and confinement did not constitute a denial of the right to a speedy trial.

We agree that the right to a speedy trial is an important issue to consider when a defendant has been found incompetent but is making continued progress toward the restoration of competency. The case-by-case basis in determining prejudice against such defendants appears to be a sound method for determining the speedy-trial issue. As we will discuss later in the chapter, however, we do not believe that this method will work for defendants who do not have any substantial probability of regaining competency. In these cases we argue that charges should be dismissed when it is determined that it is unlikely a defendant will become competent. Furthermore, we will suggest that this decision must occur within a clearly prescribed time limit.

DISPOSITION OF INCOMPETENT DEFENDANTS

The treatment and disposition of defendants found incompetent to stand trial present a significant problem to both the legal and mental health systems. Until recently, at least, the practice in the United States and Canada has been to commit incompetent defendants to mental hospitals automatically, where they remained until they regained their competency. Commitment was based solely on a finding of incompetency, resulting in a severe deprivation of liberty without even satisfying the minimal criteria provided by the civil commitment process. Our research in North Carolina (see Chapter 6) showed that incompetent defendants were held an average of nearly three years in a mental hospital. Many defendants were held for considerably longer periods, of course, including some defendants who had been hospitalized for ten years or more. The problem with such lengthy periods of confinement becomes evident when one considers some actual cases.

Ennis (1972) described the case of Alfred Curt von Wolfersdorf, who, at the time Ennis's book was written, had spent 22 years as a patient at the Matteawan State Hospital for the criminally insane. Originally charged with murder, von Wolfersdorf was found incompetent and committed to Matteawan for an indefinite period until competence was restored. An investigation of the facts of the case by Ennis revealed that the state had little evidence upon which to convict von Wolfersdorf, but the case could not be challenged because he was incompetent![4] Ennis's motion to dismiss the indictment was supported by the district attorney but, curiously, the court denied the motion and ordered a trial. The murder charge was ultimately dismissed, but not before von Wolfersdorf had spent many years in an institution because he had been deemed incompetent to defend himself on a charge for which conviction was unlikely. Gambino (1978) cited the case of Stephen Dennison, who at the age of 16 was arrested for allegedly stealing $5.00 worth of candy. He was found incompetent and hospitalized for what turned out to be 34 years of his life. As another example, Foote (1960) related the case of a military defendant, Clarence Coons, who was charged, along with three others, with murder. The charges were dismissed against Coons's three co-defendants when the court ruled that a ten-year delay in the trial was "occasioned not through the fault of the defendants but as a result of a calculated tactical gambit by the government" (p. 832). Despite the dismissal against his co-defendants, Coons, who had been found incompetent to stand trial, was ordered to remain in the institution until, according to Foote, "he should be sufficiently recovered to participate in the dismissal of the indictment against him" (p. 832). The absurdity of such a pronouncement is obvious. Perhaps the most well-known case involving an unfitness commitment is that of the poet Ezra Pound. At the end of World War II, Pound was arrested in Italy, returned to the United States, and charged with treason. Pound was never brought to trial, as he was found unfit and hospitalized for thirteen years in a mental hospital (Szasz, 1963).

While these cases may be dramatic, they are by no means atypical. Fortunately, the practice of automatically and indefinitely committing incompetent defendants in the United States was tested in 1972 in the case of *Jackson v. Indiana* (1972).

The case of Jackson v. Indiana

Theon Jackson was a 27-year-old deaf-mute, unable to read, write, or communicate in any way, save perhaps through a quite limited sign language. He was charged on two separate counts of robbery, from which he allegedly realized a total of $9.00. Following a plea of not guilty, the court ordered a psychiatric examination. The report of the two examining psychiatrists concluded that "Jackson's almost nonexistent communication skill, together with his lack of hearing and his mental deficiency, left him unable to understand the nature of the charges against him or to participate in the defense" (p. 718). One psychiatrist indicated that it was extremely unlikely that Jackson would ever develop reading, writing, or sign-language skills. The court found Jackson incompetent and ordered him committed to the Indiana Department of Mental Health until his competency was restored. Jackson's attorney promptly filed a motion for a new trial, arguing that since it was unlikely that Jackson would ever be competent, his commitment was tantamount to a life sentence without conviction of a crime (for which, even if found guilty, he would likely have served a brief sentence). His attorney argued that this commitment would deny Jackson his rights to due process and equal protection under the Fourteenth Amendment and would be considered cruel and unusual punishment under the Eighth Amendment. The motion was denied, and an appeal resulted in the Supreme Court of Indiana's affirming the trial court's decision. The Supreme Court of the United States reversed the lower court's decision, ruling that "Indiana cannot constitutionally commit the petitioner for an indefinite period simply on account of his incompetency" (p. 720).

Several points made by the U.S. Supreme Court are worth discussing in detail since they set the context for our discussion of treatment limitations and disposition of charges. The Supreme Court held that Indiana's criminal commitment statutes had deprived Jackson of due-process rights available to individuals committed under the civil commitment provisions. The Supreme Court concluded:

We hold, consequently, that a person charged by a State with a criminal offense who is committed solely on his incapacity to proceed to trial *cannot be held more than the reasonable period of time necessary to determine whether there is a substantial probability that he will attain that capacity in the foreseeable future.* If it is determined that this is not the case, then the state must either institute the customary civil commitment proceeding that would be required to commit indefinitely any other citizen, or release the defendant. Furthermore, even if it is determined that the defendant probably soon will be able to stand trial, his continued commitment must be justified by that progress toward that goal. (*Jackson*, p. 738, italics added)

Clearly the Supreme Court is concluding that limits need to be set on the type and length of commitment of incompetent defendants, and that any such commitment must be justified by treatment progress. But it left two major issues unresolved. First, it did not specify how long a period of time might be considered reasonable. Gobert (1973) suggests that, by inference, the three and one-half years of Jackson's hospitalization was unacceptable, but adds that it is unclear whether this would be considered unreasonable for all cases or only in the particular instance of Jackson. The decision left much to the interpretation of the states, and, as we will discuss, the response has varied considerably. Second, the Court gave no guidelines to help in the determination that a defendant would likely benefit from treatment and, if so, how progress toward the goal of regaining competency could be assessed.

The Court also supported Jackson's claim that equal protection was denied in that, since it was unlikely he would ever regain competency, it was unfair that the civil commitment laws were not applicable. In effect, the Supreme Court held that the Indiana statutes were defective in equal-protection terms because incompetent defendants were subject to less stringent commitment, and more stringent release, standards than were individuals committed under civil commitment procedures. The only requirement for criminal commitment was the defendant's status as incompetent to stand trial. In contrast, to justify commitment as "mentally ill," the state had to prove that the individual was (1) both mentally ill and in need of "care, treatment, training, or detention," or (2) unable to properly care for himself. There also existed substantial differences in release criteria. M. K. Pollack (1973) observed that "under an incompetency commitment one cannot be released until competent to stand trial, while both the 'feeble-minded' and the 'mentally ill' may be released when they no longer require custodial care or treatment" (p. 567). The degree of difference between the two sets of standards is evidenced by the fact that Jackson, committed and detained under the criminal provision, would probably not have been committable under either civil commitment provision and, in any case, would probably have been released under both of these civil procedures.

In finding that the existence of the differing procedures was violative of the equal-protection clause, the Court rejected the state's argument that differences in treatment could be justified by Jackson's status as a criminal defendant. Relying on *Baxstrom* v. *Herold* (1966), the Court in *Jackson* held that "if criminal conviction and imposition of sentence are insufficient to justify less procedural and substantive protection against indefinite commitment than that generally available to all others, the mere finding of criminal charges surely cannot suffice" (p. 724).

As Gobert (1973) noted, "This, of course, is the crux of the case, for it is not unequal treatment per se that is prohibited by the fourteenth amendment but unjustifiable unequal treatment" (p. 677). The Supreme Court's finding that no justification existed for differing standards for commitment established the unconstitutionality of any commitment scheme that provided for unequal treatment of individuals solely on the basis of having been accused of a crime.

The *Jackson* decision also focused upon the issue of disposition of criminal charges. Jackson's attorney argued that the charges should be dismissed because the record established his lack of criminal responsibility at the time of the alleged crimes. While the Court rejected this logic (since competency is a distinct issue from responsibility), it went on to suggest that there may be other grounds to consider dismissal of charges, including the Sixth Amendment right to a speedy trial and due-process rights related to the retention of charges against someone who is unlikely to ever have the opportunity to demonstrate innocence. Since these issues were not raised in the petition, the Court suggested that the Indiana courts should have the first opportunity to consider these issues.

Finally, the Supreme Court also touched on the issue of permitting some legal proceedings for incompetent defendants. It suggested that an incompetent defendant might be allowed to offer certain defenses or pretrial motions which could challenge the sufficiency of the indictment and thus lead to dismissal or acquittal. The decision left unclear whether incompetent defendants would be allowed to have an actual trial, but did note, seemingly with approval, that some states have procedures which allow a trial to establish innocence but do not permit a conviction. We will discuss the implications of this in subsequent sections.

Proposed limits on treatment and pending charges

Table 5.1 summarizes 12 proposals which deal with limitations on treatment and/or disposition of criminal charges. We will discuss proposals for each of these limits separately.

As can be seen by referring to the treatment limitations column in Table 5.1, most proposals call for a six-month limitation but usually provide for a possible six-month extension if a substantial probability of regaining competency exists. The American Bar Association's Commission on the Mentally Disabled proposed the briefest period—90 days with a possible 90-day extension. The Law Reform Commission of Canada, on the other hand, has essentially called for a potentially unlimited commitment. The commission suggested an initial hospitalization maximum of six months but that can be renewed indefinitely for subsequent one-year

TABLE 5.1

Proposals for Treatment
Limitations and Disposition of Charges

Source	Treatment Limitations	Disposition of Charges
American Bar Association Commission on the Mentally Disabled (1978)	90 days, with possible 90-day extension. Commission provides three alternatives for disposition after this period. First is summarized at right. Other two alternatives provide for automatic dismissal of charges with no possibility of trial, but also allow brief periods of detention to allow initiation of civil commitment proceedings against defendants charged with certain serious crimes.	At end of treatment period court can dismiss charges or set a trial, with special procedures designed to redress abilities. If convicted, new trial could be ordered if information later becomes available that was not previously introduced because of defendant's incompetency.
Burt and Morris (1972)	Six months maximum, provided court determines substantial probability exists that competency can be restored within that period.	Defendant can potentially be brought to trial even if incompetent, with special trial procedures. Charges must be dismissed at this time if trial is not set.
Engelberg (1967)	If commitment is ordered, it should be limited to a maximum of one year.	If, after one-year period has elapsed, defendant is civilly committed, charges should be dismissed. Exception to this is that charges may remain pending against defendants charged with particularly serious crimes, and reinstituted if defendant is released within specified number of years. If defendant is not civilly committed, charges would remain pending.
Federal (U.S.) Criminal Code (proposed)	Six months, with possible six-month extension provided substantial probability of recovery exists.	Not specifically addressed.
Group for the Advancement of Psychiatry, Committee on Psychiatry and Law (1974)	Six months, with possible six-month extension for questionable cases.	Same guidelines as treatment limitations.

Source	Treatment Limitations	Disposition of Charges
Report of the Governor's Commission for Review of the Mental Health Code of Illinois (1976, proposed law)	At end of one-year treatment period, or at any time prior to that if court determines there is not substantial probability that defendant will be competent within year, court shall order trial (with special provisions) or civil commitment hearing or discharge hearing. If discharge hearing does not result in acquittal, one-year treatment period can be extended for up to two years for felony charges and up to five years for defendants charged with murder (provided state has sustained its burden of proof).	Trial with special provision can be ordered, provided court is satisfied that provisions compensate for defendant's disabilities and render defendant competent. State has 160 days after end of treatment period to bring defendant to trial. If not, charges must be dismissed.
Janis (1974)	Six months, with possible six-month extension.	Charges can remain pending even after release, but court must dismiss charges when so much time has elapsed (unspecified) as to make trial unfair.
Judicial Conference of D.C. (1968)	Two years, with possible six-month extension.	Same guidelines as for treatment limitations.
Law Reform Commission of Canada (1976, proposed law)	Initial hospitalization maximum of six months, which can be renewed for subsequent one-year periods, unless charge is one which would not likely result in imprisonment, or length of hospitalization equals sentence of imprisonment defendant would have received if found guilty.	Charges can remain pending indefinitely, but suggests procedure which would allow postponement of issue of competency to end of trial. This would allow trial on merits of case, but guilty outcome could result in competency hearing. If incompetent, verdict would be set aside.
New York City Bar Association, Special Committee on the Study of Commitment Procedures and the Laws Relating to Incompetents (1968)	Limited to 12 months for defendants charged with felonies and six months for those charged with misdemeanors.	No specified limit but allows court to dismiss charges against defendants held for "so long a period as to render it unjust . . . to resume the proceedings" (p. 10).

Source	Treatment Limitations	Disposition of Charges
Roesch and Golding (1977, proposed North Carolina law)	15 months or one-half maximum sentence, whichever is less.	Same guidelines as for treatment limitations.
Stone (1976)	Six months or maximum sentence, whichever is less; possibility of six-month extension for small number of questionable cases.	Same guidelines as for treatment limitations.

Adapted from Roesch and Golding (1979).

intervals. The only restriction on commitment or renewal is that hospitalization cannot be used for charges where imprisonment is not likely or where the length of hospitalization equals the sentence of imprisonment the defendant would have received if found guilty. We believe it is problematic to have a scheme which sets a maximum in terms of probable sentence if guilty, since this links release to an offense rather than to a fixed and reasonable treatment period. An exception to this, as we will discuss, is the case that has a maximum sentence which is less than the treatment limit.

It should be noted that none of these proposals, nor the laws recently enacted by some states, indicate what is a reasonable period of time to determine if a defendant will regain competency. The reason for this is quite clear—we simply have no way of predicting, with any reasonable degree of accuracy, the probability of regaining competency. Mental health professionals have not had great success in predicting response to treatment. We do know, however, that the most frequent treatment involves the use of drugs and that positive responses to medication will occur relatively quickly if they are to occur at all. We are well aware of the potential problems when a defendant is taking medications during a trial, but most courts and state statutes allow for drug-induced competency.[5] Therefore, our current knowledge of treatment would suggest that the treatment length should be relatively brief.

It must be remembered, however, that any treatment limitation is arbitrarily set, although as Burt and Morris (1972) point out, "The time limits required need be arbitrary only in the sense that the values at stake are not reconcilable by quantification" (p. 90). There is no strong basis or data to support a six-month treatment period or a nine-month one. The point is that we need to arrive at some specified limit which would allow treatment to restore competency but would not allow indefinite confinement. Allowing this period to be too long, or tying it to a possible sentence, ignores the possibility that the defendant may be innocent or, if tried, might have been convicted of a lesser offense, have plea bargained, or been sentenced leniently. This latter set of problems is especially important given the tendency by prosecutors to overcharge and then to negotiate.

THE RESPONSE OF THE STATES

What effect have these proposals and the *Jackson* decision had on state law with respect to the treatment and charges of incompetent defendants? To answer this question, we completed a review of the state laws in effect as of March, 1979.

Treatment limitations

Only four states have not reviewed their competency statutes since 1973 (Kentucky, Louisiana, Maryland, Mississippi). Yet, as shown in Table 5.2, many states have not enacted legislation consistent with the *Jackson* decision. For example, 19 states and the District of Columbia still allow the automatic and indefinite commitment of incompetent defendants. Once admitted, under either mandatory or discretionary commitment, incompetent defendants may be held indefinitely in 24 states and the District of Columbia. Thus in about one-half of the jurisdictions there has been no effective response to the Supreme Court's decision in *Jackson* (that defendants not be held for more than a reasonable period of time necessary to determine whether competency will be regained).

The remaining states have responded by setting treatment limits of varying lengths. Eight states provide for a six-month limit, after which defendants must be released.[6] Of course, in all states such defendants may be immediately recommitted under civil commitment statutes.[7] Most of

TABLE 5.2

State Laws regarding Treatment Limitations
and Disposition of Charges

State	Is Commitment Mandatory?	Treatment Limitations	Disposition of Charges
Alabama (1975)	Yes[1]	After maximum possible sentence has expired.	Not specified
Alaska (1978)	No	No limit	Not specified
Arizona	No	Six months	Not specified; court may dismiss at its discretion at any time.
Arkansas (1977)	No	No limit	Not specified
California (1978)	No[2]	Three years or potential maximum sentence, whichever is less.	Not specified
Colorado (1973)	Yes	No limit	Not specified
Connecticut (1978)	Yes	18 months or potential maximum sentence, whichever is less.	None, except as prescribed by statutes of limitation.
Delaware (1974)	No	No limit	Not specified; court may, upon motion of defendant, conduct hearing to determine if state has probable cause; if not, court shall dismiss charge.
District of Columbia (1973)	Yes	No limit	Not specified
Florida (1978)	No	180 days	Charges *may* be dismissed after 180 days.
Georgia (1977)	Yes	Nine months	Not specified

State	Is Commitment Mandatory?	Treatment Limitations	Disposition of Charges
Hawaii (1976)	No	No limit; may request to establish defense of not guilty (other than by reason of insanity), and if court finds charges to be defective or insufficient, or that guilt is not established beyond reasonable doubt, it will dismiss and order defendant's release.	Not specified
Idaho (1978)	Yes	No limit	Charges may be dismissed if so much time has elapsed as to make criminal proceedings unjust.
Illinois (1977)	No	No limit; hearing is held after 90 days and every 12 months thereafter to determine competency.	Dismissed after period of time equal to maximum sentence which could have been imposed for offense(s) charged.
Indiana (1978)	Yes	Six months	Not specified
Iowa (1978)	No	Six months, if court determines that defendant will not regain competency within forseeable future. Civil commitment proceedings are automatically instituted.	Charges can remain pending even after civil commitment.
Kansas (1978)	No	Six months	Charges are dismissed immediately if defendant is not civilly committed at end of treatment period; if civilly committed, charges are dismissed when discharged.
Kentucky (1972)	No	No limit	Not specified

State	Is Commitment Mandatory?	Treatment Limitations	Disposition of Charges
Louisiana (1967)	Yes	Treatment period shall not exceed maximum potential sentence.	Not specified
Maine (1977)	No	One year, but can be recommitted if competency will be regained in forseeable future.	Charges are dismissed when it is determined defendant will not regain competency.
Maryland (1972)	No[3]	No limit	No upper limit, but minimum of ten years for capital offenses and five years for offenses punishable by imprisonment before dismissal may be considered.
Massachusetts (1978)	No	No limit; may request to establish defense of not guilty (other than by reason of insanity). If court grants request, evidence will be presented by both defense and prosecution. If court finds lack of evidence to support conviction, charges will be dismissed and defendant released from custody.	Dismissed after being hospitalized for a period equal to parole eligibility; minimum is one-half of the maximum potential sentence.
Michigan (1974)	No	15 months or one-third of potential maximum sentence, whichever is less. Court may extend this if progress toward regaining competency has been made.	Dismissed at same interval but may be reinstated if crime was punishable by life imprisonment, or if less than one-third of maximum sentence has expired, provided defendant has regained competency.
Minnesota (1978)	No	Defendants are subject to civil commitment laws immediately.	Three years after a finding of incompetency, except for murder cases if prosecution files an intent to prosecute when competency is restored. In this event, charges can remain pending indefinitely.

State	Is Commitment Mandatory?	Treatment Limitations	Disposition of Charges
Mississippi (1972)	No	No limit	Not specified
Missouri (1979)	Yes	No limit	Not specified
Montana (1977)	Yes	No limit	Charges may be dismissed if too much time has elapsed.
Nebraska (1975)	Yes	No limit	Not specified
Nevada (1977)	Yes	No limit	Not specified
New Hampshire[4]			
New Jersey (1978)	No	No specific limit, but should not exceed time necessary to determine if substantial probability of regaining competency exists.	Not specified
New Mexico (1975)	No	No limit	Not specified
New York (1978)	Yes	90 days for misdemeanor charges; for felony charges, maximum cannot exceed two-thirds of maximum possible sentence.	90 days for misdemeanor charges; expiration of treatment period for felony charges.
North Carolina (1978)	No	Incompetent defendants can only be committed through civil commitment procedures; release is subject to civil commitment laws; thus length of confinement is indefinite.	Court may dismiss charges: 1. If court determines defendant will not regain competency. 2. When confinement is equal to or in excess of maximum potential sentence. 3. After five years for misdemeanors and ten years for felonies.

State	Is Commitment Mandatory?	Treatment Limitations	Disposition of Charges
North Dakota (1976)	Yes	Three years or maximum possible sentence, whichever is less.	Charges dismissed after maximum treatment length has elapsed or if court determines it is obvious that competency will not be regained.
Ohio (1977)	Yes	One year, unless there is substantial probability of regaining competency.	Not specified
Oklahoma (1978)	No	No limit	Not specified
Oregon (1977)	No	Maximum is equal to maximum term of sentence if convicted, or five years, whichever is less.	Charges are dismissed after treatment limit has expired or before, if court feels that too much time has elapsed.
Pennsylvania (1977)	No	Maximum potential sentence or five years, whichever is less.	Charges are dismissed after treatment limit has expired.
Rhode Island (1976)	No	If court determines that defendant will not regain competency prior to dismissal of charges, it will order release within 30 days.	Charges are dismissed after two-thirds of potential maximum sentence has expired (life imprisonment or death penalty is considered to be 30-year sentence).
South Carolina (1976)	No[5]	See note 5 at end of table; defendant may request trial on merits and if insufficient evidence exists, charges are dismissed and defendant released.	If defendant is still unfit at end of unspecified treatment period, charges may be dismissed if hospitalization exceeds maximum sentence; court may also dismiss when defendant has regained competency but so much time has elapsed as to make prosecution not in interest of justice.
South Dakota (1978)	Yes	90 days; if still incompetent, civil commitment procedures are instituted.	Not specified

State	Is Commitment Mandatory?	Treatment Limitations	Disposition of Charges
Tennessee (1978)	No	No limit	Not specified
Texas (1978)	No	18 months	Not specified
Utah (1978)	Yes	No limit	Not specified
Vermont (1974)	No	No limit	Not specified
Virginia (1975)	Yes	No limit	Not specified
Washington (1977)	No	Six months, with possible six-month extension if defendant is found to be dangerous, or is likely to commit felony, and if substantial probability of regaining competency exists.	Charges are dismissed when treatment period has expired.
West Virginia (1976)	No	Six months, with possible three-month extension; defendant may request hearing on merits and if insufficient evidence exists, charges are dismissed and defendant released.	Dismissed at same interval.
Wisconsin (1978)	Yes	Two years	No specific time limit but depends upon determination of whether delay resulted in prejudice and denial of right to a fair trial.
Wyoming (1977)	Yes	Commitment should not exceed time necessary to determine whether there is substantial probability that defendant will regain competency. No guidelines are given to aid in this determination.	No specified limit, but court may determine that criminal proceedings would be inappropriate because too much time has elapsed.

Adapted from Roesch and Golding (1979).

[1]Commitment is mandatory only for defendants charged with felonies.

[2]If an incompetent defendant is charged with a violent or potentially violent felony, commitment will be ordered for a minimum of 90 days before possible release on an outpatient basis.

[3]Except for capital cases.

[4]New Hampshire does not specify any procedures for the commitment of incompetent defendants.

[5]If defendant is unlikely to become competent in the forseeable future, hospitalization is ordered for 60 days; a 60-day hospitalization is also ordered for defendants who are likely to become competent. In both cases the court orders the initiation of judicial admission proceedings, which will not necessarily result in continued hospitalization.

the remaining states have set limits of 18 months or less, but there are some interesting exceptions. Several states have tied treatment length with the sentence which would have been given if the defendant was convicted. Alabama, Louisiana, and Wisconsin, all of which have mandatory commitment provisions, allow incompetent defendants to be hospitalized up to a period equal to the maximum possible sentence. Oregon and Pennsylvania do not allow release until the lesser of the maximum possible sentence or five years has expired. North Dakota substitutes a three-year provision.

There are a number of problems with provisions that allow the length of confinement to be determined by type of offense. First, the underlying notion seems to be that incompetent defendants should not be released until they have been sufficiently punished for their alleged crime. Second, the period of confinement for incompetent individuals may actually be longer than for sentenced individuals, who in practice are rarely given the maximum sentence and, even if they are, are usually released early because of parole eligibility. Third, because of plea bargaining, many defendants do not actually get convicted or sentenced for the most serious charges initially filed against them.[8] A final problem with these provisions is that no attempt is made to define what reasonable treatment to restore competency would entail. A review of treatment literature would find no evidence to support the position that defendants charged with murder are more difficult to treat, or are less responsive to treatment, than, for example, a defendant charged with armed robbery. Treatment response is, of course, a highly individual matter. If it is found that no substantial probability of regaining competency exists, then defendants charged with murder should not be hospitalized (under competency laws) any longer than a defendant charged with a less serious offense. The principle of responsiveness to treatment should apply equally to all defendants.

This brings us to the issue of determining whether a substantial probability of regaining competency exists. While the *Jackson* decision and some states propose that treatment length should not exceed a period of time necessary to determine probability, no states have established any guidelines to assist in this determination. Wyoming, for example, simply states that this recommendation should be followed but does not suggest any criteria or any upper time limits. Since no one is in a scientifically defensible position with respect to making accurate predictions about response to treatment, it seems most reasonable that a specific limit be placed on length of commitment so that progress can be continuously monitored. While specification of a time limit may be somewhat arbitrary, we believe it is necessary because of our limited understanding of treatment to restore competency. As we will point out in Chapter 7, it is possible to set a reasonable limit and at the same time empirically examine the effectiveness and treatment length requirements of different kinds of treatment.

Finally, it is important to note, because of its implications for the provisional trial procedure we will propose in Chapter 7, that four states (Hawaii, Massachusetts, South Carolina, and West Virginia) allow for the possibility of a nonjury court hearing to try the merits of the case, for those defendants found incompetent. The Massachusetts statute is illustrative:

If either a person or counsel of a person who has been found to be incompetent to stand trial believes that he can establish a defense of not guilty to the charges pending against the person other than the defense of not guilty by reason of mental illness or mental defect, he may request an opportunity to offer a defense thereto on the merits before the court which has criminal jurisdiction. The court may require counsel for the defendant to support the request by affidavit or other evidence. If the court in its discretion grants such a request, the evidence of the defendant and of the commonwealth shall be heard by the court sitting without a jury. If after hearing such petition the court finds a lack of substantial evidence to support a conviction it shall dismiss the indictment or other charges or find them defective or insufficient and order the release of the defendant from criminal custody. (*Annotated Laws of Massachusetts* 123 17, p. 223)

This is not simply a probable-cause hearing, since defense counsel may present an affirmative defense. No mention is made of any special procedures such as those suggested by Burt and Morris (see Table 5.1) that would minimize or eliminate the potential effects of a defendant's disabilities, but the enactment of this statute in the four states would appear to support a provisional trial of some type. As we will argue in Chapter 7, such a provisional trial has numerous advantages, both for the protection of a defendant's rights and for the assessment and treatment of incompetency.

Before turning to the issue of disposition of charges, we want to briefly review the situation in Canada. The commitment procedures in Canada fall under the Criminal Code and are uniform across the ten provinces. Commitment is automatic and indeterminate for all defendants found unfit, regardless of offense. The Law Reform Commission of Canada has taken exception to this practice and has recommended that institutional treatment be limited to instances where such treatment is likely to help a defendant regain competency, where less restrictive alternatives are not appropriate, and where the offense is one that normally requires pretrial detention. Unfortunately, the commission did not recommend any limits on the length of commitment, nor did they offer any suggestions or guidelines for the court to use in making commitment decisions. However, the commission did advocate a provisional trial procedure in which the issue of fitness could be raised in a hearing after a verdict. If a defendant was found incompetent at this hearing, the guilty verdict would be set aside and a subsequent trial postponed, presumably for an indefinite period until competency was restored. Unlike the four states which allow for the possibility of a nonjury court hearing, the commission's proposed procedure allows for a full trial, including the use of a jury.

Disposition of charges

The issue of pending charges is an important one because it is at the heart of the debate about length of hospitalization and treatment of incompetent defendants. On the one hand, suppose it is found that an incompetent defendant is unlikely to respond to treatment. It could be argued, then, that charges should be dismissed immediately, since a trial will never be held. On the other hand, the public may be strongly opposed to brief hospitalization periods for defendants charged with serious offenses. This problem is reflected in the response of some states which allow length of confinement to be affected by type of offense. The matter of pending charges may also influence the length of hospitalization even when civil commitment is used. For these reasons it is important to consider how the states have approached the issue of the disposition of pending charges.

Twenty-seven states and the District of Columbia have no guidelines for dismissing charges (see Table 5.2). Some states tie dismissal to treatment limits (Michigan, New York, North Dakota, Oregon, Pennsylvania, Washington, West Virginia, and Wisconsin), but Michigan allows reinstatement for offenses punishable by life sentence, or if less than one-third of the maximum sentence has expired, in the event that competency is regained. In New York it should be noted (see Table 5.2) that treatment length and dismissal of charges are related only for indicted felony offenses. Charges against misdemeanants are immediately dismissed upon a finding of incompetency. A number of states allow charges to be dismissed when so much time has elapsed, making a trial not in the best interests of justice (Idaho, Montana, Oregon, South Carolina, Wyoming). No mention is made, however, of guidelines for determining how this should be decided.

Iowa and Kansas have rather curious statutes governing dismissal. In Kansas charges are dismissed immediately if a defendant is not civilly committed, but charges against those who are civilly committed are not dismissed until the person is discharged from the hospital. This procedure adds some support to the contention that pending charges are used to justify continued hospitalization. Iowa allows the charges to remain pending even after civil commitment, which can only occur, paradoxically, if a defendant is unlikely to regain competency!

The most logical direction to take with respect to dismissal of charge appears to be one which would provide for dismissal when the treatment period has expired, or when it appears that competency is unlikely to be regained. Concerns about rights to a speedy trial are amplified when charges are allowed to remain pending for indefinite periods or for lengthy periods tied to maximum sentences. The speedy-trial issue should not be the paramount concern in cases where the defendant is unlikely to become competent. We agree with the Missouri Supreme Court decision in Ex parte Kent (1973), which held that if a defendant is found incompetent with no substantial probability of regaining competency, then charges must be dismissed.

Having reviewed state law and some related constitutional issues in general, we would like to turn to a detailed examination of the competency laws and procedures as they operated in the state of North Carolina. Our purpose is to provide a context for the research we describe in the next chapter, as well as to facilitate a discussion of some problems raised at different points in the procedures.

North Carolina Competency Procedures

The following review will focus upon the North Carolina competency laws and proceedings in effect at the time of our study (1975–76). While our review focuses specifically on North Carolina, most of the procedures used there are common to most states, as was discussed in our review of state law earlier in this chapter. For clarity of presentation, we have divided the competency procedures into four major steps: (1) raising the issue of competency, (2) evaluation, (3) court hearing, and (4) disposition of incompetent defendants. Following an overview, each of the procedural steps will be discussed in detail.

Overview of procedures

The issue of competency can be raised at any time during the legal proceedings but is usually raised at a defendant's arraignment. The defense attorney, prosecution, or the court *sua sponte* may submit a motion questioning a defendant's competency. The court may deny or grant the motion. Normal legal proceedings continue if the motion is denied, but if the motion is granted, an evaluation by the forensic service staff at Dorothea Dix Hospital is typically ordered. The other two options available are rarely exercised: (1) evaluation by medical experts, presumably in a noninstitutional setting, or (2) immediate hearing without an evaluation by mental health professionals.

Defendants committed for an evaluation to the forensic unit at Dorothea Dix Hospital can be held up to 60 days but are usually returned to the court after an average of 17 days.[9] The typical evaluation procedure includes interviews by psychiatrists and other mental health professionals and the gathering of psychological test data and background information. At the end of the evaluation period a report to the court is prepared. This report includes a summary of the interview and test data and a recommendation regarding the defendant's competency to stand trial.

Following this evaluation, a court hearing is held to reach a decision about competency. The court does not have to agree with the evaluation recommendations, but, in practice, disagreement rarely occurs. Normal legal proceedings continue if a defendant is determined to be competent; incompetent defendants may be committed to an institution under either civil or criminal commitment statutes, with the latter being most commonly used. Legal proceedings are suspended until competency is regained or until any charge against an incompetent defendant is dismissed.

A more detailed discussion of the four major steps will now be presented. A flow chart of the North Carolina procedures at the time of our study has been prepared to facilitate an understanding of the system of determining competency (Figure 5.1). It will be helpful for the reader to refer to this figure while reading this material.

Raising the issue of competency

The North Carolina competency statute (G.S. 15A–1001) closely follows the language of *Dusky* v. *United States* (1960) in establishing the criteria for a determination of incompetency:[10] "No person may be tried, convicted, sentenced, or punished for a crime when by reason of mental illness or defect he is unable to understand the nature and object of the proceedings against him, to comprehend his own situation in reference to the proceedings against him, or to assist in his own defense in a rational or reasonable manner" (p. 269).

The question of competency can be raised at any time prior to sentencing but is most typically raised shortly after arrest at a defendant's arraignment (Figure 5.1, Point A). The issue of capacity to proceed can be raised by the defense, prosecution, or court; in fact, it must be raised if there is reason for an officer of the court to believe that a defendant's capacity is impaired (*Pate* v. *Robinson*, 1966).

The *Pate* v. *Robinson* decision has frequently been misinterpreted to imply that once the issue of incompetency is raised, the court must grant

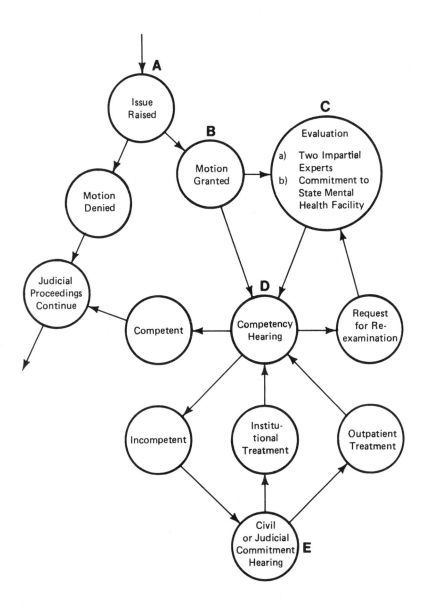

FIGURE 5–1. North Carolina Procedures for Determining Competency (1976)

the motion (Point B) and then obtain mental health evaluations and recommendations. However, North Carolina statutes indicate that the court may also (1) rule that the motion is without merit and no further action is necessary, or (2) hold a hearing immediately without obtaining a psychiatric evaluation.[11] North Carolina courts rarely exercise these two options and almost uniformly commit defendants to Dorothea Dix Hospital for evaluation.

Our review of the motions raising the issue of competency reveals that the court would have little information upon which to rule that a motion is without merit. These motions typically contain little specific information regarding the behavior of the defendant which led to raising the issue. Consider the following excerpt, taken verbatim from an actual motion written by a defense attorney:

It appears to me that this Defendant might be mentally and physically ill and deranged and, in my opinion, it is necessary that an examination be made by a psychiatrist or psychiatrists to determine the legal sanity of the Defendant and to determine further whether or not at the time of the alleged offense, he could distinguish the difference between right and wrong and know the consequences of his act, and furthermore, the Defendant needs to be examined as to his mental capacity to enter a plea when and if these cases are called for hearings, motions, and ultimate trial, and whether or not he has sufficient mental capacity at this time to assist his attorney in the presentation of and preparation of a rational defense in the case.

This motion was selected because it is typical of the information contained in the motions reviewed during the course of this study. A review of this motion raises three issues. First, it should be clear that the attorney did not attempt to justify his request for evaluation by providing specific information regarding the behavior of this defendant. The attorney only states that the defendant "might be mentally and physically ill and deranged." This vague statement gives no concrete information about the behavior of the defendant that would substantiate the validity of the request. It contains *absolutely* no information about the problems the lawyer is having with this defendant in any area of their relationship. While the use of an ambiguous term such as "deranged" may evoke some fear on the part of the court, it obviously contains little meaning and says nothing about the putative impairment of the defendant. The effect on the court, however, is clear. By making references to mental and physical illness, the attorney is suggesting that a judgment about the validity of these conclusions is not within the expertise of the court. The attorney makes this quite clear when he goes on to say that "it is necessary that an examination be made by a psychiatrist or psychiatrists." Second, the attorney makes an assumption that the alleged mental or physical illness will render the defendant incompetent, although he does not state the manner in which the defendant's behavior interfered or may interfere with the preparation of a defense. As was discussed previously, there is not necessarily a direct relationship between presence of mental illness and competency to stand trial. Third, the motion goes beyond a request for an evaluation of capacity to proceed by also requesting an evaluation of responsibility, that is, whether or not the defendant could distinguish the difference between right and wrong at the time of the alleged offense. This is an example of the confusion between two distinct legal concepts: competency to stand trial and criminal responsibility.

Typical evaluation procedures

Once a defendant's capacity to proceed is questioned and the motion is granted, the court has, according to G.S. 15A–1002 (b), three options:

a) The court may appoint one or more impartial medical experts who are required to submit a written report describing the defendant's mental health (Figure 5.1, Point C). The experts may be called upon to testify at the competency hearing (Figure 5.1, Point D), but this occurs infrequently. It is interesting to note that the statute specifies that the report describe the defendant's mental health but does not require that the report (and, of course, the evaluation) include information on the legal criteria for capacity to proceed or, indeed, the manner in which a defendant's mental health relates to the capacity to proceed.

b) The court may commit the defendant to a state mental health facility for observation and treatment, for a period not to exceed 60 days, in order to determine his/her capacity to proceed (Figure 5.1, Point C). A written report is required; the statutes do not specify whether representatives of the state facility can be called upon to testify, although such representatives have done so, albeit infrequently.

c) The court may hold a hearing immediately without additional information from medical experts or the state facility.

Options *a* and *c* are rarely exercised by the courts, since virtually all evaluations for the entire state of North Carolina are conducted by the forensic unit at Dorothea Dix Hospital. As noted above, under option *b* defendants can be committed for a period not to exceed 60 days. During the evaluation period defendants are interviewed by a psychiatrist and administered a battery of psychological tests—typically including a personality test such as the Minnesota Multiphasic Personality Inventory; the Competency Screening Test (McGarry et al., 1973); an achievement test to determine reading and comprehension level; and, in some cases, projective tests. Defendants are also seen by the social service staff, who prepare a report of the defendant's personal background and also contact the defendant's family and attorney. Routine physical examinations are also conducted. When all this information is compiled, the treatment staff meets to discuss the case. Following this meeting, a report to the court is prepared. The report typically contains demographic and background information, a psychiatric interview summary, psychological testing results, a social history, a summary of behavior while in the hospital, psychiatric opinions, psychiatric diagnosis, recommendations regarding capacity to stand trial, and, in some cases, recommendations for treatment after release from the hospital and for disposition of charges.[12] These reports form the basis of the communication to the court regarding the evaluation of competency. In practice, these reports are frequently the *only* communication with the court, since the forensic unit psychiatrists are not usually required to appear in court. The communication problems that might arise when the evaluator is not present in court to elaborate on the findings and conclusions or to explain discrepancies or misunderstandings are obvious.

Court hearing

Following evaluations and submission of a written report, a hearing (Figure 5.1, Point D) is scheduled. The court may agree or disagree with the mental health recommendations and may also request further information from other sources. As noted above, psychiatrists are infrequently called upon to testify. In fact, until 1974 defendants were often not even present at the hearing. If the hospital had reached a decision that a defendant was incompetent, they simply sent a report to the court asking for a change of status from court-ordered observation to court-ordered commitment as incompetent to stand trial. While this practice has been discontinued, the hearings are typically brief and uncontested. Following the hearing, defendants found competent are returned for the usual judicial processing (trial or other hearings). The next section will focus upon what happens to those defendants determined to be incompetent to stand trial.

Disposition of incompetent defendants

If a defendant is found incompetent at the court hearing, North Carolina statutes require the court to enter an order directing the initiation of proceedings for civil commitment (Figure 5.1, Point E). The major problem in the commitment process, as it operated in North Carolina at the time of our study, is that incompetent defendants were also *automatically* committed to an institution for treatment until they regained competency.[13] While the statutes called for a finding of both mental illness and dangerousness in order to justify commitment, all defendants found incompetent during the study period were, in fact, committed to Dorothea Dix Hospital. The fact that many of them had no histories of violence and were not charged with a violent crime suggests that dangerousness was not usually considered. If defendants did not meet the civil commitment criteria, then the court simply committed them under the criminal statutes, which allowed commitment, as specified in G.S. 122–83, of "all persons who may hereafter commit crime while mentally ill, and all who being charged with crime, are adjudged to be mentally ill at the time of their arraignment, and for that reason cannot be put on trial for the crime alleged against them" (p. 137). This procedure thus allowed for an indefinite commitment, based solely upon the defendant's status as incompetent. Furthermore, no hearing was held to determine whether defendants so committed were likely to respond to treatment and regain competency in the forseeable future, as prescribed by the *Jackson* v. *Indiana* decision. Committed defendants could remain hospitalized until either they regained the capacity to proceed or the charges against them were dismissed. The court *could* dismiss the charges:

1. When it appears to the court that the defendant will not gain capacity to proceed [no guidelines are specified to assist the court in arriving at this determination]; or

2. When the defendant has been substantially deprived of his liberty for a period of time equal to or *in excess of* the maximum permissible period of confinement for the crime or crimes charged; or

3. Upon the expiration of a period of five years from the date of determination of incapacity to proceed in the case of misdemeanor charges and a period of 10 years in the case of felony charges. (*General Statutes of North Carolina*, p. 273)

A reading of these options makes it clear that defendants could be held indefinitely, perhaps for life, since the prosecution is not bound to dismiss charges at a specified time. As we discussed earlier in this chapter, there is a definite need to develop disposition procedures which will allow for the use of less restrictive alternatives whenever appropriate, and will restrict the length of commitment for treatment of incompetency when competency is unlikely to be regained.

In this chapter we have reviewed current state law and procedures for determining competency and for the disposition of defendants found incompetent. This review and the results of the research described in the next chapter provide an understanding of the problems and issues raised by attempts to confront the issue of competency, and provide a basis for the model system we propose in Chapter 7.

Notes

1. The sample psychiatric report critiqued in Chapter 4 contains a clear statement by the evaluating psychiatrist that the defendant committed the crime for which he was charged.

2. Our examination of the psychiatric reports in North Carolina, which are sent to the courts and placed in a defendant's court record, often revealed instances of statements indicating guilt, such as "Defendant admits that he was driving under the influence of alcohol and can fully relate the circumstances of the offense," or "when asked about the charges of discharging a firearm, he stated that he was on his own property and that he was shooting at his neighbor because the neighbor was harrassing him." It should be evident that such admissions might have an affect on subsequent court proceedings.

3. See *Lessard* v. *Schmidt* (1972) for a discussion of this issue.

4. A similar circumstance occurred in the case of Donald Lang, which we discuss at length in Chapter 7. On the first of two separate murder charges Lang was found incompetent, but his attorney argued that since Lang was unlikely ever to

become competent, he should be allowed to have a trial. The Illinois Supreme Court agreed and ordered a trial, whereupon the charges were dismissed because of the unavailability of key witnesses.

5. See the section on "The Use of Drugs," in Chapter 2, for a review of legal decisions and treatment issues regarding the use of psychiatric medications during evaluation and trial.

6. Arizona, Colorado, Florida, Indiana, Iowa, Kansas, Washington, and West Virginia. Washington allows for a possible six-month extension if a defendant is found to be dangerous or likely to commit a felony, and if a substantial probability of regaining competency exists. While the statute links the first two criteria with treatment to restore competency, one wonders about its possible misuse in providing a preventive detention mechanism for the state. West Virginia provides for a three-month extension, limited to cases where substantial probability of regaining competency exists.

7. South Dakota has an interesting response to those defendants who do not meet civil commitment criteria. The statutes allow that if the civil commitment hearing fails to result in commitment, this may be regarded as evidence that a defendant is competent and the criminal proceedings may continue. This appears to be a confusion of two distinct standards. It is, of course, quite possible to meet legal definitions of incompetency but yet not meet civil commitment standards. This would especially be true in jurisdictions requiring a finding of dangerousness as well as mental illness.

8. See Alschuler (1968) and Kipnis (1976) for general discussions of the issues and problems raised by the plea bargaining process.

9. Chapter 6, Study One, presents a complete discussion of our data on the length of hospitalization for evaluation and for the treatment of incompetent defendants.

10. Chapter 2 contains a lengthy discussion of the *Dusky* criteria.

11. The degree of doubt necessary to grant a motion under the *Pate* standard is discussed in Chapter 2.

12. The content of the reports is discussed in greater detail in the Study One method section in Chapter 3; a sample report is analyzed in Chapter 4.

13. The most recent revision of the North Carolina statutes requires that, following our recommendations, the civil commitment laws be applied to incompetent defendants.

6

A Research Project on Competency: Results and Discussion

This chapter presents the results of four studies that examined various aspects of the competency issue, and were intended to provide information on how competency was defined by the principal parties in the system (judges, attorneys, and evaluators), how competency was evaluated, and how the evaluations were used by the courts. We were also interested in determining what happened to those defendants found incompetent, in terms of both treatment and subsequent return to court after restoration of competency. The information gathered as a result of these studies provided a primary base for the changes in the system we will discuss in the next chapter.

The data for each of the four studies were collected during the first six months of 1976. Study One examined the evaluation procedures used by mental health professionals to reach decisions about competency, and was based on evaluations conducted in an institutional setting. The primary data for this study were psychiatric reports completed by psychiatrists for both competent and incompetent defendants. Also included in this study was a comparative analysis of the court outcome of competent and initially incompetent defendants. The latter were, following a period of treatment, returned to court as competent. In Study Two we attempted to evaluate the usefulness of several psychological tests and ward observation techniques. However, despite collecting data for a lengthy period of time, very few defendants were found incompetent during the study period. While this precluded many statistical analyses, we were able to look more closely at those defendants found competent and thus could obtain a clearer picture of what happens to the majority of defendants referred for evaluation. In Study Three we were interested in comparing judgments about competency, based on a brief interview, with the mental health judgment, which was based on the lengthy institutional evaluation. Study Four provided some data from North Carolina judges and defense attorneys who had been involved in competency cases. These data were particularly useful in assessing the perceptions of the legal community, as well as the manner in which the competency laws and procedures are actually used in practice. We will now turn to a detailed presentation of the results and discussion of the four studies.[1]

STUDY ONE:
AN EXAMINATION OF EVALUATION PROCEDURES
IN AN INSTITUTIONAL SETTING

This study was designed to provide information about the mental health system's procedures for evaluating competency to stand trial. The study focused upon the decision-making process by obtaining data on defendants who had been evaluated for competency at Dorothea Dix Hospital. This study can be seen as an attempt to provide a better understanding of the decision rules and cues that mental health professionals have used in determining whether a defendant is competent or incompetent. During the course of evaluation hospital staff interviewed defendants, contacted families and attorneys, observed defendants' behavior on the ward, and administered psychological tests. A decision about competency was based on these sources of information. Presumably, the data from these sources will be different for those receiving recommendations of competent to stand trial and those who receive recommendations of incompetent to proceed. The present study was an attempt to analyze these differences and thus provide information about the process of reaching a decision about competency. Hospital records of defendants previously evaluated for competency, including both competent and incompetent defendants, provided the data for this study.

A related question addressed in this study was the effect that a determination of competent or incompetent had on the subsequent legal disposition of criminal charges. The incompetent defendants selected for this study were later returned to court, following a period of treatment, as competent to stand trial. Do such variables as length of hospitalization, type of determination (competent or incompetent), and treatment or dispositional recommendations (dismissal of charges, alternatives to prison) have an influence on court outcome? The analysis of court outcome involved relating the above variables to the type of legal disposition and the length and type of sentence.

Method

Subjects. The potential subject pool consisted of all persons discharged from Dorothea Dix Hospital forensic unit from fiscal year 1971 through 1975. A total of 2,055 persons were discharged during this period. Since the total number of persons found incompetent was expected to be low, it was desirable to include in the sample all persons found incompetent who were discharged during the five-year period. Rather than search the hospital records of all 2,055 cases to identify incompetent defendants, it was found that the total discharged sample could be reduced in the following manner:

a) Hospital legal status for criminal commitments was divided into three categories: (1) court-ordered observation for a competency or responsibility evaluation, (2) court-ordered commitment, usually for defendants found incompetent to stand trial, and (3) voluntary hospitalization. Defendants whose legal status was court-ordered observation and who were in the hospital for less than 45 days were eliminated from the search. This method eliminated only competent defendants, since the legal status of incompetent defendants was usually changed from court-ordered observation to court-ordered commitment and since incompetent defendants were typically held for more than 45 days.

b) Any defendants evaluated more than one time during the same fiscal year were included, even if they would have been eliminated on the basis of the criteria specified above. More than one evaluation in the same year may indicate court disagreement with the evaluation recommendations.

The initial sample of 2,055 was reduced to 642 in this way. These records were then searched by four forensic unit staff members and resulted in the identification of 130 defendants who had previously been determined by hospital staff to be incompetent to stand trial.[2] In order to evaluate differences, a control group of 140 competent defendants, matched with the incompetent group by fiscal year of admission and county of referral, was randomly selected from a list of competency evaluation admissions for fiscal years 1965 to 1975. These matching variables provided a control for potential differences in the two groups resulting from differences in judicial and hospital practices and personnel, community attitudes, and time of referral. Other potential matching variables, such as type of offense, prior record, and age, were not used because these variables may have represented real differences that contributed to a determination of competent or incompetent.

Hospital record coding. After hospital staff had identified a defendant who met the selection criteria, they coded the following information from the file: demographic data, length of present hospitalization, prior hospitalization, medications, and the psychiatric diagnosis. They then made copies of the following reports, all of which may not have been available for each defendant.

Mental Status Exam. The Mental Status Exam (MSE) was a report of an initial interview conducted by a psychiatrist. The MSE contained information about the reason for the evaluation referral, the charges against a defendant, psychiatric interview impressions, current medication, psychiatric diagnosis, and initial recommendations regarding competency and treatment in the hospital. This report was completed within one week of admission. A total of 79 competent and 91 incompetent defendants had this report.

Diagnostic Conference Report and Discharge Summary. This report (DCDS) was usually completed after the hospital staff had reached a decision about competency, usually within 60 days of admission. The DCDS was usually completed for those defendants who were to be immediately returned to court. Until recently, incompetent defendants were not discharged but, rather, were retained in the hospital. Their legal status was changed from observation to treatment for an indefinite period. These defendants had a separate Diagnostic Conference Report and a Discharge Summary (see below). The DCDS was available for all competent defendants and for 24 incompetent defendants. The DCDS is the official hospital report to the court. It typically contains the following information:

a) Identifying data—demographic information, type of offense, and county of referral.

b) Mental status on admission—a summary of the information contained in the MSE report.

c) Physical examination results.

d) Psychological testing—a summary of the tests administered and a discussion of the results and impressions.

e) Hospital course—information about the defendant's interaction with other patients and staff, and whether the defendant was disruptive or uncooperative.

f) Psychiatric opinions—an opinion about competency, and in some cases responsibility, based on the data sources described above.

g) Psychiatric diagnosis.

h) Discharge medication.

i) Recommendations—a statement of whether the defendant was competent, in some cases containing recommendations regarding further treatment after return to court. It may also have included legal disposition recommendations, such as dismissal of charges.

Diagnostic Conference Report. The DCR was completed only for incompetent defendants who were not discharged within the 60-day limit. The DCR contained information similar to the DCDS, except for post-hospital recommendations. The DCR was available for 124 incompetent defendants.

Discharge Summary. The DS was completed when an incompetent defendant was ready to be returned to the court (as competent) or after the charges had been dismissed and an incompetent defendant was to be released. The DS contained a summary of the defendant's behavior in the hospital since admission and the psychiatric opinions, diagnosis, and recommendations discussed above. The DS was available for 107 incompetent defendants.

Copies of these reports were then sent to us, with all names deleted from the reports to ensure confidentiality. A problem arose in determining a method for categorizing the information contained within the four psychiatric reports. Since the reports were narrative in form, a rating system had to be developed which could include provisions for coding as much of the information as possible.

The following method was used to develop a coding system for these data. A random sample of 40 reports not included in the study, representing eight cases per year for 1971 to 1975, was drawn by forensic unit staff. We read each report and divided the information into discrete phrases or sentences representing different behaviors. For example, a single report might include, among others, the following descriptions: "his memory and orientation were intact," "stated that he had difficulty in the past with drinking," "no evidence of hallucinations or delusions," and so on. This process was followed for all 40 reports. The descriptors (approximately 400 total) were then transcribed on 3" × 5" index cards and sorted on the basis of similar behavioral descriptions. For example, descriptors dealing with ward behavior were sorted into one pile, descriptors dealing with hallucinations into another pile, descriptors dealing with cognitive functioning into a third pile, and so on. A rating system was then devised, in the following manner, to code each of these behavioral descriptions. Items from the Psychiatric Status Schedule (Spitzer et al., 1970) were used as a guide for the wording of the behavioral descriptions to be rated. On the basis of the sort, it was found that the original 400 descriptors could be reduced to 77 distinct items. These items were divided into 12 major behavioral categories, and were used to rate the four reports described previously. Appendix A contains the complete list of items, including items from the two categories discussed below.

Eight university student raters were trained to rate the first ten categories. Another rater coded the categories of Awareness of Legal Situation and Recommendations so that these categories would not confound the other ratings. This rater also coded the diagnosis, length of hospitalization, and some other information on previous hospitalizations.

Training involved four two-hour sessions. After reviewing the rating format, the raters were asked to independently rate actual reports selected from hospital records not included in the research sample. When one report had been completed, the ratings were reviewed with one of the authors. Disagreements were discussed, and appropriate changes and clarifications were made. This procedure was followed until the investigator believed the raters understood the items to be rated and were familiar with the content and organization of the reports. A total of six reports were rated and discussed.

The raters were divided into pairs, with no rater team receiving more than one report per defendant.[3] The following scale was used to rate the items:

blank = No information on this item is available from the records. Item was left blank.

1 = Statements or other information indicate presence of the behavior.

2 = Statements or other information indicate that this behavior was not present.

Court record coding. Court outcome information was obtained by requesting the court clerks in each North Carolina county to complete a form which included information on date of arrest, charges, type of counsel, plea entered by defendant, convictions, type of sentence, and special recommendations (such as commitment to a state hospital, work release). These forms were returned for 257 of the 270 defendants in the sample, a return rate of 95%. The court record data were used to compare the court outcome for the two groups, including type of disposition (innocent or guilty) and type and length of sentence. Differences in court outcome by race were also analyzed.

Results

Demographic data. Table 6.1 summarizes the data on race, marital status, age, and educational level of the research subjects. There were 140 defendants in the competent group, ten of whom were female; the incompetent sample totaled 130, eight of whom were female. Approximately 41% of the total sample was black, a figure which is consistent with the North Carolina arrest rate for blacks. A slightly higher percentage of blacks were found incompetent, but the difference between groups was not significant. Only about 27% of the total sample were married when referred for a competency evaluation. Differences between the groups for these two variables were not significant. The incompetent group was significantly older, with a mean age of 36, as compared with 29 years for the competent group ($t[268] = -3.91$, $p<.01$). The incompetent sample also had significantly fewer years of education, although only about 19% of the total sample had completed high school ($t[267] = 3.70$, $p<.01$).

Psychiatric treatment history and diagnosis. Over one-half of the incompetent defendants had previous admissions to psychiatric facilities, compared to only 14% of those defendants found competent. As shown in Table 6.2, incompetent defendants were, compared to competent defendants, significantly more likely to have previous psychiatric admissions to Dorothea Dix Hospital ($t[268] = -2.98$, $p<.01$); they were also significantly more likely to have a history of admissions to other psychiatric facilities ($t[265] = -2.43$, $p<.05$). Following discharge, incompetent

TABLE 6.1
Demographic Information

	Competent Defendants (N = 140)	Incompetent Defendants (N = 130)
Sex		
Male	130	122
	(93%)	(94%)
Female	10	8
	(7%)	(6%)
Race		
White	85	69
	(61%)	(53%)
Black	51	60
	(36%)	(46%)
Indian	4	1
	(3%)	(1%)
Marital status		
Single	59	64
	(42%)	(49%)
Married	43	32
	(31%)	(25%)
Divorced	14	9
	(10%)	(7%)
Separated	15	14
	(11%)	(11%)
Widowed	8	11
	(6%)	(9%)
Mean age**	29.62	36.17
Mean educational level**	8.65	6.88

Percentages of column total are given in parentheses.
**$p < .01$

defendants continued to have more involvement with Dorothea Dix Hospital. Fifty-six of the 130 incompetent defendants were readmitted to Dix, compared with only 14 of the 140 competent defendants. Twenty-five incompetent defendants had more than one subsequent admission, compared with only five competent defendants. The statistical significance of such differences is visually apparent.

TABLE 6.2

Psychiatric Treatment History

	Competent	Incompetent
Mean number of admissions to Dorothea Dix Hospital prior to evaluation	.27	.63**
Mean number of admissions to other psychiatric facilities	.30	.62*

*$p < .05$
**$p < .01$

Table 6.3 shows the psychiatric diagnosis for the two groups. Examination of this table reveals clear and striking differences between the two groups. Incompetent defendants typically received a psychotic label (schizophrenia, other diagnoses of psychosis, organic brain syndrome), while the competent defendants usually received a label of "without psychosis." Mental retardation accounted for almost all of the remaining psychiatric diagnoses of incompetent defendants. If the 23 incompetents diagnosed as mentally retarded are added to the psychosis diagnosis cases, the two labels account for 87% of the diagnoses for the incompetent group. On the other hand, the competent group rarely received a psychosis label. In fact, 101 competents (72%) received a diagnosis of without psychosis, and only nine were considered to be mentally retarded. When the diagnostic categories are collapsed into two categories (psychotic labels and mental retardation versus nonpsychotic labels), the difference was highly significant (chi-square [1] = 141.77, $p < .001$).

Length of hospitalization. Defendants found incompetent at the end of the evaluation period were almost uniformly retained in the hospital until competent. Thus a longer length of hospitalization would be expected for

TABLE 6.3

Psychiatric Diagnosis

| | Final Diagnosis | |
	Competent (N = 140)	Incompetent (N = 130)
Mental retardation	9 (6%)	23 (18%)
Organic brain syndrome—psychosis	2 (1%)	5 (4%)
Organic brain syndrome—nonpsychotic	2 (1%)	6 (5%)
Schizophrenia	8 (6%)	71 (55%)
Other diagnoses of psychosis	3 (2%)	13 (10%)
Neuroses	3 (2%)	2 (2%)
Personality disorder	5 (4%)	2 (2%)
Alcohol/drug abuse	5 (4%)	0
Without psychosis	101 (72%)	8 (6%)
Deferred or nonspecified	2 (1%)	0

Adapted from Roesch (1979). Percentages of column total are given in parentheses.

the incompetent group. In fact, this was true, but the difference was far greater than expected. Competent defendants remained in the hospital for an average of 43 days, while incompetent defendants remained an average of almost three years. Table 6.4 shows, by year of discharge, the mean, median, and range for length of hospitalization for the incompetent group. Because there are a number of extreme cases (defendants held for considerable periods of time), it is more appropriate to refer to both the mean and median figures to obtain a clear picture of length of hospitalization.

TABLE 6.4

Length of Hospitalization
for Incompetent Defendants (in days)

| | Year of Discharge | | | | |
	1971	1972	1973	1974	1975
Mean	668	874	1,132	1,445	911
Median	453	820	635	893	572
Range	230–1,598	27–2,437	91–4,632	151–3,014	10–5,123

Incompetent defendants discharged in 1971 were held for an average of almost two years. The length of hospitalization increased dramatically in 1973 and 1974. It appears that this was due to the release of several defendants held for many years, most notably one defendant who had been held for nearly 13 years. As can be seen by looking at both mean and median figures, incompetent defendants were generally held for two to three years.

Converting the length of hospitalization into one score, such as a mean or a median, obscures some important information about extreme cases. There were many instances in which incompetent defendants were held for much of their adult life. The ranges of hospitalization shown in Table 6.4 make this evident. One individual, charged with murder, was admitted in 1961 and finally discharged in 1975, nearly 14 years later. Many other individuals were held ten years or more.

One hypothesis regarding length of hospitalization is that incompetent defendants charged with violent crimes will be held in the hospital longer than those defendants charged with less serious offenses. Table 6.5 shows the type of offense at referral to Dorothea Dix Hospital. If a defendant was charged with more than one offense, the most serious offense was used. Type of offense was obtained for 253 of the 270 cases in the sample. Offenses were divided into the following categories: (1) murder, (2) assault, (3) rape/sex offenses, (4) other violent offenses, (5) property crimes, and (6) other nonviolent offenses.

TABLE 6.5

Type of Offense at Referral

	Competent (N = 131)	Incompetent (N = 126)
Murder	35 (27%)	48 (38%)
Assault	16 (12%)	25 (20%)
Rape	17 (13%)	18 (14%)
Other violent offenses	20 (15%)	6 (5%)
Property crimes	36 (28%)	28 (22%)
Other nonviolent offenses	7 (5%)	1 (1%)

Table 6.5 shows that incompetent defendants were significantly more likely to be charged with murder and assault, while competent defendants had a higher proportion of property crimes and other nonviolent offenses (chi-square [5] = 16.99, $p<.01$). The frequency of murder charges was, relative to arrest rates, high in both groups, accounting for 27% of the offenses in the competent group and 38% in the incompetent group. The majority of the defendants were charged with violent offenses (murder, assault, rape, and other violent offenses). Violent offenses accounted for 67% of the offenses in the competent group, compared with 77% in the incompetent group. The remainder were charged with property crimes or other nonviolent offenses. The percentage of violent crimes was considerably out of proportion to the arrest rates for violent crimes in North Carolina. The FBI Uniform Crime Report showed that in 1972 violent offenses accounted for only 20% of the total arrests. Since 1972, this figure has declined to only about 11% of the total arrests in 1975. The finding that referrals for competency evaluations are disproportionately charged with violent offenses is consistent with the findings of studies reviewed in Chapter 3.

Table 6.6 shows the mean length of hospitalization by type of offense at referral. There was little variation in length of hospitalization for competent defendants, although those defendants charged with murder tended to stay slightly, but not significantly, longer than defendants charged with other offenses. However, it is clear that incompetent defendants charged with murder were held much longer than incompetent defendants charged with any other offense. However, the type of offense does not appear to have any controlling influence on the length of stay for all other incompetent defendants.

TABLE 6.6

Type of Offense at Referral
by Mean Length of Hospitalization Days

	Murder		Assault		Rape		Other Violent Offenses		Property Crimes		Non-violent
	Mean	Median	Mean	Median	Mean	Median	Mean	Median	Mean	Median	Mean
Compe-tent	49	37	38	40	42	36	35	34	41	37	35
	(N = 35)		(N = 16)		(N = 17)		(N = 20)		(N = 36)		(N = 7)
Incompe-tent	1,354	868	616	230	854	713	361	134	721	698	965
	(N = 48)		(N = 25)		(N = 18)		(N = 6)		(N = 28)		(N = 1)

Psychiatric medication. Psychiatric medication, especially tranquilizers, was used extensively for incompetent defendants. During the last four months of hospitalization, 97 of 130 (75%) incompetent defendants were taking medication, all but six of whom were on some form of tranquilizer. The remaining six defendants were taking antidepression medication. Thorazine was used in over half the cases, making it the most frequently used tranquilizer. Only 22 competents (16%) were taking medications during the last few months of hospitalization. Again, tranquilizers were most frequently used. Many defendants were taking more than one drug. In fact, 42 defendants were taking two or more tranquilizers simultaneously, and ten defendants were taking an antidepressant and a tranquilizer at the same time. Forty-eight incompetent defendants (37%) were instructed to continue taking medication at discharge. Again, most defendants were taking tranquilizers. Thirty-four defendants were also taking a second medication. Only 15 competent defendants (11%) were to continue taking medication following discharge.

Psychiatric reports. The reliability of the ratings on the four psychiatric reports described in the method section was calculated in the following manner. In order to analyze all sources of unreliability, the ratings were arranged into the following three combinations: (1) ratings of blank and 2 versus 1 (this indicates the reliability of rating presence versus absence of negative behaviors), (2) 1 versus 2 (this indicates the degree of reliability when a statement was made about behavior), and (3) 1 and 2 versus blank (this indicates the reliability of observing a statement in the report). Finally, percent agreement for all three ratings was calculated. A summary of the results will be described here for each report. Appendices B, C, D, and E contain the complete set of reliability coefficients and percent agreement for each report.

The analyses of the psychiatric reports described later in this chapter use the blank and 2 versus 1 dichotomized ratings. This indicates, as noted above, the presence versus absence of negative behaviors (the three items scored in the positive direction were reverse coded). Therefore, only these reliability coefficients (Pearson product-moment correlation coefficients) and percent agreement will be described here. Before turning to this description, it should be noted that the percent agreement for each item will be inflated because of the large number of blank ratings. This is due to the fact that, while the reports contain a large amount of information, very little information is consistently noted in all reports. For some items no information was available or was available in fewer than 10% of the cases. These items were dropped for all analyses. The percent agreement and reliabilities for each report are as follows:

Mental Status Exam. Percent agreement ranged from 71.7% to 96.4%, with a median of 88.0%. Reliability coefficients ranged from .37 to 1.00, with a median of .75.

Diagnostic Conference Report and Discharge Summary. Percent agreement for the ratings on this report ranged from 79.4% to 98.8%, with a median percent agreement of 90.7%. Reliability coefficients for the blank and 2 versus 1 ratings ranged from .11 to .91, with a median of .66.

Diagnostic Conference Report. Percent agreement ranged from 69.1% to 98.4%, with a median of 84.6%. Reliability coefficients ranged from .28 to .91, with a median of .61.

Discharge Summary. Percent agreement ranged from 52.3% to 100%, with a median of 89.7%. Reliability coefficients ranged from .37 to 1.00, with a median of .73.

Since it was not appropriate to average ratings of this kind on items in which there was disagreement, each report was reviewed after each pair of raters had completed their ratings. Disagreements were resolved by Roesch, who reviewed each disagreement and decided whether the item was actually present or absent; he was not aware of the initial ratings. The revised ratings were used for all other analyses.

As discussed in the method section, the four psychiatric reports were combined to facilitate the comparison of the two groups. The Mental Status Exam (MSE) was completed on both groups at the same time and was available for 75 of the 140 competent defendants and 83 of the 130 incompetent defendants. The MSE ratings for each group could thus be compared directly. The remaining three reports were completed at different times. The Diagnostic Conference Report and Discharge Summary (DCDS) was completed for all competent defendants but for only 20 incompetent defendants. In contrast, most incompetent defendants had two separate reports: the Diagnostic Conference Report (DCR), and the Discharge Summary (DS). The DCR was completed about 50 days after the initial evaluation (MSE) and at approximately the same time as the DCDS for competent defendants. The DCR reflects the information and impressions which influenced the determination of incompetent. The DS was completed at discharge for incompetent defendants, usually when defendants had regained competency and were returned to court. The DS reflects changes in the defendants which supported a change in the judgment of competency.

Given the above organization of the reports, the following three comparisons would yield information on differences between the two samples at various times in the evaluation process: (1) the Mental Status Exam for each group; (2) the Diagnostic Conference Report for incompetent defendants and the Diagnostic Conference Report and Discharge Summary for competent defendants; (3) the Discharge Summary for incompetent defendants, and the DCDS for competent defendants.

The purpose of this study was to determine if there was information contained in the hospital reports which would identify differences between competent and incompetent defendants. The ratings for each report were subjected to a principal component analysis to determine if they could be reduced to a smaller set of variables to be used in a discriminant analysis. Prior to the principal component analysis of the three combined reports, items in which less than 10% of the sample had a score indicating deviance or pathology on that item were eliminated. In this manner, 29 items from the MSE, 29 items from the DCR/DCDS combination, and 37 items from the DS/DCDS were eliminated. The reduced set of items was then subjected to a principal component analysis. The results of this analysis will be considered separately for each of the three combined reports.

The 31 items which were retained from the MSE were subjected to a principal component analysis. Using the scree test criterion (Cattell, 1966), nine components, accounting for 54% of the total variance, were retained and rotated to the varimax criterion.[4] The nine components, their respective items, and the salient loadings for each item (± .40) are presented in Appendix F. The nine components were labeled (1) Alcohol Abuse, (2) Speech Disorganization, (3) Drug Abuse, (4) Inappropriate Behavior, (5) Depression, (6) Delusions, (7) Affect/Legal Involvement, (8) Hallucinations, and (9) Cognitive Functioning.

The 31 items from the DCR/DCDS combination, were subjected to a principal component analysis.[5] Seven components were retained and are presented, along with their respective items and the salient loadings for each item, in Appendix G. The seven components were labeled (1) Delusions, (2) Speech/Affect, (3) Alcohol Abuse, (4) Hostility, (5) Hallucinations, (6) Interactional Behavior, and (7) Anxiety.

Finally, the 23 items from the DS/DCDS combination were also analyzed by the same series of methods. Seven components, using the scree test criterion, accounting for 52% of the total variance, were retained. The seven components, their respective items, and the salient loadings for each item (± .40) are presented in Appendix H. The seven components were (1) Alcohol Abuse, (2) Hallucinations/Past Delusions, (3) Hostility, (4) Depression, (5) Cognitive Functioning, (6) Delusions, and (7) Drug Abuse.

These components were then used as variables in a discriminant analysis for each report.[6] The following summarizes the results of these analyses.

Predicting Competency from the Mental Status Exam. The nine components were entered into a stepwise discriminant analysis[7] ($F < .05$) con-

trasting the competent group (N = 75) with the incompetent group
(N = 83). Table 6.7 presents the component means and the discriminant
function coefficient column. Six of the components received significant
weights. In descending order, the following variables were of most importance in making the discrimination between the two groups: (1) Delusions, (2) Speech Disorganization, (3) Alcohol Abuse, (4) Inappropriate
Behavior, (5) Cognitive Functioning, and (6) Drug Abuse. These results
may be interpreted as implying that individuals who are classified as incompetent tend to have Mental Status Exams which indicate the presence
of delusions, confused and incoherent speech, and uncooperative behavior; they are, however, unlikely to have a history of alcohol and drug
abuse.

Based upon the discriminant analysis, Table 6.8 compares the results of
the prediction of group membership (competent or incompetent) with the
actual hospital determination made approximately four to six weeks after

TABLE 6.7

Mental Status Exam:
Component Means and Discriminant
Function Coefficients

Component	Competent (N = 75)	Incompetent (N = 83)	Discriminant Function Coefficients
Alcohol Abuse	.96	.48	.34
Speech Disorganization	.11	.52	− .36
Drug Abuse	.13	.04	.32
Inappropriate Behavior	.08	.34	− .34
Depression	.19	.37	
Delusions	.15	.72	− .50
Affect/Legal Involvement	.67	.72	
Hallucinations	.39	.76	
Cognitive Functioning	.69	1.09	− .35

Adapted from Roesch (1979).

TABLE 6.8

Mental Status Exam:
Prediction Results[1]

Actual Group	Number of Cases	Predicted Group Membership	
		Competent	Incompetent
Competent	75	62	13
		(82.7%)	(17.3%)
Incompetent	83	23	60
		(27.7%)	(72.3%)

[1]Percent of "grouped" cases correctly classified = 77.22%.

the Mental Status Exam. This prediction resulted in the correct classification of 83% of the competent sample and 72% of the incompetent sample. Conversely, the discriminant function incorrectly classified 17% of the competent sample and 28% of the incompetent sample. This result implies that the outcome of the evaluation can be predicted on the basis of the initial psychiatric evaluation.

Predicting Competency from the Diagnostic Conference Report and Discharge Summary/Diagnostic Conference Report. The seven principal components from this report were entered into a stepwise discriminant analysis. Table 6.9 presents the component means and discriminant function coefficients. As can be seen by referring to the last column, five of the component means received significant weights. In descending order of discriminating power, these were: (1) Speech/Affect, (2) Interactional Behavior, (3) Delusions, (4) Hallucinations, and (5) Alcohol Abuse. Incompetent defendants tended to have reports which characterized them as having confused and incoherent speech, as being isolated, and as having impaired insight and judgment, delusions, and hallucinations; they were unlikely to have a history of alcohol abuse.

The report was the hospital's first communication to the court. It was at this point that a recommendation about competency was made. This report was based on information obtained during a defendant's hospitalization, including a social history, psychological testing, and additional interviews by psychiatrists and others. Thus the report included more information than the Mental Status Exam. *However, the prediction of the*

TABLE 6.9

Diagnostic Conference Report and Discharge Summary
Diagnostic Conference Report:
Component Means and Discriminant Function Coefficients

Component	Competent (N = 136)	Incompetent (N = 130)	Discriminant Function Coefficients
Delusions	.19	.95	−.38
Speech/Affect	.16	1.18	−.47
Alcohol Abuse	.90	.62	.14
Hostility	.10	.35	
Hallucinations	.30	.93	−.16
Interactional Behavior	.23	1.13	−.46
Anxiety	.45	.45	
Prior Felonies	.37	.20	

Adapted from Roesch (1979).

group membership, based on information contained in the report, was not any more accurate than the prediction based on information contained in the Mental Status Exam. Table 6.10 shows that the discriminant function correctly classified 90% of the competent group and 74% of the incompetent group. Approximately the same number of incompetent defendants were incorrectly classified as competent, when compared to the Mental Status Exam. The accuracy of the competent sample prediction was slightly improved. As we discuss below, this suggests that the additional information collected during hospitalization did not significantly affect the decision, at least for the vast majority of cases.

Predicting Competency from the Diagnostic Conference Report and Discharge Summary/Discharge Summary. The seven principal components resulting from the analysis of these combined reports were entered into a stepwise discriminant analysis. Table 6.11 shows that five components received significant weights. In descending order of discriminating power, these were: (1) Drug Abuse, (2) Alcohol Abuse, (3) Hallucinations/Past Delusions, (4) Depression, and (5) Cognitive Functioning. It should be remembered that this report was the discharge report for both competent

TABLE 6.10

Diagnostic Conference Report and
Discharge Summary/Diagnostic Conference Report:
Prediction Results[1]

Actual Group	Number of Cases	Predicted Group Membership	
		Competent	Incompetent
Competent	136	122 (89.7%)	14 (10.3%)
Incompetent	130	34 (26.2%)	96 (73.8%)

[1]Percent of "grouped" cases correctly classified = 81.95%.

TABLE 6.11

Diagnostic Conference Report and
Discharge Summary/Discharge Summary:
Component Means and Discriminant Function Coefficients

Component	Competent (N = 138)	Incompetent (N = 128)	Discriminant Function Coefficients
Alcohol Abuse	.93	.20	−.54
Hallucinations/Past Delusions	.30	.47	.30
Hostility	.09	.13	
Depression	.43	.16	−.22
Cognitive Functioning	.37	.26	−.21
Present Delusions	.13	.18	
Drug Abuse/Legal Involvement	.49	.04	−.63

Adapted from Roesch (1979).

and incompetent defendants. Thus incompetent defendants were being
returned to the court as competent. As a consequence, the incompetent
sample appeared much less pathological at the time of this report. The

incompetent end of the dimension was characterized primarily by hallu-cinations, both in the present and in the past, and by delusions in the past. The competent group was characterized primarily, as with other re-ports, by a history of alcohol and drug abuse.

Since the incompetent sample was reported to be less deviant and pathological on this report, the prediction of group membership showed that nearly 38% of the competent sample were misclassified as incompe-tent, based on the information available in the report (Table 6.12), while less than 10% of the incompetent group were placed in the competent group.

TABLE 6.12

Diagnostic Conference Report and
Discharge Summary/Discharge Summary:
Prediction Results[1]

Actual Group	Number of Cases	Predicted Group Membership	
		Competent	Incompetent
Competent	138	86	52
		(62.3%)	(37.7%)
Incompetent	128	12	116
		(9.4%)	(90.6%)

[1]Percent of "grouped" cases correctly classified = 75.94%.

In summary, the discriminant analyses of the psychiatric reports re-vealed that the information available from the initial psychiatric inter-view alone is sufficient for making a decision about competency, at least for the majority of cases. In other words, the data collected from a variety of other sources which necessitate a lengthy and institutional evaluation, such as ward evaluations, psychological tests, and social histories, do not seem to be of critical importance in reaching a decision about compe-tency.

Court outcome. The collection of court follow-up data was discussed earlier in the method section. Court follow-up was obtained for 131 competent and 126 incompetent defendants, a return rate of 95%. The majority of the sample were represented by court-appointed attorneys (72.7% of the competent and 72.1% of the incompetent group).

Five defendants (four incompetent and one competent) were found not guilty by reason of insanity. These defendants were not included in the court outcome analyses, since there were no compelling reasons for placing them in either the innocent or the guilty category. Defendants found not guilty by reason of insanity were, in a sense, guilty of the offense but not responsible for it. While they did not receive a prison sentence, they were usually involuntarily committed to a mental hospital. Two of these incompetent defendants were charged with murder, one with auto theft, and one with assault with intent to commit rape, and they were held in the hospital for 1,059, 867, 1,193, and 635 days respectively (mean = 939 days). All were committed to a mental hospital following disposition. The one competent defendant was charged with breaking and entering, was held for 36 days, but was not committed following disposition of charges. One other defendant's case was pending and was also excluded from the court outcome analyses. This defendant had been found incompetent but was returned to court to stand trial after being in the hospital for over 12 years. Despite this lengthy hospitalization, the court recommitted him as incompetent to stand trial, with the charges against him still pending. Thus, with these exclusions, court outcome data were available for 130 competent and 121 incompetent defendants.

The analysis of court outcome was complicated because of the use of plea bargaining, conviction on one charge but not on other charges, or conviction on one count but not on other counts. Thus any analysis cannot simply look at whether a defendant was convicted of the original charge(s). The present analysis takes these possibilities into account in the following manner. If a defendant was not convicted of the most serious offense against him, we then determined whether he entered a plea to a reduced charge, or was convicted on a second, third, or fourth charge. If a plea of guilty was entered to a reduced charge, or if a second, third, or fourth charge resulted in a conviction, then this offense was used as the disposition offense. Offenses were grouped into six categories: (1) murder (first and second degree), (2) assault (aggravated assault, assault with a deadly weapon), (3) rape (rape, attempted rape), (4) other violent offenses (manslaughter, kidnapping, armed robbery), (5) property offenses (burglary, larceny, vandalism, breaking and entering), and (6) nonviolent offenses (possession of marijuana, disorderly conduct, check offenses).

The court outcome analyses are presented in sequential order beginning with the determination of guilt or innocence and following all defendants until they are no longer in the legal system. Table 6.13 shows the type of offense at disposition. The percentage of cases in each offense category will not be the same as shown in Table 6.5 (offense at time of referral to Dorothea Dix Hospital), since many defendants entered a plea to a reduced charge or were convicted of another charge. Table 6.13 shows that many defendants with murder charges entered a plea to a reduced offense, usually to assault or manslaughter. This was true for nine competent and 16 incompetent defendants. Many of the defendants charged with assault were also allowed to enter a plea to a less serious violent offense. The difference between the competent and incompetent groups for type of offense at disposition was significant. As can be seen by referring to Table 6.13, incompetent defendants were significantly more likely to be charged with a violent offense at disposition, and less likely to be charged with property crimes or other nonviolent offenses. When the offenses were collapsed into two categories (murder and assault versus property crimes and other nonviolent offenses), this difference was clear (chi-square [1] = 6.86, $p<.01$). This finding was expected, since the incompetent group

TABLE 6.13

Type of Offense at Disposition

	Competent (N = 130)	Incompetent (N = 121)
Murder	26 (20%)	32 (26%)
Assault	18 (14%)	26 (22%)
Rape/sex offenses	15 (11%)	13 (11%)
Other violent offenses	22 (17%)	21 (17%)
Property crimes	39 (30%)	28 (23%)
Other nonviolent offenses	10 (8%)	1 (1%)

TABLE 6.14
Court Outcome[1]

	Murder*		Assault*		Rape/Sex Offenses		Other Violent Offenses		Property Crimes		Other Nonviolent Offenses	
	Innocent	Guilty	Innocent	Guilty	Innocent	Guilty	Innocent	Guilty	Innocent	Guilty	Innocent	Guilty
Competent	2 (8%)	24 (92%)	1 (6%)	17 (94%)	7 (47%)	8 (53%)	3 (14%)	19 (86%)	10 (26%)	29 (74%)	1 (10%)	9 (90%)
Incompetent	12 (38%)	20 (62%)	11 (42%)	15 (58%)	5 (39%)	8 (61%)	4 (19%)	17 (81%)	11 (39%)	17 (61%)	1 (100%)	0

[1]An innocent outcome includes defendants found innocent in a trial, those who had charges dismissed, and those released after no probable cause was found. A guilty outcome includes those found guilty in a trial and those who plea bargained.

*p < .05

had a higher percentage of murder and violent offenses when they were referred for evaluation.

Table 6.14 summarizes the court outcome for the two groups. The results for each offense category will be considered separately.[8] An innocent outcome includes defendants found innocent at trial, those who had charges dismissed, and those released owing to a finding of no probable cause. Most defendants in the innocent category had their charges dismissed. A guilty outcome includes those found guilty in a trial and those who entered a guilty plea.

As can be seen by referring to Table 6.14, incompetent defendants charged with murder were significantly more likely to obtain an innocent disposition (chi-square [1] = 5.43, $p<.05$), although the majority of defendants in both groups received a guilty disposition. In order to determine if length of hospitalization had an influence on the court outcome, a t-test was computed (Table 6.15). The 12 incompetent defendants receiving an innocent disposition had a mean length of hospitalization of 2,279 days, compared with a mean of 886 days for those defendants found guilty. The difference was significant ($t[30] = 2.63$, $p<.01$). Table 6.16 shows that incarceration was the most frequent outcome for those defendants found guilty of murder. All competent defendants were incarcerated, while only three incompetent defendants were not incarcerated. These data suggest that the length of hospitalization may be a significant factor

TABLE 6.15

Length of Hospitalization by Disposition
for Incompetent Defendants[1]

	Murder**	Assault	Rape/Sex Offenses	Other Violent Crimes	Property Crimes
Innocent	2,279	456	893	402	632
	(N = 12)	(N = 11)	(N = 5)	(N = 4)	(N = 11)
Guilty	886	719	869	888	823
	(N = 20)	(N = 15)	(N = 8)	(N = 17)	(N = 17)

[1]Only one incompetent defendant was charged with an offense in the sixth category. He was found innocent and had been hospitalized for 965 days.

**$p < .01$

TABLE 6.16

Type of Sentence by Offense

	Murder		Assault		Rape/Sex Offenses		Other Violent Offenses		Property Crimes[1]		Other Nonviolent Offenses	
	Prison	Nonprison	Prison	Nonprison	Prison	Nonprison	Prison	Nonprison	Prison	Nonprison	Prison	Nonprison
Competent	24 (100%)	0	9 (53%)	8 (47%)	7 (88%)	1 (12%)	18 (95%)	1 (5%)	15 (52%)	14 (48%)	3 (33%)	6 (67%)
Incompetent	17 (85%)	3 (15%)	7 (47%)	8 (53%)	4 (50%)	4 (50%)	12 (71%)	5 (29%)	3 (18%)	14 (82%)	0	0

[1]Incompetent defendants convicted of property crimes were significantly less likely to receive a prison sentence (chi-square = 3.89, $p < .05$). No sentencing differences were found for the remaining offense categories.

in determining whether a defendant charged with murder will be prosecuted. However, incompetent defendants found guilty were no less likely than competent defendants to be sent to prison, regardless of length of hospitalization. Thus lengthy hospitalization had an influence only on prosecution, not on type of sentence.

Incompetent defendants charged with assault were also significantly more likely to have charges dismissed or to be found innocent (chi-square [1] = 5.50, $p<.05$; see Table 6.14). Length of hospitalization did not appear to be a factor, as the 11 incompetent defendants receiving an innocent disposition had a mean length of hospitalization of 456 days, compared with 719 days for guilty incompetent defendants. This difference was not statistically significant. Table 6.16 shows that there was no difference in the incarceration rates.

Table 6.14 shows that there were no significant differences in court outcome for the remaining offense categories, nor were there any differences in incarceration rates (Table 6.16), with the exception of defendants charged with property crimes, in which incompetent defendants were significantly more likely to receive a nonprison sentence (chi-square [1] = 3.89, $p<.05$). Comparisons of length of hospitalization for the two groups showed no significant differences (Table 6.15).

Length of hospitalization of incompetent defendants had no influence on the use of prison or nonprison sentences for any offense category. Table 6.17 summarizes these data for the incompetent guilty group.

TABLE 6.17

Length of Hospitalization by Type of Sentence
For Incompetent Defendants (Mean Number of Days)[1]

	Murder	Assault	Rape/Sex Offenses	Other Violent Crimes	Property Crimes
Prison	891	845	1,058	858	376
	(N = 17)	(N = 7)	(N = 4)	(N = 12)	(N = 3)
Nonprison	856	608	681	961	919
	(N = 3)	(N = 8)	(N = 4)	(N = 5)	(N = 14)

[1]No significant differences between prison and nonprison sentences were found for length of hospitalization by type of offense.

Table 6.18 shows the length of prison sentence. The length of sentence, for both minimum and maximum sentences, was about the same for the two groups, although the incompetent group tended to have somewhat shorter sentences. However, with the exception of the maximum sentence for the category of "other violent offenses," none of these differences was significant.

The final logical analysis of the court outcome data would be an analysis of the relationship between length of hospitalization and length of prison sentence. The appropriate statistic would be the Spearman rank correlation coefficient. However, with the exception of the offense categories of murder and other violent crimes, the number of subjects in each offense category was not large enough to carry out the analysis. The analysis of the categories of murder and other violent crimes revealed no significant relationship between length of hospitalization and length of sentence.

TABLE 6.18
Average Length of Prison Sentence (in Years)[1]

	Competent	Incompetent
Murder		
Minimum	21	18
Maximum	32	26
Assault		
Minimum	7	9
Maximum	7	9
Rape/sex offenses		
Minimum	9	9
Maximum	15	10
Other violent crimes		
Minimum	15	13
Maximum	24	15
Property crimes		
Minimum	6	2
Maximum	8	3

[1]With the exception of the maximum sentence for violent crimes, none of the differences in sentence between competent and incompetent defendants was significant.

Some defendants were recommitted to Dorothea Dix Hospital following disposition of charges. This rehospitalization reflects the influence of the mental health recommendation on court outcome and sentencing. The recommendation was usually of the form, "if no active prison sentence is given, this defendant should be involuntarily committed to Dorothea Dix Hospital." The hospital had recommended commitment of three competent and 40 incompetent defendants. As part of the disposition, the court ordered hospitalization for three competent (two of whom had commitment recommendations) and 21 incompetent defendants (12 of whom had recommendations). Thus the rate of agreement between hospital recommendation and court disposition was 67% and 30% respectively. It is of interest to note that the 40 incompetent defendants had already been in the hospital for an average of 1,192 days and a median of 722 days!

In summary, the analyses of court outcome revealed that incompetent defendants charged with serious violent crimes, including murder, assault with intent to kill, and assault with a deadly weapon, were more likely, when compared to competent defendants, to receive an innocent disposition. Length of hospitalization appeared to be a significant factor only in determining whether an incompetent defendant would be prosecuted for murder. Incompetent defendants not prosecuted had been hospitalized significantly longer than prosecuted defendants. Furthermore, with the exception of property crime offenders, incompetent defendants were no less likely than competent defendants to receive incarceration sentences.

Court outcome by race. The court outcome data were available for 143 white defendants (78 competent, 65 incompetent) and for 103 black defendants (48 competent, 55 incompetent). Table 6.19 shows, by race, the type of offense at referral.

Analysis of the competent group by race revealed no significant differences. Therefore, only the analysis of the incompetent group will be discussed. A chi-square analysis revealed a significant difference between black and white incompetent defendants for referral offense (chi-square [5] = 10.87, $p<.05$). This difference appears to be due to the differences in murder charges. As Table 6.19 shows, 49% of the white incompetent group were charged with murder at referral, compared with only 23% of the black group. This difference in murder charges becomes more clear by inspecting the first row of Table 6.20. A chi-square analysis of both groups

TABLE 6.19

Offense at Referral by Race

	Competent		Incompetent[*]	
	White (N = 78)	Black (N = 48)	White (N = 65)	Black (N = 55)
Murder	15 (19%)	19 (40%)	32 (49%)	12 (22%)
Assault	9 (12%)	6 (13%)	10 (15%)	15 (27%)
Rape	12 (15%)	3 (6%)	8 (12%)	9 (16%)
Other violent offenses	14 (18%)	6 (13%)	3 (5%)	3 (5%)
Property offenses	24 (31%)	11 (23%)	12 (18%)	15 (27%)
Nonviolent offenses	4 (5%)	3 (6%)	0	1 (2%)

[*]$p < .05$

by race for those charged with murder revealed a significant difference (chi-square [1] = 6.56, $p<.05$). A lower proportion of whites charged with murder were found in the competent group; conversely, a higher percentage of whites were found in the incompetent group. Analyses of the remaining offense categories revealed no significant differences.

Table 6.20 shows type of offense at disposition. Again, the differences in type of offense between black and white incompetent defendants were significant (chi-square [5] = 14.03, $p<.05$). As would be expected from the analysis described above, chi-square analyses of both groups by race and offense category indicated that the difference was due to murder charges (chi-square [1] = 8.56, $p<.01$). Of particular interest is the fact blacks were more likely to have a murder charge reduced. Only eight of 32 (25%) white incompetent defendants had a murder charge reduced, compared with seven of 12 (58%) black defendants.

There were few race differences in court outcome. Blacks charged with assault were more likely to receive an innocent disposition (Fisher's Exact

TABLE 6.20

Offense at Disposition by Race

	Competent		Incompetent[*]	
	White (N = 78)	Black (N = 48)	White (N = 65)	Black (N = 55)
Murder	11 (14%)	14 (29%)	26 (40%)	6 (11%)
Assault	12 (15%)	5 (10%)	11 (17%)	15 (27%)
Rape	10 (13%)	3 (6%)	6 (9%)	7 (13%)
Other violent offenses	12 (15%)	10 (21%)	10 (15%)	10 (18%)
Property offenses	27 (35%)	12 (25%)	12 (19%)	16 (29%)
Nonviolent offenses	6 (8%)	4 (3%)	0	1 (2%)

[*]$p < .05$

Test = .004). Ten of 15 blacks charged with assault were found innocent versus only one of 11 white incompetents. Whites charged with other violent offenses were significantly more likely to receive an innocent disposition (Fisher's Exact Test = .043). Four of ten whites were found innocent, compared with none of ten blacks. No other differences in innocent/guilty determinations were found.

The use of prison and nonprison sentences showed no significant race differences for any offense category. It is interesting to note, however, that the three defendants convicted of murder but not sent to prison were white. There was a tendency for white defendants to receive longer minimum and maximum sentences. However, the low number of defendants precluded statistical analysis.

Finally, only one difference in length of hospitalization by referral offense was significant. White incompetent defendants charged with murder were held for an average of 1,605 days, compared with 781 days for black incompetent defendants ($t[45] = 2.60$, $p<.01$).

In summary, few differences in court outcome and length of hospitalization by race were found, with the primary exception of defendants
charged with murder. Blacks were much less likely to be charged with
murder and, if so charged, were much more likely to have the charge
reduced. Furthermore, blacks with murder charges were held in the hospital for a significantly shorter period and were less likely to be found
incompetent.

Discussion

The purpose of this study was to identify the legal and mental health
procedures for confronting the issue of competency to stand trial. This
study was designed to determine the characteristic differences between
competent and incompetent defendants that emerged at the mental
health evaluation or court processing stages of competency determination,
since such information might lead to a better understanding of the process
of making decisions about competency. The identification of differences
between competent and incompetent defendants could lead to improvements in the evaluation process.

Several differences between competent and incompetent defendants
were found. Incompetent defendants often had a history of psychiatric
hospitalization prior to their evaluation for competency. Our figure of
slightly more than one-half with previous hospitalizations is not quite as
high as the 81% figure reported by Steadman (1979) in his study of incompetent defendants in New York, but it does suggest, as Steadman points
out, that many incompetent defendants have shifted back and forth between the criminal justice and mental health systems.

In terms of psychiatric diagnosis, incompetent defendants were typically viewed as psychotic or mentally retarded, while competent defendants were usually seen as being nonpsychotic. This finding supports the
conclusions of earlier researchers (e.g., McGarry, 1965) that psychiatrists
tend to view psychotics as incompetent to stand trial. However, this does
not necessarily suggest that the diagnosis was made first, which then led
to a determination of incompetency. It is possible that the incompetency
determination was made first, after which the psychiatrist attached a diagnostic label consistent with the prevailing views about incompetency.

Some comments need to be made about the reliability of competency
decisions. The fact that there is such a strong relationship between com-

petency determinations and gross diagnostic categories (e.g., psychosis) suggests that the reliability of competency decisions might correspond closely to psychiatric diagnostic reliability, which is generally in the neighborhood of .70 for gross categories (see Helzer et al., 1977, for a recent review). More directly related to the competency issue, McGarry et al. (1973) reported reliabilities in the .70 and .80 range for raters making judgments about various aspects of competency, based on a brief interview. One of our own studies (Study Three), reported later in this chapter, showed similarly high agreement and also demonstrated that judgments made on the basis of a brief interview were highly related to judgments based on more lengthy institutional evaluations. But the strong relationship between psychiatric diagnosis and competency suggests a problem with the validity of the decision, particularly the construct validity of the competency criterion (see Chapters 2 and 4). Are defendants who may be reliably judged to be incompetent actually incapable of participating in their defense? Such a relationship has been assumed but has yet to be empirically demonstrated. We will keep this issue in mind in our discussion, later in the book, of various alternatives to present methods of assessing competency.

Discriminant analyses of the psychiatric reports revealed a number of significant differences between the two groups. Incompetent defendants were described as being delusional, hallucinating, confused, uncooperative, and having impaired judgment and insight. Competent defendants were described as having no major symptoms, with the frequent exception of histories of alcohol and/or drug abuse. The most interesting finding with respect to the psychiatric reports was that the prediction of group membership (competent or incompetent) based on information contained in the Mental Status Exam was about as accurate as the prediction based on information contained in the Diagnostic Conference Report. The Mental Status Exam was based entirely on an interview by a psychiatrist and occurred within two or three days of admission. The Diagnostic Conference Report, on the other hand, was prepared four to six weeks after admission and was based on more information about a defendant, including psychological tests, behavior on the ward, interviews by social workers, and family contacts. This finding suggests that the additional information contained in the Diagnostic Conference Report was not critical to the determination of competency, at least for most referrals. Obviously, this is in part due to the fact that many defendants are inappropriately referred for evaluation, as we discussed in Chapter 3. Nevertheless, this finding does suggest that the amount of time spent in the hospital for evaluation (up to 60 days in the past and currently about 17 days in North Carolina) may not add to the decision-making ability of the evaluators. The deprivation of liberty and expense of hospitalization may well be unnecessary. It appears that an interview alone, which could be conducted in a noninstitutional setting, might provide sufficient information for making a decision about the majority of referrals. In the next chapter we will propose such a noninstitutional, community-based screening evaluation.

Incompetent defendants were often held for extreme periods in the hospital prior to their return to court. Many defendants were held ten years or more, with the longest being a defendant charged with murder who was held for 14 years, after which charges were dismissed. Most of the defendants in this study were hospitalized prior to *Jackson* v. *Indiana* (1972), which held that incompetent defendants could not be held longer than a reasonable period of time necessary to determine if they could be restored to competence. Unfortunately, the Supreme Court did not define "reasonable period of time"; therefore, the lengthy hospitalizations found for the incompetent defendants in this study are still possible. The recommendations proposed in the final chapter attempt to provide a more ethically and legally defensible system for the commitment of incompetent defendants.

Despite the lengthy hospitalization of incompetent defendants, there were few differences between the two groups in court outcome. In fact, the majority of defendants, both competent and incompetent, in every offense category were found guilty. This finding provides some support for the hypothesis that the competency issue is more likely to be raised when there is a high probability of conviction. Mental health recommendations and the use of mitigating circumstances as part of the defense would be more desirable and possibly advantageous for the defense in such cases. The most consistent differences were for murder and assault charges. Incompetent defendants charged with murder or assault were significantly more likely to receive an innocent disposition, usually the result of a dismissal of charges by the prosecutor. Length of hospitalization may have been a determining factor for dismissing murder charges, since incompetent defendants found innocent had been hospitalized nearly three times longer than guilty incompetent defendants. This finding may be due to the fact that too much time had transpired from arrest to hospital release, and therefore the prosecutor's case was diminished owing to witness unavailability. This hypothesis is supported by the fact that no length-of-hospitalization differences were found in the comparisons of charges other than murder. Defendants in the remaining offense categories had been held less than three years, on the average. Thus the prosecution would be more likely to have witnesses and victims available, and more confidence in the successful prosecution of a case. However, length of hospitalization did not appear to influence the outcome of these defendants charged with assault. In fact, incompetent defendants found guilty of assault tended to have longer periods of hospitalization. Once a determination of guilt had been made, the fact that a defendant had previously been found competent did not significantly influence the use of prison sentences. The only exception to this was for incompetent defendants found guilty of property crimes. These defendants were significantly more likely to receive a suspended sentence, usually because defendants were given credit for time spent in the hospital. This time often exceeded the prison sentence which could have been given.

The fact that many charges were ultimately dismissed points to the problems of lengthy trial delays. Witnesses and victims become unavailable, memories fade, the prosecution's case is diminished, and the defense is made more difficult. These data suggest that lengthy delays should be avoided, to protect the interests of both prosecution and defendant.

Study Two:
A Prospective Study of the Decision-Making Processes
Involved in the Determination of Competency

The previous study provided an analysis of the mental health decision-making procedures for reaching a determination of competency. However, the study had to rely upon information available in hospital records and was necessarily based upon evaluations which had already been completed. Thus different assessment techniques could not be evaluated. The present study was an attempt to assess the usefulness of several psychological tests and ward observation techniques in order to determine possible changes and improvements in the decision-making process. However, despite a lengthy data collection period, there were very few defendants found incompetent. While this result precluded most statistical comparisons between competent and incompetent defendants, the study did provide us with some very useful information on the characteristics of competent defendants, a group which accounted for 93% of the referrals during the study period. We will now turn to a description and discussion of the results of this study.

Method

Subjects. The subjects were 151 defendants referred to the forensic unit between February 20 and April 30, 1976, for competency evaluations.

Procedure. These defendants completed the following self-report measures, which were collected within three days of admission in order to minimize the influence of institutionalization on responses.

a) Competency Screening Test (Lipsitt, Lelos, and McGarry, 1971). This measure was routinely administered to all defendants and was used in the decision-making process. However, during the study the CST score was not reported to the forensic unit staff, in order that the predictive validity of the measure could be evaluated (see Chapter 3 for a review).

b) A questionnaire designed to obtain demographic and other background data and information about the present charges against the defendant.

c) Psychological Screening Inventory. The Psychological Screening Inventory (PSI) is a self-report measure of psychopathology developed by Lanyon (1970). The PSI consists of five scales, including a defensiveness scale designed to assess the validity of responses.

d) Slosson Intelligence Test. This measure was in current use by the forensic unit.

e) Internal-External Locus of Control Scale. This measure was developed by Rotter (1966) and was intended to measure the degree to which individuals perceive events in their lives as largely controlled either by themselves or by forces outside their control. When events in an individual's life are perceived as being the result of luck, chance, fate, or under the control of other, more powerful individuals, the belief is labeled *external control*. On the other hand, persons who view events as being largely contingent on their own behavior and influence are considered to have a high degree of *internal control* (Rotter, 1966). The scale developed to measure this dimension is a 29-item forced-choice test, including six filler items designed to disguise the purpose of the measure. The remaining items require an adoption of either a statement representing internal control or a statement representing external control.

f) Social Desirability. The Marlowe-Crowne Social Desirability Scale (MC-SD) was adopted to obtain a measure of the extent to which defendants attempt to present themselves in either a positive or a negative fashion. The MC-SD is a 33-item, self-report test in true-false format, with satisfactory test-retest reliability and internal consistency (Crowne and Marlowe, 1964).

In addition to the self-report measures, hospital record and court data were obtained, using the same method of collection as described in Study One. The Psychotic Inpatient Profile (PIP) was also administered (Lorr and Vestre, 1969). The PIP is a 96-item inventory measuring 12 dimensions of psychopathology based on ward observations. The first eight dimensions were rated by nursing personnel (see Table 6.21). Items were rated on a four-point scale, ranging from never present to nearly always present.

Nine raters (Dorothea Dix Hospital forensic unit nursing personnel) were trained by Roesch in three separate one-hour sessions. The purpose

TABLE 6.21

Psychotic Inpatient Profile

Scale	Representative Item
Excitement	Talks in a loud voice
Hostile belligerence	Loses temper when dealing with other patients
Paranoid projection	Acts as though the hospital is persecuting him
Anxious depression	Looks worried and nervous
Retardation	Moves quite slowly
Seclusiveness	Mixes with other patients
Care needed	Needs help in dressing
Psychotic disorganization	Makes up new or unusual words

of the PIP as well as the items and factor scores were explained to the raters. The raters were then asked to rate a patient with whom they were all familiar. The ratings were reviewed and any disagreements were discussed. This procedure was followed until three patients were rated by each rating team. Raters were divided into pairs, with each pair independently completing a PIP at two time intervals: (1) the first three days following admission, and (2) three weeks after admission. Each rating was based on the behavior of the defendant during the preceding three-day period. If a defendant was discharged prior to three weeks, the second rating was completed at discharge.

Results

Background data. The sample included 151 defendants, only 11 of whom were determined to be incompetent. Based on these figures, it is estimated that the rate of incompetency determinations is approximately 7%. Projections from the rate of admissions suggest a very low annual rate of incompetency determination.

The sample included only two females, both of whom were found to be competent. The breakdown by race was approximately the same as found in Study One, with 58% of the population being white. Only 31 competent defendants and one incompetent defendant had completed high school. The mean age for competent defendants was 28, for incompetents, 32. Over one-half of the sample (54%) were 25 years old or less. In fact, almost one-third of the sample were less than 21 years old. The youngest was 12 years old. This defendant was found competent, but the court case was pending at the time of this study. One 14-year-old and two 16-year-olds were charged with murder, declared competent, found guilty, and sentenced to prison for periods ranging from ten to 80 years.

Many defendants had prior arrest and conviction records. Forty percent of the competent group had at least one prior arrest, while 31% had two or more previous arrests. Twenty percent had at least one prior felony conviction, and 21% had one or more prior misdemeanor convictions. Arrest history was available for only eight of the 11 incompetent defendants. Two had been arrested previously; one had a prior felony conviction and one had a prior misdemeanor conviction.

The competency evaluation was usually suggested or initiated by the defense attorney (78%), but was also suggested by relatives (9%), by the defendant (6%), or by arresting officers or jailers (3%). The remaining four referrals were initiated by prosecutors or judges.

Only 13 competent and one incompetent defendants had been previously hospitalized at Dorothea Dix Hospital. Twenty-two competent and one incompetent defendants had previous admissions to other psychiatric facilities.

Defendants are currently being held in the hospital for brief periods of time. The mean length of hospitalization was approximately 17 days. Only 17 of the 151 defendants in the sample were held longer than three weeks. Thus, with few exceptions, the determination of competency appeared to be a straightforward process.

Psychiatric diagnosis. Incompetent defendants were again primarily viewed as psychotic or mentally retarded. These diagnoses, however, did not automatically lead to an incompetency determination. Many competent defendants were considered to be psychotic, but the psychosis was apparently not considered to interfere with competence. Defendants with alcohol and drug abuse histories were uniformly viewed as competent. This was also true for the defendants in Study One.

Psychiatric report. The only psychiatric report available for these defendants was the Diagnostic Conference Report and Discharge Summary. This report was available for all defendants in the sample. Owing to the low number of incompetent defendants, statistical comparisons were not possible. However, an item analysis of the ratings produced some interesting, but tentative, information about the decision-making process. The description of each group which follows summarizes information from the report in which at least 10% of the group had the behavior present. The actual percentage of each group for a given description is reported in parentheses.

The competent group was described as being anxious (25%), depressed (21%), and having an inappropriate affect (27%). Approximately 32% were reported to have histories of alcohol abuse, while only 11% had a history of drug abuse. Finally, it was reported that 30% had impaired judgment or insight. On the other hand, the incompetent group was described as being uncooperative (33%) and having an inappropriate affect (42%). Two-thirds of the group were reported to have impaired judgment or insight and poor memory for recent and past events. Finally, 50% were described, in the all-too-present psychiatric jargon, as being not oriented to time, place, or person.

The item analysis of this report revealed, first of all, the paucity of information communicated to the court. The reports were usually quite brief and frequently contained only vague descriptors of a defendant's behavior, such as "defendant is depressed," "defendant is uncooperative," "affect is inappropriate," "insight and judgment is impaired," or unsupported comments about past behavior, such as "defendant has a history of alcohol abuse." Very little information seemed to distinguish the two groups. The most important items seemed to be uncooperative behavior in the hospital, memory, insight and judgment, and orientation. Yet many competent defendants were described in similar terms and, perhaps more important, some incompetent defendants did not have any difficulties in these areas.

Psychological tests. Table 6.22 summarized the psychological test data. Since the incompetent group was small, comparisons of test scores would be inappropriate. Therefore, only brief descriptions of the test results will be presented. It is interesting to note that incompetent defendants were unable or unwilling to complete many of the tests. This may have been due to reading ability, as supported by scores on the Wide Range Achievement Test, or perhaps due to uncooperativeness. Both of these factors may have contributed to a hospital determination of incompetent to stand trial.

Scores on the Slosson Intelligence Test and the Wide Range Achievement Test were consistent with the educational and demographic background of the defendants. Psychological Screening Inventory scale scores were consistent with the profiles of psychiatric inpatients, but were not similar to the profiles of prison inmates. This finding is consistent with the fact that many defendants are referred for a competency evaluation because of a history of psychiatric treatment.

Pre- and postfactor scores[9] for the Psychotic Inpatient Profile are shown in Table 6.23. Although the low number of incompetent defendants makes statistical comparisons impossible, it is interesting to note that the incompetent defendants scored much higher on all eight factors. Incompetent defendants were perceived by ward personnel to be much more deviant and pathological. It should be noted that the pre- ratings were

TABLE 6.22

Psychological Test Scores

	Competent	Incompetent
Competency Screening Test	24	13
	(N = 123)	(N = 5)
Psychological Screening Inventory[1]		
Alienation	10.6	—
Social nonconformity	12.1	—
Discomfort	13.5	—
Expression	11.2	—
Defensiveness	10.3	—
Intelligence	84	60
	(N = 125)	(N = 7)
Wide Range Achievement Test[2]		
Reading	7.6	3.4
Spelling	5.6	3.2
Arithmetic	5.3	2.8
Marlowe-Crowne Social Desirability Scale	18.3	—
	(N = 79)	
Internal-External Locus of Control Scale	10.5	—
	(N = 77)	

[1]Data available for 75 competent defendants only.
[2]Data available for 121 competent defendants and four incompetent defendants.

made three days following admission, prior to the hospital judgment about competency. The post- ratings of incompetent defendants may be slightly inflated because they were usually completed just prior to discharge, after a determination had been made. The knowledge that a defendant was incompetent (or, conversely, competent) may have influenced the post-ratings. The large differences in the ratings of competent and incompetent defendants provide some support for the notion that ward personnel have the ability to make significant contributions to the decision-making process. Given that defendants being evaluated spend the vast majority of their time on the ward, it seems apparent that information about ward behavior should be more systematically incorporated into the decision-making process. The PIP may be a useful measure for including this information. The data summarized here provide some support for its use, although more data are needed before it can be more confidently used. The low item reliabilities clearly point to the need for more training in the use of the PIP.

TABLE 6.23

Psychotic Inpatient Profile Mean Scores

	Competent		Incompetent	
	Pre- (N = 124)	Post- (N = 97)	Pre- (N = 7)	Post- (N = 6)
Excitement	1.39	1.58	4.71	7.00
Hostile belligerence	1.30	1.25	3.64	6.66
Paranoid projection	1.32	1.32	5.28	10.00
Anxious depression	1.97	1.59	3.07	1.83
Retardation	1.42	1.12	3.78	1.91
Seclusiveness	20.98	20.02	26.28	25.66
Care needed	1.72	1.41	4.07	4.25
Psychotic disorganization	1.15	1.08	7.85	6.50

The social desirability measure and the internal-external locus of control measure were administered to determine their relationship to the Competency Screening Test. The results are discussed in the remainder of this section.

The Competency Screening Test (McGarry et al., 1973) was completed by 123 competent defendants and five incompetent defendants, but was not used in the decision-making process. McGarry et al. (1973) suggest a cut-off score of less than 20 as a basis for identifying possibly incompetent defendants. High scores would be associated with competence. The low number of incompetent defendants only allows for tentative conclusions.

The CST score correctly grouped 101 of the 123 competent defendants and three of the five incompetent defendants. Thus the prediction based on the CST score was wrong for 22 (of 123) competent and two (of five) incompetent defendants. Competency Screening Test data collected as part of Study One showed that six of 11 competents and only five of ten incompetents scored below 20. Generalization from data would be unwarranted because of the low number of incompetent defendants, although they do cast some doubt on the validity of the CST as a screening device. In addition, it should be noted that these data were collected under realistic base rate conditions, in which the actual percentage of persons found incompetent is quite low. The finding that about one-half of the defendants ultimately found incompetent would have been missed by the CST does not lend support to its use in making initial decisions about competency.

It is possible, however, to examine the relationship of the CST to other measures. As discussed in Chapter 3, high scores on the CST may reflect an unfounded belief in the fairness of the criminal justice system and/or an attempt to respond in a socially desirable fashion. Table 6.24 shows the correlations between the CST and several other measures completed by the sample.[10] Intelligence level appears to be a significant factor in the CST score. Defendants with lower intelligence scores, as measured by the Slosson Intelligence Test, also received lower scores on the CST. Low arithmetic scores on the Wide Range Achievement Test were also associated with low CST scores. Defendants who scored high on the Internal-External Locus of Control Scale (a high score indicates a belief that events in one's life are primarily controlled by forces outside one's control) also tended to receive lower scores on the CST. Further, the defendants were asked how fairly they believed the criminal justice system operates. A perception that the system was unfair was associated with a low score on the CST, as was a perception that the prosecutor was unfair. Finally, the correlation between social desirability and the CST approached significance ($p < .10$). Defendants who attempted to present themselves in a socially desirable manner tended to have higher scores on the CST.

Court outcome. Court data were obtained for 137 of the 151 Study Two defendants, a return rate of 90%. Twenty-two cases were pending and were dropped from further analysis. One defendant was found not guilty by reason of insanity and also was not included in the analysis. This de-

TABLE 6.24

Correlations Between the Competency Screening Test
and Other Measures

	Competency Screening Test
Intelligence	.42[a]
Wide Range Achievement Test:	
Arithmetic Score	.21[d]
Internal-External Locus of	
Control Scale	−.35[b]
Marlowe-Crowne Social Desirability	
Scale	.16[c]
Perceived fairness of the criminal	
justice system	−.16[d]
Perceived fairness of prosecutor	−.18[d]

[a]N = 122, $p < .001$ [c]N = 76, $p < .10$
[b]N = 74, $p < .001$ [d]N = 116, $p < .05$

fendant was charged with rape and assault and was involuntarily committed to a state hospital. Thus complete court data were available for 109 competent and five incompetent defendants.

Table 6.25 shows the type of offense at disposition. Compared with the Study One offenses (see Tables 6.5 and 6.13), the present offense data showed a drop in murder charges and an increase in property crimes. This difference may reflect an increase in the number of referrals charged with misdemeanors as a result of a 1975 change in the statutes allowing such referrals.

The court outcomes for competent and incompetent defendants will be considered separately, since there were only five incompetent defendants. One incompetent defendant was charged with murder. He was returned to court from the hospital with the recommendation that the charges against him be dismissed and that he be civilly committed back to the hospital. The court concurred and committed this defendant following dismissal of charges. The other four incompetent defendants were charged with property crimes. All had charges against them dismissed. One of

TABLE 6.25

Type of Offense at Referral and Disposition

	Competent (N = 109)		Incompetent (N = 5)	
	Referral	Disposition	Referral	Disposition
Murder	15	12	1	1
	(14%)	(11%)	(20%)	(20%)
Assault	15	16	0	0
	(14%)	(15%)		
Rape/sex offenses	14	13	0	0
	(13%)	(12%)		
Other violent offenses	7	8	0	0
	(6%)	(7%)		
Property crimes	47	51	4	4
	(43%)	(47%)	(80%)	(80%)
Other nonviolent offenses	11	9	0	0
	(10%)	(8%)		

these defendants, who was charged with auto theft, had the following recommendation from the hospital: "I suggest that the court consider the possibility of disposing of his charge and involuntarily commit him back to Dorothea Dix Hospital for further evaluation and treatment. Both a petition and medical certificate for such commitment are enclosed." The court followed this recommendation. A second defendant, charged with larceny, received a recommendation for commitment to a mental retardation center. Again, the court concurred. The third defendant was sent to a home for the elderly, also upon recommendation of the hospital. Disposition after dismissal of charges for the fourth defendant was not noted in the court records.

The court outcome for competent defendants is summarized in Table 6.26. Slightly more than four-fifths of the defendants were found guilty, with 60% of these receiving a prison sentence. Minimum and maximum sentences for each offense are shown in the last two columns of Table 6.26.

TABLE 6.26

Court Outcome for Competent Defendants

	Innocent	Guilty	Prison	Nonprison	Length of Sentence (in years)	
					Minimum	Maximum
Murder	1	11	1	10	26.5	40.7
Assault	4	12	5	7	17.4	21.7
Rape	3	10	2	8	8.0	12.3
Violent offenses	1	7	1	6	19.8	22.0
Property offenses	10	41	19	22	9.4	11.8
Nonviolent offenses	2	7	2	5	3.4	4.0

The disposition of cases resulting in an innocent verdict provided additional information about the mental health system's influence on court outcome. The hospital report had recommended dismissal of charges and civil commitment of five defendants who had received recommendations of competent to stand trial. All five were subsequently committed to a state hospital. Over one-half of the competent defendants received recommendations for outpatient mental health treatment. The court agreement is unknown, although it would be low since most defendants received prison sentences. Fourteen defendants received hospital recommendations for voluntary referral to a state hospital. The court concurred in only one of these cases, in which an agreement was made with the defendant that if he completed a 90-day "voluntary" commitment, the charges against him would be dismissed.

Two additional analyses were performed on the court outcome data. An analysis of court outcome by race for the competent group revealed no significant differences. The final analysis involved an examination of prior arrest history and court outcome. Number of arrests and number of felony convictions were not related to whether a defendant was found guilty or whether he received a prison sentence. Number of prior misdemeanor convictions was significantly but moderately related to prison sentences, but this finding may have been due to chance.

Discussion

While the low number of incompetent defendants in this study precluded many statistical analyses, some interesting aspects of the data support our recommendations for change and will be briefly discussed. The evaluation length at Dorothea Dix Hospital was found to be much shorter than in the past. The mean length of hospitalization for evaluation was only 17 days, compared with 43 days for the Study One sample. Only 17 of the 151 defendants were held longer than three weeks, perhaps reflecting increased efficiency during the period of evaluation. This finding also suggests that, for the vast majority of referrals, the evaluation of competency is a straightforward process. In fact, it is likely that perhaps all but these 17 defendants could have been evaluated in a much shorter period of time in a noninstitutional setting. The 17 cases held longer than three weeks could be considered the more difficult cases, either because the decision about competency was not clear or because the staff believed that brief treatment was necessary. In either case the 17 cases (11% of the total sample) may be considered a rough estimate of the percentage of cases requiring evaluation beyond a brief, immediate, and locally administered screening interview.

The Diagnostic Conference Report and Discharge Summary was the only report prepared as a result of the evaluation and was the official report to the court. The finding that there was little information available in a documented fashion points to the need for improvement in the communication to the court (see extended discussion of this point in Chapter 4). These reports, in order to be useful to the court and allow it to take an increased decision-making role, must be behaviorally specific, citing in detail the information upon which conclusions are made and, most important, describing how these behaviors would affect a defendant's competency to stand trial. Recommendations for achieving this goal are set forth in the last chapter of this book, as well as in Chapter 4.

The psychological test data revealed some differences between the two groups, but again the low number of incompetent defendants did not allow for any specific recommendation for use in future evaluations. How-

ever, data on the Competency Screening Test, a measure which purports
to be useful for evaluating competency, did cast some doubt on its validity.
Preliminary data on the CST suggested that scores on this measure may
be significantly affected by intelligence level, reading ability, perceived
ability to control one's life, a tendency to respond in a socially desirable
fashion, and a perception about the fairness of the criminal justice system.
These relationships raise some doubts about the CST. Defendants with
poor reading skills, for example, may nevertheless be competent to stand
trial, since motions and other information could be read and explained by
their attorneys. Our data on error rates using the CST, particularly the
misclassification of one-half of the incompetent defendants, also point to
a limited usefulness of the CST as a screening device. These data suggest
that the CST may not be measuring competence to stand trial, and support the conclusions which were reached following the review of the CST
in Chapter 3, namely that the Competency Screening Test is of questionable validity and should not be used in the determination of competency
to stand trial until further empirical support is obtained.

The court outcome data clearly indicated the degree of influence of the
mental health recommendations. Court data were available for five incompetent defendants. The disposition of one of the cases was unknown,
but the remaining four defendants had their charges dismissed, yet were
committed to institutions. All four had hospital recommendations for dismissal of charges and commitment. The influence of the hospital recommendation should be apparent. A review of the hospital records of the
two defendants committed to a mental hospital revealed no clear information that either defendant was presently dangerous to himself or others.
Both defendants were described as being hostile and belligerent while in
the hospital, but neither actually physically assaulted or even threatened
to assault staff members or other patients. It is perplexing, then, that the
court so readily concurred with the hospital recommendation, except that
commitment may have seemed to be the most efficient way to reach a
disposition of the case.

The mental health recommendation even had considerable influence
on the court outcome of defendants found competent to stand trial. For
example, five defendants receiving recommendations from the hospital
that they were competent to stand trial also received recommendations
for dismissal of charges and involuntary commitment. All five defendants

were subsequently committed following dismissal of charges. These hospital recommendations clearly go beyond the purpose of a competency evaluation, yet appear to be supported by the courts. This finding suggests that statutory changes which more clearly define the nature and scope of the competency evaluation, as well as the commitment of incompetent defendants, are necessary.

STUDY THREE:
A PILOT STUDY OF THE UTILITY OF A BRIEF, IMMEDIATE COMPETENCY SCREENING INTERVIEW

This study was considered a pilot study designed to provide some preliminary information on the feasibility of a brief interview as a substitute for hospital evaluation. The study attempted to determine whether a brief interview could provide a sufficient amount of information to reach a decision about competency, at least for the majority of cases. Defendants referred to Dorothea Dix Hospital for competency evaluations were interviewed within 24 hours of admission by members of the Wake County Mental Health Association. Ratings were completed by interviewer pairs, and these ratings and predictions of competency were compared with the determinations resulting from the lengthier hospital evaluation.

Method

Subjects. Thirty defendants referred to Dorothea Dix Hospital for a competency evaluation between March 1 and May 15, 1976, were interviewed within 24 hours after admission.

Procedure. The defendants were interviewed by eight members of the Wake County (North Carolina) Mental Health Association. The interviewers were trained in the following manner. The training session began with a one-hour lecture summarizing the issues and literature discussed earlier in this book. The lecture was followed by a review of the Competency Assessment Instrument (McGarry et al., 1973), a 13-item rating scale designed to measure a defendant's awareness and understanding of legal issues (see Chapter 3 for a review). The interviewers used the CAI along with questions designed to assess overall evaluations of competency and responsiveness to treatment. Interviewers were given a copy of the manual for the CAI, which provides definitions and suggested interview questions for each item. As a supplement to these questions, a copy of the appendix of an article by Bukatman, Foy, and deGrazia (1971), which contains a series of questions focusing upon legal issues, was reviewed and given to the interviewers. In addition, copies of several articles which discuss issues in determining competency were given to the interviewers as a supplement to the formal lecture (Eizenstat, 1968; Hess and Thomas, 1963; Kaufman, 1972; McGarry, 1965; Slovenko, 1971; *Dusky* v. *United States*, 1960). The final part of the training session involved a role-playing situation; two staff members of Dorothea Dix Hospital who had previous experience with competency evaluations played the roles of interviewer and defendant. The interview lasted approximately 30 minutes. The interviewers then rated each item on the scale. Each rating was reviewed by discussing conflicts and disagreements. The entire training session took approximately three hours.

Results and Discussion

Thirty interviews were conducted by the rater pairs, after which they independently completed the rating scale. Item percent agreement ranged from 68.8% to 96.7%, with a median of 81.2%. The item ratings were highly correlated with the judgment about competency, and therefore only the interviewers' global judgments and the hospital staff determinations will be compared.

The evaluation results of the trained interviewers compared with those of the hospital were as follows (see Table 6.27). Four defendants of the total 30 interviewed were identified by the interviewers as possibly incompetent to stand trial. There was agreement among interviewers on three of these defendants. The fourth defendant was viewed as incompetent by only one interviewer. There was complete agreement between the interviewer pairs for 26 competent defendants. In comparison, the Dorothea Dix Hospital evaluation of these same 30 defendants resulted in three determinations of incompetent to stand trial. Twenty-five of the 27 defendants judged competent by hospital staff were the same individuals found competent by the trained interviewers. The interviewers and hospital were in agreement for two of the three defendants found incompetent by the hospital. Thus the interviewers and hospital evaluators were in agreement in 27 of the 30 cases, for an overall rate of agreement of 90%.

TABLE 6.27

Relationship of Interviewer
and Hospital Determinations of Competency

Hospital	Interviewer[1]	
	Competent	Incompetent
Competent	25	2
Incompetent	1	2

[1]In the one case where interviewer disagreement occurred, the defendant was included in the incompetent group.

The results of this study should be considered tentative owing to the small sample size. However, it appears that a brief interview has the potential for screening competent defendants prior to a lengthier evaluation. The high rate of agreement between the interviewers' and the hospital's determination of competency points to the facts that most decisions about competency are straightforward and that hospitalization is not necessary. Thus the amount of time spent in the hospital may not add to the decision-making ability of the evaluators. As was suggested from the results of our analyses of the psychiatric reports described in Study One, it appears that ward observations, psychological tests, and other data collected during hospitalization have little influence on the determination. An interview alone, which might focus almost entirely on legal issues, may provide a sufficient basis for reaching decisions, at least for the vast majority of cases. The Competency Assessment Instrument appeared to be particularly useful in this respect, providing a structure and direction to the interview. However, the high correlation between the individual CAI item ratings and the global judgment about competency suggests that the interviewers may have made the global judgment first and then rated items consistent with this judgment. Obviously, further investigation of the scale itself is necessary but, nevertheless, the CAI was quite helpful as a guide to the interviewers. This study provides some initial support for a community-level evaluation in a noninstitutional setting to reduce both the delay and the cost of competency evaluations. A small percentage of cases would still require further evaluation, but as we shall suggest, even this evaluation does not have to occur in an institutional setting.

STUDY FOUR:
LEGAL AND JUDICIAL INTERPRETATION
OF COMPETENCY STATUTES AND PROCEDURES

This study was designed to obtain information from the legal community (judges and defense attorneys) with respect to the interpretation and actual use of the competency statutes and procedures. Of particular interest are (1) the manner in which the issue of competency is raised in the courts, (2) how judges decide to grant (or not grant) competency motions, (3) what attorneys' motivations are for requesting an evaluation, (4) how the evaluation report is used by the court, and (5) how decisions are made about the treatment of defendants found incompetent to stand trial.

Method

Subjects. There were two groups of subjects. The first group was composed of district and superior court judges in North Carolina. The second group included defense attorneys representing clients who were admitted to Dorothea Dix Hospital for a competency evaluation between February 25 and April 30, 1976.

Procedure. A total of 163 judges were mailed a questionnaire (Appendix I) designed to obtain information regarding their views on the process of determining competency to stand trial. The 55 judges responding to this questionnaire represented a return rate of approximately 37%. The 111 attorneys were contacted by telephone by forensic unit staff at Dorothea Dix Hospital as part of their routine procedure for obtaining social history and background information on all referrals. The attorneys were asked to specify their reasons for requesting an evaluation and their expectations for the outcome of the evaluation.

Results

Judge questionnaire. The judges were asked to indicate the factor which they believed contributed to motions for competency evaluations. Table 6.28 shows that 67% of the judges believed that defense attorneys misunderstood the competency criteria (20% felt that this was true of the prosecution); about 50% of the judges also believed that another contributing factor was an attempt by the defense to build a case for diminished responsibility.

TABLE 6.28

Judge Questionnaire:
Factors Which Contribute to Motions for Competency Evaluations[1]

Misunderstanding on part of defense counsel as to criteria for capacity to proceed	Misunderstanding on part of prosecutors as to criteria for capacity to proceed	Attempt to obtain treatment recommendations from mental health professionals	Attempt by defense counsel to delay trial	Attempt by prosecutor to build a case for diminished responsibility	Attempt by prosecutor to circumvent pretrial release	Attempt by prosecutor to build a case against diminished responsibility
53%	20%	14%	67%	51%	12%	10%
(N = 27)	(N = 10)	(N = 7)	(N = 34)	(N = 26)	(N = 6)	(N = 5)

[1]Percentage of judges responding yes to each factor are reported.

Despite the fact that the judges believed that many motions were unjustified and/or unsupported, most of these judges indicated that they would order an evaluation unless they believed the motion was being used as a transparent delay tactic. The majority of judges (56%) indicated they granted the motion immediately, while the remaining judges stated they would request additional facts not included in the motion.

Once the motion was granted and the evaluation completed, defendants were returned to court for a hearing to reach a decision about competency. The hospital recommendations appear to carry considerable weight in this decision. Thirty-five percent of the judges stated that they never disagreed with the evaluation recommendations, while the remaining 65% only rarely or occasionally disagreed. Furthermore, 59% of the judges indicated that they typically did not hold a formal hearing, relying entirely upon the evaluation recommendation.

The judges were also asked about the procedures for the commitment of incompetent defendants. Almost one-half (47%) of the judges indicated that commitment should be automatic (Table 6.29), regardless of offense. Over three-fourths (76%) of the judges stated that a violent or potentially violent offense was sufficient grounds for involuntary commitment. It was also found that 60% of the judges would commit incompetent defendants if the charge was a nonviolent felony, and that 43% would commit incompetent defendants even if the charge was only a misdemeanor.

TABLE 6.29

Judge Questionnaire:
Institutional Commitment of Defendants
Found Incompetent to Stand Trial

Commitment should be automatic	Discretion of person or groups rendering verdict	Separate hearing before a jury should be held	Medical experts should determine
47%	18%	20%	16%
(N = 21)	(N = 8)	(N = 9)	(N = 7)

The judges were about equally divided in their responses when asked to specify the most important commitment criterion other than type of offense. While slightly over one-half stated that dangerousness was the most important commitment criterion, there was an almost equal number of judges who believed that the fact a defendant was mentally ill and in need of treatment was the most important criterion for initiating commitment proceedings.

Attorney contacts. Table 6.30 reveals that most of the attorneys responded in noninformative phrases when questioned about their reasons for requesting a competency evaluation. Approximately 79% wanted to know whether their client was competent, but they were unwilling or unable to do more than make this general request; 51% also wanted to know whether their client was responsible for the alleged offense. A few attorneys were more specific and consistent with the competency criteria (see items 3, 4, and 5, Table 6.30), but their responses were little more than a paraphrasing of the statute. When the attorneys did provide more information, the reasons frequently had no relationship to competency. For example, two attorneys requested an evaluation solely on the advice of the arresting officers, while 11 attorneys made the motion at the request of the defendant's family. A prior history of psychiatric treatment or alcohol/drug abuse was a motivation in many cases.

TABLE 6.30

Reasons Given by Defense Attorneys
for Requesting a Competency Evaluation

Item	Number[1] (N = 111)	Percent
1. Whether client is competent to stand trial	79	71.2
2. Whether defendant was responsible for crime	51	45.0
3. Did not appear to have sufficient present ability to consult with attorney; could not communicate	15	13.5
4. Does not have a recollection of events re offense	8	7.2
5. Does not have a rational as well as factual understanding of the proceedings	6	5.4
6. Is not oriented to time and place	6	5.4
7. Incoherent	2	1.8
8. Confused	2	1.8
9. Unusual behavior	7	6.3
10. Mentally disturbed	2	1.8
11. History of alcoholism	4	3.6
12. History of drug abuse	4	3.6
13. History of mental illness	6	5.4
14. Prior psychiatric hospitalizations or treatment by psychiatrist	8	7.2
15. Nature of offense—seriousness of charges	11	9.9
16. Frequency of criminal activity	2	1.8

Item	Number[1] (N = 111)	Percent
17. Advice of arresting officers	2	1.8
18. Family requested or recommended evaluation	11	9.9
19. Explosive or aggressive behavior in jail or court or interview	1	0.9
20. Suicide threats, attempts	5	4.5
21. Avoid basis for postconviction appeal	1	0.9
22. Damage to jail	2	1.8
23. Need for treatment (need of help)	5	4.5
24. Does not understand seriousness of charges	6	5.4
25. Represented client in the past	1	0.9
26. Upset, distressed, depressed	4	3.6
27. Client's age	2	1.8
28. During interview, showed an outburst of temper	2	1.8
29. Recommendation of jailer	2	1.8
30. Receiving treatment at present time	1	0.9
31. Need a "break from jail"	1	0.9
32. Minister's recommendation	1	0.9
33. Limited intelligence (intellectual ability)	3	2.7
34. On drugs	1	0.9
35. Car accident (as a child)	1	0.9
36. Doubt as to responsibility of client	1	0.9
37. Previously judged incompetent	1	0.9
38. Recommendation of psychiatrist from another facility	1	0.9

[1]The number of responses does not equal the number of attorneys contacted, since many attorneys gave multiple reasons for requesting an evaluation of their client.

Table 6.31 summarizes the attorneys' expectations for the outcome of the evaluations. An inspection of this table makes it clear that many other reasons apart from a question of competency may have motivated the motion. For example, requests for treatment recommendations and sentencing alternatives were frequently made by attorneys. Furthermore, several attorneys desired recommendations for dismissal of the charges against their clients.

TABLE 6.31

Expectations for Evaluation/Recommendations
Given by Defense Attorneys

Item	Number[1] (N = 111)	Percent
1. Whether defendant appreciates seriousness of charges	9	8.1
2. Remorse feelings for crime—realizes consequences of behavior	2	1.8
3. Treatment alternatives to prison	7	6.3
4. Treatment recommendations	19	17.2
5. Treatment for drug abuse	2	1.8
6. Recommendations for treatment of alcoholism	2	1.8
7. Special facilities, rehabilitation (not specifically treatment)	3	2.7
8. Unspecified requests for recommendations	23	20.7
9. Whether client is committable to a psychiatric hospital	2	1.8
10. Legal disposition of case (charges should be dismissed, nol pros)	4	3.6
11. Indications of mental illness, presence of psychosis *diagnosis*	16	14.4
12. Is client dangerous to self or others?	2	1.8
13. How easily is client led by others?	2	1.8
14. Client's mental makeup, psychiatric evaluation	8	7.2
15. If client was suffering from mental block	1	0.9
16. Does client have a drug problem?	1	0.9
17. Would like client to be *aware* of his problem	1	0.9
18. Effect drinking activity had on alleged offense	7	6.3
19. Kind of drugs he was on at time of crime, what condition his mind would be in (effect of drugs)	6	5.4
20. State of mind at time of crime (effect on crime)	6	5.4
21. Impaired judgment	1	0.9
22. I.Q. evaluation	15	13.5
23. Suitability for pretrial release	1	0.9
24. Information about past psychiatric hospitalizations	1	0.9
25. Physical evaluation	1	0.9
26. Is client in need of brain surgery?	1	0.9

[1]The number of responses does not equal the number of attorneys contacted, since many attorneys gave multiple reasons for requesting an evaluation of their client.

Discussion

This study was designed to provide some supplemental information about the legal and judicial views of the competency statutes and procedures. The analysis was intended to identify possible areas of disagreement or misunderstanding about the way in which the competency procedures are used. The low return rate for the judge questionnaires may be partially explained by the fact that many judges, especially recently appointed ones or judges in rural counties, have never been involved in a competency hearing and therefore could not properly complete the questionnaire. Nearly one-half of the 100 North Carolina counties did not make any referrals to Dorothea Dix Hospital in 1976 (Roesch and Golding, 1977).

Analysis of the judge questionnaire revealed several problems and concerns which can be raised regarding the procedures for confronting the issue of competency to stand trial. Most judges revealed that they uniformly grant competency motions even though they frequently question the legitimacy of the motions. This may reflect a feeling on the part of the judges that they lack the expertise to evaluate competency and must defer the issue to mental health professionals. Some judges also indicated that they grant motions to avoid any basis for postconviction appeals. Apart from the possible reasons for the fact that few motions are denied, the problem is compounded by the fact that the motions typically contain little specific information about a defendant's behavior which justify the motion.

Responses from attorneys provide some support for the judges' concerns about the legitimacy of the motions. While the issue of competency is frequently raised as a result of a legitimate concern that a defendant is not able to assist in the defense, it has been pointed out, as we reviewed in Chapter 3, that the motion is sometimes raised by the defense either to delay the trial or to lay the foundation for the introduction of mitigating circumstances. Many attorneys in the present study indicated reasons for requesting an evaluation which were not directly related to a question of competency (such as history of alcohol or drug abuse, prior psychiatric hospitalizations, requests from family, need for treatment). Furthermore, many attorneys expressed a desire to obtain recommendations for treatment, alternatives to prison, and for the legal disposition of the case. These recommendations could presumably be used by the defense attorneys in the plea bargaining or sentencing process, but clearly go beyond the intention of competency evaluations.

The transfer of decision-making responsibility from the court to mental health professionals is evidenced by the finding that two-thirds of the judges only rarely or occasionally disagreed with the mental health recommendations, while the remaining judges reported that they never disagreed. A majority of judges indicated that a formal hearing is not even held. These findings suggest that North Carolina judges have often relinquished their decision-making responsibility to mental health professionals, despite the fact that at least two legal decisions (*People* v. *Greene*, 1952; *United States* v. *David*, 1975) have held that the final determination of competency must rest with the court.

The final point in the competency procedures is the disposition of defendants found incompetent. Questionnaire responses indicated some conflict about commitment criteria. North Carolina statutes provide that civil commitment must be based on a finding of dangerousness *and* mental illness. Yet 47% of the judges indicated that commitment of incompetent defendants should be automatic, regardless of the perceived dangerousness of such defendants. Since such commitments in North Carolina are for unspecified periods of time, important questions can be raised about the protection of rights of defendants committed in this manner.

Several procedural and statutory changes could be instituted to increase the decision-making ability of judges and minimize the number of inappropriate referrals for a competency evaluation. The motions should be written in very specific terms, detailing the behaviors observed by the defense attorney (or prosecution or court) that provide the basis for questioning the defendant's competency to stand trial. The court can exercise its decision-making responsibility by not granting motions which are not supported by specific information in the reports and/or testimony by attorneys or others. The evaluation reports could be limited to the issue of competency only and not contain any treatment or dispositional recommendations.

With respect to the commitment of incompetent defendants, it is clear that a finding of incompetency is perceived by many judges as providing a sufficient basis for involuntary commitment, regardless of perceived dangerousness or availability of less restrictive alternatives for treatment to restore competency. As we have pointed out elsewhere (Roesch and Golding, 1978), these issues demand further attention and resolution if competency procedures are to accomplish their intended goal without jeopardizing defendants' rights.

Notes

1. Some of the data analyses and discussion presented in this chapter represent revised versions of previously published material (see Roesch, 1978a,b, 1979; Roesch and Golding, 1978).

2. It should be noted that, upon discharge, these defendants received recommendations of competent to proceed with trial.

3. Attempts were made to keep the raters blind as to the group membership (competent or incompetent) of the defendant, as well as to the purpose of the study. As discussed previously, the part of the report dealing with court recommendations regarding competency and posthospital treatment were independently coded by another rater. However, many of the reports contained references to competency in other sections of the report. These references would have revealed the group membership to the rater. Also, the length of hospitalization, brief for competent defendants and lengthy for incompetent defendants, allowed the raters to determine group membership. It is not believed, however, that this knowledge significantly influenced the ratings. The nature of the rating scale was such that items were rated only if specific mention of a behavior was made.

4. Oblique rotations of the components, as well as a principal axis factor analysis with varimax and oblique rotations, resulted in similar solutions. This was true for all three reports. Thus only the principal component analyses with varimax rotation will be reported.

5. The standard methods for determining the number of components to retain were not used because they led to the retention of many minor factors that did not appear warranted by the data. Kaiser's criterion resulted in 12 components, and the scree test criterion resulted in approximately the same solution. Based on the psychological meaningfulness of the components, only seven rather than 12 components were retained, accounting for 46% of the total variance.

6. The components resulting from the principal component analysis are potential discriminating variables on which the groups may differ. These components are new variables made up of linear combinations of the items on a particular report. The new variables allow a reduction of the information present in the report to fewer variables. A discriminant analysis attempts to assign a weight to each variable in terms of its significance in distinguishing between the two groups. The goal is to find the optimal combination of variables that maximally distinguishes the two groups. Variables that receive the highest weights (positive or negative) can be understood as being more important in distinguishing the groups. One can also compute a score for each individual based on these weights and then use this score to "predict" whether a given individual had received a hospital

recommendation of competent or incompetent. The accuracy with which one can predict group membership based upon the discriminant functions can be used to index the importance of the functions.

7. At each step of the discriminant analysis a component was retained or deleted contingent on whether it added significantly to the discriminant function ($p < .05$).

8. Since only one incompetent defendant was charged with a nonviolent offense resulting in an innocent disposition, this category was not included in the subsequent statistical analyses.

9. The item ratings for each rater pair were averaged and then scored for each factor. Item reliabilities ranged from .11 to .70, with a mean of .27. The low reliabilities point to the need for more training of nursing personnel with respect to the use of the PIP and the identification of ward behavior. Furthermore, this lack of reliability casts some doubt on other forms of recorded observations (most commonly in the form of nursing notes) by nursing personnel. Since such notes are sometimes used as a basis for decisions about hospital privileges, release dates, and so on, it may be quite valuable to look more closely at their reliability.

10. Since the incompetent N was low, and because many of them did not complete the tests, the subjects in this analysis were largely competent defendants.

A Model System

The empirical and scholarly research described in the preceding chapters formed the basis of a series of recommendations for creating change in North Carolina's approach to the issue of competency. While these recommendations, involving major changes in both the legal and the mental health systems,[1] were initially intended specifically for North Carolina, our review of the law and procedures in other states clearly suggests that the recommended system may have a greater applicability. For this reason, we will present our recommendations for a model system in a generalized form. In the following sections we consider changes at each step in the process, from raising the issue of competency through the disposition of defendants found incompetent. Figure 7.1 presents the model system in schematic form.

RAISING THE ISSUE OF COMPETENCY

As discussed in the review of North Carolina procedures, one of the major problems inherent in the current method of raising the issue of competency (Figure 7–1, Point A) is that the motions requesting an evaluation are typically vague, containing little information about the basis of the request. The court typically has little information upon which to base a decision and consequently can usually do little more than simply grant the motion. As our research suggests (Study Four, Chapter 6), competency evaluations are sometimes used by defense attorneys for reasons other than a concern for a defendant's competency. These data are convergent with the high base rate for a finding of competency in defendants who are evaluated (see Chapter 3). If these inappropriate uses are to be curtailed, it is necessary for the courts to deny motions which are not supported by relevant facts. To accomplish this purpose, we propose that the courts require that motions submitted to them be written in very specific terms, detailing the following information:

a) What behaviors did the defense attorney (or the prosecution or court) observe that led to requesting the motion? This part of the motion should describe in some detail the interaction between the attorney and client which suggested that the defendant may be incapable of assisting in the defense.

b) How do these behaviors hinder the preparation of a defense? It is not enough, for example, to state that a defendant was hostile and belligerent during an interview. The motion must show that there is a probable relationship between this behavior and the capacity to assist in the defense.

In order to illustrate how the above kinds of information can be incorporated into a competency motion, we have written a sample motion (Appendix J). It is imperative, if the competency procedure is to be used properly, that the court exercise its authority by denying those motions which have not been substantiated in the manner described above.

Given that the motion contains the necessary information, the court will grant the motion if there is sufficient reason to believe that a *Pate*-level doubt is justified.[2] If the court does not believe there is sufficient reason to question a defendant's competency, the motion should be denied and judicial proceedings should continue. When the motion is granted, we propose that court refer the defendant to a screening panel (Figure 7.1, Point B).

COMMUNITY-BASED EVALUATION

Our analysis of the typical decision-making process (Study One, Chapter 6) indicated that the amount of time spent by the defendant in the hospital, during which psychological tests were administered, ward observations were made, and families and attorneys contacted, did not add to

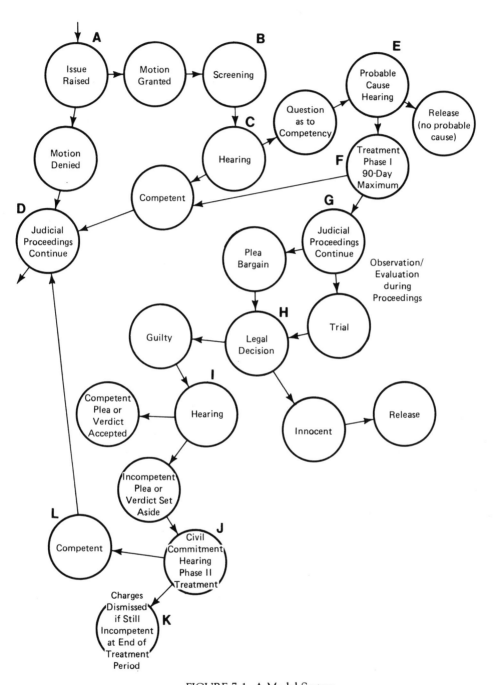

FIGURE 7.1. A Model System

the decision-making ability of the evaluators. Discriminant analyses of the information available in the psychiatric reports suggested that a prediction of competency status made on the basis of the intake interview alone (the Mental Status Exam) was about as accurate as predictions based on information contained in later reports. In other words, information from such sources as psychological tests, ward observations, and additional interviews seems to have had little influence on the final decision about competency. At least for the majority of cases, the decision-makers seemed to base their decision on information obtained in a single interview, which typically lasted less than an hour and was completed within the first few days of admission.[3] This finding suggests that an interview alone (which could, of course, be conducted in a noninstitutional setting) could provide sufficient information for making decisions about the majority of referrals. Furthermore, the results of Study Three that indicated a high rate of agreement between the determination based on a brief interview and the hospital determination suggest that most decisions about competency are straightforward and that a restrictive and expensive hospitalization is not necessary. The data obtained from judges and attorneys (Chapter 6, Study Four) provide additional support for a community-based evaluation. Many judges indicated a belief that the competency evaluation was used for a number of purposes unrelated to competency, such as delay of trial and attempts to obtain recommendations which could be used in plea bargaining or sentencing. The responses of defense attorneys support the judges' perceptions. Many attorneys indicated a desire to obtain treatment recommendations as the basis for requesting a competency evaluation.

The converging results of all these studies suggest that a community-based evaluation would provide a sufficient basis for making a determination of competency, at least for the vast majority of cases. The transfer of responsibility from the hospital to the community would reduce both the delay and the cost of competency evaluations. Furthermore, community evaluations may actually decrease the number of referrals, since some of the less legitimate reasons for referral, such as delaying the trial or removing a defendant from the community, would be eliminated. In order to discourage the use of competency evaluations for the purpose of obtaining treatment recommendations, the request for evaluation should be limited to the issue of competency to stand trial. If other mental health services need to be provided to the courts (e.g., sentencing recommendations), it may be necessary that statutes be written which specify the nature and scope of these services rather than continuing the misuse of competency statutes, with the associated infringement of a defendant's rights.

The following section discusses a procedure for conducting community-based evaluations through the use of screening panels responsible for the initial evaluation of all defendants referred for competency evaluations.

SCREENING PANELS

The use of screening panels responsible for conducting evaluations at the community level is a critical feature of the model system we propose (Figure 7.1, Point B). The screening panel would consist of representatives of both the legal and mental health professions and would be responsible for conducting an initial evaluation of all defendants referred by the court. Based on our contention that legal issues are often overlooked in competency evaluations, we believe that an interviewing team comprised of both professions would provide an effective complement of training and expertise, would lead to a more appropriate focus on *both* mental health and legal issues, and might serve to increase understanding and communication between the two professions. The need for professional interaction has been argued by a number of authors.[4] It seems clear that involvement of lawyers in the screening process is critical to a balanced approach to the evaluation of competency. Mental health professionals can play a crucial and valuable role in competency evaluations when they testify in nonconclusory terms, giving the judge and/or jury as concrete and specific a picture of the defendant's mental state and capabilities as possible. It is, however, the responsibility of the court to decide if such "facts," in the given legal context, lead to a determination of incompetency.

The screening panel we propose would consist of two to three individuals: a trial lawyer (but not the defense attorney), and at least one, but perhaps two, mental health professionals. The screening panel would complete an evaluation within three to five days following referral and would then submit a report to the court within ten days. Screening would take place in suitable surroundings, in a conference room at the jail, at the local mental health center, or in the offices of the court and/or the screening panel members. Defendants would not be hospitalized unless their behavior justified such action under current civil commitment standards.[5] Following the spirit of recent court decisions (Diamond and Louisell, 1965; Golten, 1972; *Lessard v. Schmidt*, 1972), the defendant's counsel would be permitted to observe the evaluation if he/she so desired. Based upon projections from the current rate of incompetency determinations, approximately 80 to 90% of defendants so evaluated would be found by the court to be competent to stand trial. Since this screening procedure is considerably less expensive and involves less delay than sending the defendant to a mental hospital for an inpatient evaluation, the state would be saved considerable time and expense[6] and defendants would not be unnecessarily detained.

There are several precedents for the use of a community-based screening procedure, although few of them directly involve the use of lawyers in the evaluation. Laben et al. (1977) developed a competency screening procedure in Tennessee, using an evaluation team consisting of a psychologist, a psychiatrist, and a psychiatric social worker. Most of the evaluations were conducted in the county jail, using the Competency Assessment Instrument as a basis for making initial decisions.[7] The team members also conducted more comprehensive evaluations on those defendants not immediately found competent. The results of this two-stage evaluation process were quite promising.[8] During the first six months of operation only one of 45 defendants required long-term hospitalization as incompetent. Another 15 defendants required short-term interventions (less than ten days), which usually occurred in the jail. After this brief intervention all of these defendants were able to stand trial. Connecticut (Fitzgerald, Peszke, and Goodwin, 1978) and Massachusetts (Rosenberg and McGarry, 1972) also used an evaluation team and have achieved similar results, as has the New York City Forensic Psychiatry Clinic (Goldstein, 1973). It appears that a screening procedure results in speedier determinations, fewer inpatient evaluations, and few determinations of incompetency.

The screening panel procedure does not, by itself, satisfactorily deal with the problem created by those defendants who are not immediately found competent. To the extent that one can generalize from the work of researchers like Laben and her colleagues (Laben et al., 1977; Laben and Spencer, 1976), as well as our own research, it would appear that a very small percentage would not be immediately found competent or respond to intervention within a very brief period. We are in strong agreement with the Laben procedure and urge that all attempts at brief treatment be encouraged. But what of those defendants who do not respond to brief treatment? We propose a brief treatment period (not more than three months), but only if there is clear and convincing evidence that treatment may improve a defendant's condition within the treatment period limitation. This treatment does not, of course, have to occur in an institutional setting. If a defendant is eligible for bail, then treatment should occur on an outpatient basis. Defendants who do not respond to treatment should be afforded the opportunity for a trial despite their alleged incompetency. We will elaborate on this proposal in a subsequent section.

COMPETENCY HEARING

After the screening evaluation is completed, a hearing (Figure 7.1, Point C) would be held to review the findings and recommendations of the screening panel. This hearing might be waived, with the consent of the court, if neither the defense nor the prosecution contests the findings of the evaluation, but it may be in the best interests of all parties to uniformly require a hearing. The court should weigh the findings of the initial evaluation and arrive at a determination, which may be based primarily but not necessarily entirely on the findings of the screening panel. Within its proper discretion, the court should require the production of all evidence properly related to the issue, question expert evaluators as well as other witnesses, and order whatever other procedures and/or examinations are necessary to satisfy the requirement that a full hearing be granted once a substantial doubt about competency has been raised.[9] The court should operate on the assumption that the defendant is competent unless there is clear and convincing evidence to the contrary.[10] If the court finds the defendant competent, then judicial proceedings would immediately resume (Figure 7.1, Point D). It is estimated that the majority of defendants (perhaps as high as 90%) will be determined to be competent at this point. The remaining defendants will be considered to be questionably competent, so that evaluation beyond the relatively brief screening evaluation is necessary. These defendants will proceed to a probable-cause hearing.

Probable-Cause Hearing

A mandatory probable-cause hearing is recommended for all defendants who, as a result of the competency hearing, remain in a questionably competent status. Probable-cause hearings have been proposed by many writers (Eizenstat, 1968; Engelberg, 1967; Schroeder, 1974; Comment, *Harvard Law Review*, 1967) for defendants determined by the court to be incompetent. The probable-cause hearing (Figure 7.1, Point E) must be held prior to commitment (for a *limited* period) of such defendants. This recommendation is based on two related factors. First, in order to prevent the confinement of possibly innocent defendants, the state should be required to show that, based on available evidence, there is sufficient reason to believe the defendant committed a crime. Second, and highly related to the first issue, most defendants (incompetent or otherwise) never have an actual trial. Plea bargaining, in which an agreement is reached between the prosecution and defense that a defendant will enter a plea of guilty in exchange for a lesser sentence or reduced charges, is the most frequent disposition of criminal cases.[11] Therefore, no trial or hearing is ever held to determine guilt or innocence. A modified probable-cause hearing, in which both the prosecution *and* the defense could present evidence, is thus a necessary preliminary step to the *in situ* evaluation we will propose later in this chapter. If no probable cause exists, the charges would be dismissed; if probable cause exists, defendants would be assessed to determine their likely response to treatment. We will elaborate upon this in the next section. Finally, it should be noted that in addition to a probable-cause hearing, the defense should be allowed to introduce any evidence or submit any motions which might lead to the dismissal of charges.

Treatment of Incompetent Defendants

We propose two possible periods of treatment for allegedly incompetent defendants. The first period might occur immediately after a finding of probable cause (Figure 7.1, Point F). A hearing would be held in which the court would determine whether it seems likely that a defendant would respond to treatment within a three-month period. If not, the provisional trial described in the next section could immediately be held. If treatment is appropriate, the screening panel would provide the court with a specific treatment plan, detailing both the kinds of treatment and the anticipated outcome. This treatment plan should indicate the manner in which the specified treatment is expected to allow the defendant to stand trial. The plan should also indicate the least restrictive alternative necessary to restore competency, with hospitalization used only when all less restrictive alternatives are not feasible.[12] Thus, if a defendant would otherwise be eligible for bail, treatment should occur on an outpatient basis if the type of treatment necessary can be carried out in this fashion. We recommend that this initial treatment period be limited to not more than three months. If a defendant is not likely to respond to treatment, or remains incompetent at the expiration of the treatment period, we propose that a trial be allowed nevertheless. We will elaborate upon this, as well as the possibility of a second treatment period, in the next two sections.

Provisional Trials

A critical and central part of the changes that we believe are necessary is the introduction of a provisional trial. At the end of the treatment period described in the preceding section (or immediately after the probable-cause hearing if treatment response is unlikely), we propose that a defendant be allowed to participate in a trial or other judicial proceeding (Figure 7.1, Point G). Since this may be the most controversial aspect of our model system, we will discuss its rationale at length. The screening panel would continue to evaluate and observe a defendant during the proceeding, with a hearing held at the end of trial for a defendant found guilty.[13]

The idea of allowing a provisional trial for incompetent defendants is not a new one. As early as 1960, Foote proposed a restricted form of a provisional trial in which incompetent defendants would be given the opportunity to test the merits of the cases against them. Foote (1960) cited three instances in which a defendant might have valid grounds for questioning the merits of the case:

The first is the instance . . . where the defendant can show that the prosecution is barred as a matter of law; another example would be an indictment which on its face discloses that the statute of limitations has run. Second are cases where the defendant alleges that he can show an intrinsic defect in the prosecution's factual case which will prevent conviction, for example, that essential evidence was obtained by an unlawful search and seizure or that the prosecution's evidence shows entrapment as a matter of law. Third, counsel for an incompetent defendant may wish to assert an affirmative defense which can be established without participation of the defendant. In a robbery prosecution based on identification evidence, for example, counsel may be able to establish from employment records and the testimony of third parties that the defendant was at work in another city at the time of the crime. (p. 841)

Since Foote, more expanded provisions for the trial of incompetent defendants have been suggested by Burt and Morris (1972), Ennis and Hansen (1976), Gobert (1973), Janis (1974), Kaufman (1972), and by comments in both the *Harvard Law Review* (1967) and the *Fordham Law Review* (1972). Most of these proposals are based on the premise that guilty verdicts of those defendants ultimately found incompetent would be set aside, although, as we will discuss shortly, the Burt and Morris proposal calls for special pretrial and trial procedures designed to compensate for a defendant's incompetency. One objection to this, as a comment in the *Harvard Law Review* (1967) pointed out, is that the state has an interest in maintaining the "dignity and rationality of the proceeding and the assurance of its determination" (p. 467). The same article comments, "Society may be justified in forbidding the trial of an accused who is incompetent if it is willing to release him or to provide treatment, but it is not so justified if the result for the defendant is indefinite commitment under conditions often as punitive as a prison" (p. 468), and goes on to conclude that "ideally, the determination of the defendant's competency would be deferred until after the trial on the merits of the case. Then if the defendant was found incompetent, a guilty verdict would be set aside; if competent, the verdict would stand" (p. 469). The recommendations set forth in this chapter propose that the evaluation occur *during* rather than following the trial.

Burt and Morris (1972) have proposed, following a six-month maximum period, a trial of incompetent defendants with special pretrial and trial procedures. These include pretrial disclosure of evidence that the prosecution might use at trial, a higher burden of proof, corroboration of issues on which defendants may be prevented from effective rebuttal, and special jury instructions to take into account favorably any disabilities of the defendant. Furthermore, Burt and Morris allow convicted defendants a new trial if evidence not available because of their incompetency is brought forth.

The recommendation that a trial be allowed for possibly incompetent defendants may, at first glance, appear to be in opposition to statutory provisions regarding the conviction of incompetent defendants. *Pate* v. *Robinson* (1966) and *Bishop* v. *United States* (1956), for example, held that the conviction of a legally incompetent defendant violates due process. However, a series of lower court decisions lends support to our contention that a provisional trial is permissible. In *Drope* v. *Missouri* (1975) the Missouri Court of Appeals had concluded that it would be permissible to defer a competency evaluation until after a trial had been completed. Upon appeal to the Supreme Court, Chief Justice Burger, speaking for a unanimous Court, stated that "such a procedure may have advantages, at least where the defendant is present at the trial and the appropriate inquiry is implemented with dispatch" (*Drope*, p. 182). The federal circuit courts have repeatedly approved of competency hearings during postconviction proceedings.[14]

A defendant who, subsequent to trial, is found to have been incompetent has a due-process right to have the result of the trial set aside. The courts have considered the problem of the timing of a competency hearing under circumstances that, while factually dissimilar to what we propose, lend some further support to the use of a provisional trial. The problem of timing usually arises during postconviction proceedings in the following way. The record shows that there was sufficient evidence at the trial to raise a *bona fide* doubt as to the competency of the defendant, and the defendant on appeal contends that the trial judge erred. The difficulty for the appellate court is whether to order a *nunc pro tunc* hearing on the defendant's competency to stand trial or to set aside the conviction and remand the case for a new trial. The critical element for determining the fairness of the *nunc pro tunc* competency hearing is the availability of contemporaneous knowledge (*Bowers* v. *Battles*, 1977; *Carroll* v. *Beto*, 1970; *Rose* v. *United States*, 1975; *United States ex rel. McGough* v. *Hewitt*, 1975; *United States* v. *Makris*, 1976). Contemporaneous knowledge includes not only the availability of expert testimony based upon findings made at or near the time of trial but also the trial judge's impressions gathered from the defendant's appearance and demeanor at the trial.

These cases are not direct authority for the use of a provisional trial because they arise to remedy a constitutional error committed at the trial. Nevertheless, if the court is satisfied that sufficient contemporaneous knowledge of the defendant's competency at trial is available, the *nunc pro tunc* hearing is treated as the functional equivalent of a pretrial hearing. Our recommendation that the screening panel should, during the trial of a defendant who has not responded to treatment and may never respond, evaluate a defendant's competency ensures the availability of contemporaneous knowledge for the postconviction hearing. Thus the posttrial hearing procedure (Figure 7.1, Point I) as recommended guarantees the fundamental element required by the courts for the fairness of a *nunc pro tunc* hearing. Moreover, we believe the use of the provisional trial and postconviction hearing procedure can be demonstrated to lessen the deprivation of liberty of incompetent but innocent defendants, and to have at worst no effect on the deprivation of liberty of incompetent but uncertain-as-to-innocent defendants.

The case of Donald Lang, an illiterate deaf-mute, lends further support to this procedure. Although Lang had been found to be physically unfit for trial, his attorney moved that he be allowed to waive his constitutional right to bar his trial on the basis of incompetency, and thus be able to proceed to trial. Lang was subsequently committed to an institution. On appeal, the Illinois Supreme Court, in *People ex rel. Myers* v. *Briggs* (1970), reversed the lower court decision and held that "this defendant, handicapped as he is and facing an indefinite commitment because of the pending indictment against him, should be given an opportunity to obtain a trial to determine whether or not he is guilty as charged or should be released" (p. 288). The *Myers* court cited *Regina* v. *Roberts* (1953), a case no longer in force in England, as one basis for its decision. The *Roberts* decision held that it was legally permissible to try an individual who was incompetent. A second basis was the fact that, under the Illinois statutes in effect at the time, Lang was subject to an indefinite commitment without a determination of guilt.[15] Since *Jackson* v. *Indiana* (1972), however, most states (including Illinois) do not allow indefinite commitment of incompetent defendants. As a result, a later Illinois decision (*People* v. *Lang*, 1975), involving a new charge against the same defendant, held that if Lang was incompetent, a trial could not be held and he must be remanded to the Department of Mental Health for a commitment hearing.[16] However, Ryerson (1975) pointed to the ambiguity of the court's decision in *Lang*: "The court found that if a person is handicapped to the extent that modifications in trial procedure cannot be devised, he cannot be constitutionally tried. Implicit in this finding is that if special trial procedures can be devised to compensate for a defendant's handicap, a trial can be held consistent with due process" (p. 699). Thus it remains unclear whether a trial for incompetent defendants in Illinois would be permitted. Nevertheless, it appears that the court decisions cited above, especially *Myers*, have established the potential basis for a provisional trial.

As we discussed in Chapter 5, several states already allow a provisional trial, although no state to our knowledge has actually held such a trial. The Texas statutes allow a defendant the option of an immediate evaluation of competency. Section 4(d) of the Texas statutes states:

If the competency hearing is delayed until after a verdict on the guilt or innocence of the defendant is returned, the competency hearing shall be held as soon thereafter as reasonably possible, but a competency hearing may be held only if the verdict in the trial on the merits is "guilty." If the defendant is found incompetent to stand trial after the beginning of the trial on the merits, the court shall declare a mistrial in the trial on the merits. A subsequent trial and conviction of the defendant for the same offense is not barred and jeopardy does not attach by reason of a mistrial under this section. (p. 271)

Massachusetts statute allows for the trial of persons already determined to be incompetent:

If either a person or counsel of a person who has been found to be incompetent to stand trial believes that he can establish a defense of not guilty to the charges pending against the person other than the defense of not guilty by reason of mental illness or mental defect, he may request an opportunity to offer a defense thereto on the merits before the court which has criminal jurisdiction. The court may require counsel for the defendant to support the request by affidavit or other evidence. If the court in its discretion grants such a request, the evidence of the defendant and of the commonwealth shall be heard by the court sitting without a jury. If after hearing evidence to support a conviction it shall dismiss the indictment or other charges or find them defective or insufficient and order the release of the defendant from criminal custody. (p. 151)

In conclusion, it would seem that a provisional trial may be allowable under current court guidelines. In our model system the procedures for a provisional trial would be as follows. Based on the Burt and Morris (1972) proposal, special pretrial and trial procedures would be used if necessary to compensate for the possible negative effects of a defendant's incompetency. The screening panel would continue to evaluate and observe the defendant during the proceeding. Defendants found guilty (Figure 7.1, Point H) would proceed to a hearing (Figure 7.1, Point I). The screening panel would submit its report detailing their observations. The court has several options at this point. It can find a defendant competent, in which case the verdict would stand. It can find the defendant incompetent and the verdict would be set aside. In the latter instance the defendant would be subject to the treatment guidelines described in the next section and might be subject to a new trial if there was a positive response to treatment. The court, in its third option, could concur that the defendant was incompetent but, because the defendant's participation was not critical or because the special trial procedures compensated for the incompetency, would allow the guilty verdict to stand.

There are two equally important reasons for recommending a trial of possibly incompetent defendants. First, the trial would force the state to demonstrate its case against a defendant, and the defense would have the opportunity to present evidence in its behalf. Since a trial requires evidence beyond that required in a probable-cause hearing, this would minimize the problems of confining defendants for significant periods even when the state does not have a very good case or when the defense could present evidence to establish innocence. That this can be a problem is evidenced by such cases as the von Wolfersdorf one described in Chapter 5. Second, and perhaps most important, it would allow for a direct evaluation of competency. Our current evaluation procedures, whether they are implemented in an institution or in the community, must rely on a verbal interaction with defendants, and evaluators usually have little information about the circumstances surrounding the charges or the nature of the defense. Yet we ask these evaluators to make a prediction about how defendants will respond and behave during the legal proceedings. The consequences of a finding of incompetency are quite severe indeed, even in those states which limit the length of treatment and hospitalization. We are suggesting that our knowledge of the construct of competency is too tentative to be able to make this kind of prediction with reasonable certainty. However, we could begin to understand this construct better if we were to allow a trial for possibly incompetent defendants, and if we also continued the evaluation during the trial.[17] Evaluation of defendants during the legal proceedings assesses competency on the basis of actual performance and behavior within the criterion situation (the proceedings) rather than on the basis of large inferences drawn, for example, from a defendant's behavior in a mental hospital or from psychological tests. As Meehl (1971) points out, "Behavior science research shows that, by and large, the best way to predict anyone's behavior is his behavior in the past" (p. 88). It is well known that the circumstances of a particular case vary considerably. In some cases the participation of the defendant is critical to the defense; in other cases the degree of participation required may be minimal. It may also be, for example, that a client cannot communicate with a particular attorney but could communicate quite effectively with another attorney.[18] If the screening evaluators continued to observe and evaluate a defendant during the trial, they would have a considerably more complete assessment of the defendant's capabilities. The evaluators could also assess the degree to which various methods to compensate for the potential incompetency were successful. The trial and evaluation would thus allow for the functional approach to the issue of competency we have discussed throughout this book.

Our proposal for a provisional trial builds on earlier proposals by providing for the continued involvement of the screening panel. Information gained from this additional evaluation has uses which go beyond its relationship to a particular case. At a minimum, as we note above, it will provide a potentially more appropriate assessment of competency. It could also provide us with an opportunity to assess the predictive validity of the initial decision that a defendant might be incompetent. As we have previously discussed, decisions about competency are heavily related to traditional diagnostic categories and untested assumptions about the relationship between severe mental illness and incompetency. One wonders how well these allegedly incompetent defendants would have performed if they had been brought to trial. We are suggesting that we need to allow a provisional trial not only to better protect defendants' rights but also to provide us with important validity data regarding the construct of competency. A trial, for instance, could provide us with information about the relationship between certain symptoms or behaviors and a defendant's conduct at the trial. It could tell us more about the kinds of skills and participation a defendant would need to have a fair trial. Thus a provisional trial could result in improving the evaluation as well as making the consequences of a finding of incompetency fair to both the defendant, who is given an opportunity for a trial but not penalized if truly incompetent, and the public, who are concerned about a fair decision. Essentially, we are advocating a functional approach to the assessment of competency. In Chapter 2 we discussed the case of *Wilson v. United States* (1968), in which the court held that a trial judge should, at the end of trial, assess the actual effects of the defendant's amnesia on the trial proceedings. The U.S. Court of Appeals suggested six factors to aid in this decision, all of which provide a contextual basis (the actual trial) for determining the effects of the amnesia. We are suggesting that it is logical to apply this same reasoning to the question of competency in general. The procedures we discuss in this chapter allow such a functional approach to the evaluation of competency during trial and would provide a more reasonable and effective method for addressing the issue of competency. As in the case of amnesia, this would allow a direct assessment of a defendant's abilities, or lack of abilities, during the actual trial.

DISPOSITION OF INCOMPETENT DEFENDANTS

Defendants who are tried and found guilty, but because special procedures did not compensate for their incompetency or because the defendant's participation was critical to the case, would be subject to civil commitment laws (Figure 7.1, Point J). As we discussed in Chapter 5, most treatment limitation proposals have suggested a six-month maximum for treatment of incompetent defendants, but these proposals usually allow for a possible six-month extension if a substantial probability of regaining competency exists. We concur with this recommendation, with the provision that treatment occur in the least restrictive alternative possible. Prior to the commitment hearing under the civil commitment laws applicable in a given state, treatment personnel should provide the court with a specific treatment plan, detailing the proposed type and place of treatment and the manner in which it is likely to restore a defendant's competency. Defendants who regain competency during this treatment period would be returned to court for trial or other judicial proceedings (Figure

7.1, Point L). Charges against defendants who remain incompetent should be dismissed at the end of the specified treatment period (Figure 7.1, Point K). Of course, these defendants might be subject to continued confinement and/or treatment under civil commitment statutes.

We specifically reject the idea that special commitment procedures are necessary to deal with incompetent defendants who (1) have been found "guilty" and (2) have little possibility of regaining competency. In many cases such defendants would be committed under current civil statutes that require a showing of mental disorder and dangerousness and/or grave inability to care for oneself. It seems unwise to provide for a "lesser" commitment standard that would allow for either dangerousness or mental illness as the sole criterion. Cases such as Donald Lang's are so unusual that almost no statute could properly cover the range of circumstances. Given the tendency for mental health legislation to be misused, such statutes would seem to be unwarranted. We recognize the political problems that arise when a defendant who is charged with a particular heinous or violent crime is unable to stand trial. This is a problem analogous to, but not identical with, the disposition of individuals found "innocent" by reason of insanity. In cases where defendants have been shown to have committed an act that may have been quite violent and reprehensible, it seems morally "unfair" to let such individuals "evade" punishment. But under most current commitment statutes such a defendant would be easily committable and would likely end up "serving" as much time as similarly charged, but competent, defendants. On balance, to pass a law that would allow commitment to cover an extremely rare event (defendants who were charged with serious offenses but who do not meet civil commitment criteria) would seem unwise, especially in light of the probability that it would be applied more frequently to less unusual circumstances as part of society's concern about the mentally disordered, especially those who have allegedly committed a crime.

CONCLUSION

The model system presented in this chapter is the culmination of several years of empirical research, in the form of the series of studies we discussed in Chapter 6, as well as an integration of other research and literature and our perceptions of the adequacy of present models for confronting the issue of competency. The model system is one which we hope will minimize infringement of defendants' rights and deprivation of liberty, minimize costs, but maximize the quality of decision-making. We hold that this could be accomplished by conducting evaluations in the community rather than in an institution, by drawing upon the expertise of both legal and mental health professionals in evaluating competency, by allowing a trial procedure for allegedly incompetent defendants, and by providing additional safeguards and alternatives for defendants found incompetent. A major part of this model system involves an examination of the decision criteria, in which we propose that functional behaviors be the primary criteria. A defendant's behavior, including the common diagnostic descriptors such as delusions, must be specifically related to the particular circumstances of the individual's case. This is a critical basis for our recommendation that a provisional trial be held, since it would allow a direct assessment of the extent to which a defendant's behavior interfered (or did not interfere) with a fair trial.

We would like to conclude this book with a final caution. The model system is, from our perspective, potentially a more effective method for determining competency. Nevertheless, it is presented as an empirically testable system which will require substantial evaluation and critique if it is implemented. Such a process of evaluation will help to refine and extend the system, since it will provide a more substantial data base on the reliability and validity of legal–mental health decision-making in the context of competency to stand trial.

Notes

1. Our recommendations specifically for North Carolina were contained in a report (Roesch and Golding, 1977) submitted to the North Carolina Department of Mental Health, the North Carolina Administrative Office of the Courts, and the North Carolina legislature.

2. See Chapter 2 for a discussion of the proper grounds for determining if a sufficient doubt about competency exists.

3. This finding parallels earlier work on the incremental validity of various clinical assessment instruments. Typically, clinicians reach a conclusion (however

valid) very rapidly, and an increase in the information available to them rarely results in changes in their decisions (Meehl, 1960; Sines, 1959; Wiggins, 1973).

4. See Chapter 4 for a lengthy discussion of the importance of professional interaction. While some, such as Schulman (1973), have taken the extreme position that lawyers are the group most capable of evaluating the legal issue of competency (adding that the role of the behavioral scientists be eliminated), we believe that both professions have important contributions to make.

5. Such standards vary from jurisdiction to jurisdiction, and we do not believe that the present text is an appropriate focus for a lengthy discussion of civil commitment laws. We are aware that attempting to create a change in one system (e.g., incompetency commitment laws) often opens up an entire new area of study and possible reform. Since an examination of these issues is beyond the present scope, let us simply state that what we are suggesting is that commitment of defendants for evaluation and/or treatment should be subject to some constitutional safeguards rather than, as is often the case, be an *automatic* outcome (see Monahan and Wexler, 1978, and *Addington v. Texas*, 1979, for discussions of procedural issues and burden of proof in civil commitment).

6. Based on an average length of hospitalization of 17 days at Dorothea Dix Hospital, and an estimated cost of $47.27 per day, the cost of one evaluation was approximately $804.00 in North Carolina at the time of our study. This figure does not include the cost of transportation to and from Dorothea Dix. The cost of an evaluation by a screening panel was estimated to be $300 to $400, based on two professionals spending two hours each per evaluation and court testimony. If the evaluations were conducted by staff from local mental health centers, the cost reduction would be even greater.

7. See Chapter 3 for a review of the Competency Assessment Instrument.

8. Laben also demonstrated a significant cost reduction. The evaluation team's assessment cost approximately one-third that of the institutional evaluations conducted prior to the establishment of her team.

9. In Chapter 2 we review the criteria necessary to raise doubt (*Pate*) as opposed to the criteria for competency *per se* (*Dusky*).

10. We recognize the difficulty in determining the standard of proof necessary to reach a decision about competency. Since there has never been a case questioning the standard of evidence in competency cases, there is no legal tradition upon which we can rely. The logic we have applied here is similar to the logic the Supreme Court followed in *Addington v. Texas* (1979) (see Chapter 4). Unlike the insanity plea, incompetency is not a defense and need not be overcome by the reasonable-doubt standard. In balancing the interests of the states and the rights of a defendant, the middle ground seems appropriate, particularly if considered with the other changes we propose in this chapter.

11. Some writers (e.g., Alschuler, 1968) have argued that because of some serious problems inherent in the plea bargaining process, it should be abolished. While such arguments may be persuasive, the current reality in the legal system is that plea bargaining is used for the majority of criminal cases (see Finkelstein, 1975; Mather, 1974; Newman, 1956).

12. An efficient mechanism of judicial review is necessary at this point, since recent experience in the area of civil commitment reform suggests that the principle of the least restrictive alternative may not always be followed (Hiday, 1977).

13. As we have discussed in the preceding text, it is recognized that most defendants do not have a trial; rather, cases are disposed of through some form of plea bargaining. The evaluation of possibly incompetent defendants may well be easier if there is a trial, but plea bargaining does not preclude the evaluation procedure we discuss in this section. The screening panel would simply assess the degree to which the defendant understood and participated in the plea bargaining arrangement.

14. See *United States ex rel. McGough* v. *Hewitt* (1975); *Carroll* v. *Beto* (1970); *United States* v. *Makris* (1976); *Sieling* v. *Eyman* (1973).

15. Lang's case on this first charge never came to trial, however, since after the decision in *Myers* v. *Briggs* the state dropped its charges on the grounds of insufficient evidence.

16. Lang is currently in jail, pending the outcome of a recently ordered civil commitment proceeding to determine if he meets the dangerousness criterion. It is of interest to note that a recent Illinois Supreme Court decision held that Lang met the requirements to be classified as mentally ill by virtue of the fact that he had been found incompetent (*People* v. *Lang*, Supreme Court of Illinois Opinion, May 24, 1979).

17. It is important to remember that this proposed trial procedure be considered in conjunction with the screening procedures we recommend. The screening evaluation will remove competent defendants as well as defendants who are quite clearly incompetent (such as cases similar to Theon Jackson's). The number of cases reaching the provisional trial stage would be quite low in most jurisdictions, since the vast majority of defendants referred for evaluations are found competent (see Chapter 3).

18. This situation is analogous to attempts in psychotherapy to match therapists and clients, on the assumption that there is an optimal match between characteristics of therapists and characteristics of clients.

APPENDIX A

North Carolina Psychiatric Reports Coding System

The following information may be obtained from the Mental Status Exam, Diagnostic Conference Report and Discharge Summary, Diagnostic Conference Report, and/or Discharge Summary.

NOTE: *The following scale should be used to code each item:*
β = No information on this item is available from the records.
1 = Statements or other information indicate presence of behavior.
2 = A statement was made indicating this behavior was not present.

VARIABLE

I. Inappropriate Behavior and Mannerisms
    1. Personal appearance is markedly unkempt or bizarre.
    2. Laughs, grins, or giggles inappropriately.
    3. Exhibits peculiar, inappropriate, or bizarre gestures, manneristic body movements, or postures.

II. Speech Disorganization
    4. Exhibits flight of ideas (that is, abruptly and/or rapidly changes the topic of conversation so that ideas are not completed).
    5. Exhibits loose associations (that is, says things together which have little or no logical or inherent relationship to each other).
    6. Exhibits clang associations (that is, combines unrelated words or phrases because they share similar sounds).
    7. Talks, mutters, or mumbles to self without apparent provoking stimulus.
    8. Speech is, at least some of the time, disorganized, incoherent, or confused.
    9. Speech is either frequently blocked or perseverative (that is, the patient frequently either abruptly stops talking in midsen-

tence or repeats his end words or phrases over and over in a mechanical manner).

10. Speech is aimless or wandering or rambling (that is, the subject tends to drift off or away from the point at issue while responding to questions or topics).

11. Speech is filled with words or phrases that are not found in the ordinary language or dictionary (that is, neologisms; word salad).

III. Affective State

12. While in the hospital, preoccupied or shows little or no interest or attention to what is going on around him.

13. Speech is depressed (that is, speaks rarely or not at all or in a faint voice or weakly, etc.).

14. Talks of the circumstances surrounding his present arrest with little or no emotion or concern.

15. Is sleepy or without energy most of the time.

16. Admits to a variety of fears or worries.

17. Admits to or appears to be often anxious or anxious most of the time.

18. Is restless or is unable to stay still.

19. Is often sad or depressed.

20. Exhibits negative self-appraisal (that is, accuses himself of being unworthy, sinful, or evil, or feels inadequate, doesn't like himself, bothered by feelings of having done something terrible, etc.).

21. Affect is described as inappropriate.

IV. Interactional Behavior

22. Is deliberately evasive in answering questions.

23. Is verbally abusive (that is, shouts, yells, or screams at people, curses, or uses obscene language frequently).

24. Expresses hatred, contempt, or anger for staff and other patients.

25. Engages in nonverbal hostile behavior not directed toward others (that is, bangs fist against walls or tables, stamps his feet, slams around the ward, etc.).

26. Is argumentative (that is, tries to start arguments with staff, patients, visitors, etc.).

27. Makes menacing gestures or engages in physical attacks on staff or patients.

28. Expresses objections to interviewer or resentment at having to answer questions or resentment at being in the hospital.

29. Is hostile, belligerent, sarcastic, contemptuous, or insulting toward staff or patients.

30. Report indicates that the individual has engaged in physical attacks on person or persons.

31. While on ward person attacks or hits some person or persons.

32. The person or the person's family, associates, or other authorities fear that he may physically injure another person.
33. Individual indicates that he often avoids or fears contact or social involvement with others.
34. Behaviorally, the individual is socially isolated on the ward (stays by self; doesn't interact with others).
35. Patient is described as cooperative, quiet, well-mannered, no behavior problem, etc.

V. Self-Destructive Behavior

36. Patient indicates that he has thoughts about killing himself or desires or intends to kill himself.
37. Patient indicates that he has, in the near or recent past (that is, within the past six months), made a suicidal gesture or attempt.
38. Patient indicates that he has deliberately physically mutilated himself, or thinks about it.
39. Patient or hospital report indicates that the person has tried to commit suicide in the distant past (that is, six months ago or more).

VI. Alcohol and Drug Abuse

40. The patient, a hospital report, or others indicate that he has had difficulty with alcohol abuse.
41. Person has alcoholic history to the point that he has either lost consciousness, had delirium tremens, or become physically ill because of alcohol usage.
42. Individual has been arrested in the past for public drunkenness.
43. History of drug abuse (this does not include occasional or social usage of drugs).
44. Patient or report indicates history of excessive drug abuse to the point where a person was hospitalized or became physically ill.
45. Patient or report indicates that he has been arrested in the past for drug abuse.

VII. Cognitive and Perceptual Disorganization

46. Patient admits, in the past, to having had olfactory, auditory, visual, or somatic hallucinations.
47. Patient complains, in the present (that is, in the hospital), of having olfactory, auditory, visual, or somatic hallucinations.
48. In the past, patient admitted to having thought processes which are delusional (that is, overt delusions, ideas of reference, ideas of persecution, people engaged in a conspiracy against him, people are controlling him, external sources are controlling him, etc.).
49. In the present, the individual indicates thought processes which could be classified as delusional (that is, overt delusions, ideas of reference, ideas of persecution, people engaged in a con-

spiracy against him, people are controlling him, external
sources are controlling him, etc.).

50. Patient communicates to others ideas or delusions of grandiosity.

51. Report indicates that the staff has noted behavioral patterns
which are consistent with hallucinatory or delusional processes.

VIII. Past Criminal Behavior (Note: This does not refer to the charges
which are currently pending against the individual.)

52. Report indicates that he has been arrested in the past for misdemeanors.

53. Report indicates that he has been arrested in the past for felonies.

IX. Organic Involvement

54. Patient has a history of (or has exhibited in the hospital) epileptic behavior.

55. Psychological and/or medical examination indicates the presence of mild and/or mild and diffuse brain damage.

56. Psychological and/or medical examination indicates the presence of moderate or severe brain damage.

57. Patient, while on ward, has had neurological symptoms traceable to an external source, such as alcohol (for example, DTs,
seizures, loss of consciousness, etc.).

X. Intellective and Cognitive Functioning

58. Note: Only one of the following descriptions will be valid. Indicate which one is accurate by writing the number corresponding to that item in column.
1. Psychological tests indicate that the person is classifiable as severely retarded (35 or less).
2. Psychological tests indicate that the person is classifiable as moderately retarded (36–51).
3. Psychological tests indicate that the person is classifiable as mildly retarded (52–84).
4. Psychological tests indicate that the person is classifiable as of normal intellectual ability (85–115).
5. Psychological tests indicate that the individual is
classifiable as above average or of superior intellectual
ability (116 and above).

59. Patient has intact memory for recent and past events.

60. Psychiatric reports indicate that the patient's insight and/or
judgment are impaired.

61. Psychiatric reports indicate that the patient is oriented as to
time, person, or place.

XI. Awareness of Legal Situation

62. Patient is able to give an adequate account of circumstances
surrounding crime of which he is accused.

63. Patient appears able to cooperate with the defense.
64. Patient appreciates the nature of the court proceedings against him and the possible consequences of conviction.
65. Patient is apprehensive about the nature of the legal difficulty he is in. (I.e., patient expressed a desire to return to court = 2; patient expressed a desire *not* to return to court = 1.)

XII. Recommendations

66. Defendant is competent to stand trial.
67. Defendant *presently* knows right from wrong.
68. It is recommended that charges be dismissed against this person.
69. If the patient receives no active prison sentence, it is recommended that this person be referred for outpatient mental health care (mental health center, private practitioner, etc.). Also includes participation in industrial programs, sheltered workshops, counseling centers, and AA programs.
70. If the patient receives no active prison sentence, patient should be referred back to Dorothea Dix or other state mental hospital, on a *voluntary* basis.
71. If the patient receives no active prison sentence, patient should be judicially or civilly committed back to Dorothea Dix or other state mental hospital.
72. Patient should remain in hospital until time of trial.
73. Patient should receive psychiatric care if imprisoned.
74. Patient should be continued on psychiatric medications.
75. Patient is incompetent to stand trial and should be committed to Dorothea Dix until such time as mentally capable to plead to the indictment.
76. Patient should be transferred to a VA hospital or other psychiatric facility.
77. Defendant knew right from wrong at the time of the alleged crime. Patient should be viewed as responsible for his/her actions.

APPENDIX B

Mental Status Exam: Reliability Coefficients

Item	1 v. 2 Ratings	(Blank, 2) v. 1 Ratings	(1, 2) v. Blank Ratings	Percent Agreement
1	1.00	.88	.83	92.1
2	1.00	.81	.75	93.9
3	1.00	.41	.67	89.2
5	1.00	.65	.78	93.9
8	.91	.65	.66	82.5
10	1.00	.75	.41	86.1
12	1.00	.37	.36	88.5
13	1.00	.42	.33	88.5
16	1.00	.56	.48	89.1
17	.91	.75	.78	89.1
19	.92	.83	.82	91.1
21	.86	.72	.77	85.5
22	1.00	.71	.50	83.7
34	1.00	.58	.59	94.0
35	.82	.70	.47	71.7
39	1.00	.61	.71	94.5
40	.90	.63	.63	85.5
42	.94	.89	.83	92.8
43	.91	.61	.80	91.6
44	1.00	.66	.84	94.6
46	.92	.75	.59	79.5
47	.82	.69	.70	85.0
48	.91	.55	.66	81.9
49	.93	.68	.67	84.3
51	.88	.36	.58	80.1
52	.92	.69	.66	86.2
53	.92	.70	.65	85.0
54	1.00	1.00	.70	96.4
59	.73	.70	.70	83.2
60	.91	.79	.70	88.0
61	.76	.72	.58	86.2

The following items were dropped from all analyses owing to less than a 10% endorsement frequency: 4, 6, 7, 9, 11, 14, 15, 18, 20, 23, 24–33, 36–38, 41, 45, 50, 55–57.

APPENDIX C

Diagnostic Conference Report and Discharge Summary:
Reliability Coefficients

Item	1 v. 2 Ratings	(Blank, 2) v. 1 Ratings	(1, 2) v. Blank Ratings	Percent Agreement
1	.84	.74	.88	97.0
2	.71	.66	.81	97.6
3	**	**	.42	85.6
8	.65	.41	.70	83.1
10	1.00	.86	.37	90.1
12	1.00	.57	.53	90.7
13	.75	.49	.56	92.0
14	.84	.55	.68	90.7
15	1.00	.57	.73	93.2
16	**	.70	.57	95.6
17	1.00	.69	.74	90.7
18	**	.51	.41	93.8
19	.79	.57	.68	88.8
21	.95	.84	.80	90.0
22	.87	.65	.68	91.3
29	1.00	.11	.18	90.6
34	.86	.40	.80	90.0
35	.32	.22	.52	79.4
39	1.00	.77	.84	98.8
40	.97	.79	.77	88.2
41	.91	.79	.86	92.5
42	1.00	.86	.86	93.8
43	.95	.88	.91	95.6
44	1.00	.91	.96	98.8
46	.94	.85	.88	93.2
47	.94	.80	.92	95.6
48	1.00	.73	.87	93.8
49	1.00	.47	.85	93.1
51	.89	.38	.66	82.5
52	.62	.60	.56	80.1
53	.90	.81	.65	83.2
56	.64	.57	.86	92.6
59	.87	.78	.73	85.7
60	.86	.66	.72	85.6
61	1.00	.66	.58	81.9

The following items were dropped from all analyses owing to less than a 10% endorsement frequency: 4–7, 9, 11, 20, 23–28, 30–33, 36–38, 45, 50, 54, 55, 57.

** Reliabilities could not be calculated, since there were no ratings for this combination of ratings.

APPENDIX D

Diagnostic Conference Report: Reliability Coefficients

Item	1 v. 2 Ratings	(Blank, 2) v. 1 Ratings	(1, 2) v. Blank Ratings	Percent Agreement
1	.89	.83	.79	92.6
2	**	.77	.78	92.7
3	1.00	.28	.45	88.6
8	.89	.60	.56	76.4
10	**	.57	.54	88.6
12	1.00	.58	.56	80.5
13	1.00	.45	.48	88.6
14	**	.61	.48	84.5
15	1.00	.61	.60	95.2
16	**	.38	.36	80.4
17	1.00	.50	.52	84.6
18	**	.55	.50	87.0
19	.68	.58	.54	84.6
21	.76	.65	.66	80.5
22	.62	.61	.50	85.3
27	1.00	.82	.79	97.6
29	0.00	.76	.72	85.1
34	.82	.69	.65	82.2
35	.87	.61	.48	74.8
39	**	.76	.69	95.1
40	.92	.75	.71	83.7
41	.90	.74	.64	87.0
42	1.00	.83	.66	88.6
43	1.00	.91	.88	96.7
44	**	**	.56	94.3
46	.92	.74	.64	80.5
47	.91	.79	.64	80.5
48	.76	.43	.44	69.1
49	.70	.63	.59	73.2
51	1.00	.45	.41	74.0
52	.80	.56	.60	83.8
53	1.00	.62	.58	82.1
56	1.00	.81	.69	94.3
59	.87	.56	.54	73.9
60	.12	.41	.53	72.3
61	.90	.75	.50	77.3

The following items were dropped from all analyses owing to less than a 10% endorsement frequency: 4–7, 9, 11, 20, 23–26, 28, 30–33, 36–38, 45, 50, 54, 55, 57.

** Reliability could not be calculated, since there were no ratings for this combination of ratings.

APPENDIX E

Discharge Summary: Reliability Coefficients

Item	1 v. 2 Ratings	(Blank, 2) v. 1 Ratings	(1, 2) v. Blank Ratings	Percent Agreement
1	1.00	1.00	.87	97.2
3	••	••	.61	89.7
8	1.00	.81	.65	82.3
12	••	••	(−) .061	52.3
13	••	••	.49	97.2
14	.79	.62	.23	64.5
15•				
17	1.00	.26	.49	80.3
19	.78	.66	.79	93.5
21	.88	.64	.76	90.7
22	1.00	.70	.24	76.6
29	.64	.34	.60	91.6
34	.71	.30	.29	69.1
35	1.00	1.00	.77	90.6
36•				
40	••	.96	.96	99.1
41	••	1.00	1.00	100.0
42•				
43	••	1.00	1.00	100.0
44, 45•				
46	.81	.73	.70	86.0
47	.56	.34	.75	85.9
48	.75	.39	.52	76.7
49	.63	.41	.59	74.7
50	1.00	1.00	.76	96.2
51	1.00	.20	.33	71.1
52	••	1.00	1.00	100.0
53	••	.70	.70	99.0
55	••	1.00	1.00	100.0
59	.63	.52	.55	79.4
60	1.00	.35	.21	73.9
61	••	.77	••	88.8

The following items were dropped from all analyses owing to less than a 10% endorsement frequency: 2, 4–7, 9–11, 16, 18, 20, 23–28, 30–33, 37–39, 54, 56, 57.

• This item was included in subsequent analyses because data were available from the Diagnostic Conference Report and Discharge Summary.

•• Reliability could not be calculated, since there were no ratings for this combination of ratings.

APPENDIX F

Mental Status Exam: Principal Components

Component	Items
Alcohol Abuse	The patient, a hospital report, or others indicate that he has had difficulty with alcohol abuse.
	Individual has been arrested in the past for public drunkenness.
	Report indicates that he has been arrested in the past for misdemeanors.
Speech Disorganization	Exhibits loose associations.
	Speech is, at least some of the time, disorganized, incoherent, or confused.
	Speech is aimless or wandering or rambling.
	While in the hospital, patient is preoccupied or shows little or no interest or attention to what is going on around him.
Drug Abuse	History of drug abuse.
	Patient or report indicates history of excessive drug abuse to the point where patient was hospitalized or became physically ill.
Inappropriate Behavior	Exhibits peculiar, inappropriate, or bizarre gestures, manneristic body movements, or postures.
	Speech is depressed.
	Patient is described as cooperative, quiet, well-mannered, no behavior problem, etc.
Depression	Is often sad or depressed.
	Behaviorally, the individual is socially isolated on the ward.
	Patient has a history of epileptic behavior.
Delusions	Personal appearance is markedly unkempt or bizarre.
	Admits to a variety of fears or worries.
	In the past, patient admitted to having thought processes which are delusional.

Component	Items
	In the present, the individual indicates thought processes which could be classified as delusional.
Affect/Legal Involvement	Affect is described as inappropriate.
	Patient or hospital report indicates that the person has tried to commit suicide in the distant past.
	Report indicates that he has been arrested in the past for felonies.
Hallucinations	Laughs, grins, or giggles inappropriately.
	Patient admits, in the past, to having had olfactory, auditory, visual, or somatic hallucinations.
	Patient complains, in the present, of having olfactory, auditory, visual, or somatic hallucinations.
	Report indicates that the staff has noted behavioral patterns which are consistent with hallucinatory or delusional processes.
Cognitive Functioning	Admits to or appears to be often anxious or anxious most of the time.
	Patient has intact memory for recent and past events.
	Psychiatric reports indicate that the patient's insight and judgment are impaired.
	Psychiatric reports indicate that the patient is oriented as to time, person, or place.

Mental Status Exam: Item Loadings on Principal Components

Item[1]	1	2	3	4	5	6	7	8	9	h²
				Component						
40	78									63
42	85									77
52	81									72
5		50								44
8		61								43
10		64								46
12		49								54
43			83							70
44			77							63
3				61						52
13				59						45
35				67						56
19					69					68
34				42	49					56
54					58					42
1						64				51
16						51				51
48						62				54
49						66				67
21							55			48
39							60			48
53							56			51
2								63		52
46								54		52
47								71		55
51								40		47
17									39	32
59									48	55
60									44	54
61									71	57

[1]Appendix A contains the complete list of items.

APPENDIX G

Diagnostic Conference Report and Discharge Summary/Diagnostic
Conference Report: Principal Components

Component	Items
Delusions	Admits to a variety of fears or worries.
	In the past, patient admitted to having thought processes which are delusional.
	In the present, the individual indicates thought processes which could be classified as delusional.
	Report indicates that the staff has noted behavioral patterns which are consistent with hallucinatory or delusional processes.
Speech/Affect	Laughs, grins, or giggles inappropriately.
	Speech is, at least some of the time, disorganized, incoherent, or confused.
	Speech is aimless or wandering or rambling.
	Is sleepy or without energy most of the time.
	Affect is described as inappropriate.
Alcohol Abuse	The patient, a hospital report, or others indicate that he has had difficulty with alcohol abuse.
	Person has alcoholic history to the point that he has either lost consciousness, had delirium tremens, or become physically ill because of alcohol usage.
	Individual has been arrested in the past for public drunkenness.
	Report indicates that he has been arrested in the past for misdemeanors.
Hostility	Makes menacing gestures or engages in physical attacks on staff or patients.
	Is hostile, belligerent, sarcastic, contemptuous, or insulting toward staff or patients.
	Patient is described as cooperative, quiet, well-mannered, no behavior problem, etc.
Hallucinations	Personal appearance is markedly unkempt or bizarre.

Component	Items
	Patient admits, in the past, to having had olfactory, auditory, visual, or somatic hallucinations.
	Patient complains, in the present, of having olfactory, auditory, visual, or somatic hallucinations.
	Patient has intact memory for recent and past events.
Interactional Behavior	While in the hospital, patient preoccupied or shows little or no interest or attention to what is going on around him.
	Talks of the circumstances surrounding his present arrest with little or no emotion or concern.
	Behaviorally, the individual is socially isolated on the ward.
	Psychiatric reports indicate that the patient's insight and judgment are impaired.
Anxiety	Admits to or appears to be often anxious or anxious most of the time.
	Is restless or is unable to stay still.
	Is often sad or depressed.

Diagnostic Conference Report and Discharge Summary/Diagnostic Conference Report: Item Loadings on Principal Components

| Item[1] | Component | | | | | | | h² |
	1	2	3	4	5	6	7	
16	68							56
48	82							71
49	82							73
51	47							29
2		51						31
8		60						52
10		52						38
15		46						27
21		48						36
40			75					25
41			50					59
42			79					38
52			67					26
27				71				57
29				75				63
35				69				65
1					−45			47
46					74			20
47					73			66
59					41			35
12						67		65
14						37		25
34						67		47
60						45		30
17							59	37
18							43	40
19							70	56

[1]Appendix A contains the complete list of items.

APPENDIX H

Diagnostic Conference Report and Discharge Summary/Discharge
Summary: Principal Components

Component	Items
Alcohol Abuse	The patient, a hospital report, or others indicate that he has had difficulty with alcohol abuse.
	Person has alcoholic history to the point that he has either lost consciousness, had delirium tremens, or become physically ill because of alcohol usage.
	Individual has been arrested in the past for public drunkenness.
	Report indicates that he has been arrested in the past for misdemeanors.
Hallucinations/ Past Delusions	Patient admits, in the past, to having had olfactory, auditory, visual, or somatic hallucinations.
	Patient complains, in the present, of having olfactory, auditory, visual, or somatic hallucinations.
	In the past, patient admitted to having thought processes which are delusional.
	Report indicates that the staff has noted behavioral patterns which are consistent with hallucinatory or delusional processes.
Hostility	Is hostile, belligerent, sarcastic, contemptuous, or insulting toward staff or patients.
	Patient is described as cooperative, quiet, well-mannered, no behavior problem, etc.
Depression	Speech is, at least some of the time, disorganized, incoherent, or confused.
	Admits to or appears to be often anxious or anxious most of the time.
	Is often sad or depressed.
Cognitive Functioning	Affect is described as inappropriate.
	Patient has intact memory for recent and past events.
	Psychiatric reports indicate that the patient's insight and judgment are impaired.
	Psychiatric reports indicate that the patient is oriented as to time, person, or place.

Component	Items
Present Delusions	Is deliberately evasive in answering questions.
	In the present, the individual indicates thought processes which could be classified as delusional.
	Psychological and/or medical examination indicates the presence of mild and/or mild and diffuse brain damage.
Drug Abuse/Legal Involvement	History of drug abuse.
	Report indicates that he has been arrested in the past for felonies.

Diagnostic Conference and Discharge Summary/Discharge Summary: Item Loadings on Principal Components

Item[1]	Component							h²
	1	2	3	4	5	6	7	
40	73							62
41	56							55
42	83							74
52	72							67
46		74						58
47		58						55
48		68						50
51		41						49
29			69					51
35			66					50
8				50				48
17				73				60
19				79				64
21					54			39
59					49			33
60					50			33
61					65			46
22						78		64
49						51		43
55						52		61
43							71	54
53							63	61

[1]Appendix A contains the complete list of items.

Appendix I

*Competency to Stand Trial in North Carolina: A Survey
of Legal Opinions*

The National Clearinghouse for Criminal Justice Planning and Architecture is currently assisting the state of North Carolina in evaluating the legal and mental health process of determining competency to stand trial. We are working closely with the Department of Mental Health and Office of Courts Administration. The information we are asking you to provide in this survey will assist us in our analysis of the present procedures regarding the issue of competency to stand trial. Any additional comments you have about changes in current practices will be appreciated. We have tried to design the survey to be as brief as possible by using a short-answer or multiple-choice format.

1. Motions requesting a determination of the capacity of a defendant to proceed can, by North Carolina statutes (15A-1002), be raised by the prosecutor, the defendant, the defense counsel, or the court on its own motion. The following questions relate to the decisional criteria that you typically employ in dismissing or granting such a motion.

    a) In general terms, what information do you seek before making your decision?

    b) Do you have any implicit or explicit decisional schemes by which you combine this information in arriving at a decision?

    c) Do you routinely grant such a motion? .... Yes ( ) 1
                                                                    No ( ) 2

    (1) If yes, what factors lead you to adopt such a decisional scheme?

    (2) If no, on what basis do you typically deny such a motion?

2. If you grant the motion, North Carolina statutes permit you three alternatives: a) to conduct a hearing immediately, b) to commit the de-

fendant to a state mental health facility for observation and evaluation, or c) to appoint one or more impartial medical experts to observe
and evaluate the defendant.

a) Do you ever conduct a hearing immediately? .... Yes ( ) 1
                                                                  No ( ) 2

    If yes, approximately what percentage of cases? .... _____%

b) Do you ever commit the defendant to a state .... Yes ( ) 1
   mental health facility?   No ( ) 2

    If yes, approximately what percentage of cases? .... _____%

    If commitment is to a facility other than Dorothea Dix,
    please specify._____

c) Do you ever appoint impartial medical experts? .... Yes ( ) 1
                                                        No ( ) 2

    If yes, approximately what percentage of cases? .... _____%

d) If you use *more than one* of the alternatives, what aspects
    of the case contribute to your decision?

3. When a defendant has been returned to court following evaluation
   (whether at a state mental health facility or by a group of medical
   experts),

a) Where do you typically hold the .... In your chambers ( ) 1
   hearing to reach a decision about   In open court ( ) 2
   a defendant's capacity to proceed?   At other location ( ) 3
                                 If another location, please
                                   specify._____

b) Who is present at such a hearing? .... Prosecuting attorney ( ) 1
                                           Defense counsel ( ) 2
                                                Defendant ( ) 3
                        Author of medical report ( ) 4
                                               Other ( ) 5
                           If other, please specify.

    _____

c) Do you ever make a determination solely on the .... Yes ( ) 1
   basis of the mental health recommendations   No ( ) 2
   without conducting a formal hearing?

If yes, approximately what percentage of cases? .... _____%

d) How frequently does your decision about the ....Never ( ) 1
defendant's capacity to proceed differ from the   Rarely ( ) 2
court-ordered evaluation recommendations?   Occasionally ( ) 3
                                             Frequently ( ) 4

If you have checked rarely, occasionally, or frequently, what factors usually contribute to your disagreement with the recommendations?

e) What information from the evaluation-recommendations do you find most useful in making your decision?

4. A preliminary statistical analysis of records at Dorothea Dix indicates that a very large proportion of defendants sent for evaluation are recommended as competent to stand trial. This would seem to suggest that factors other than the defendant's apparent competency or incompetency are involved in motions for evaluation of competency. Based upon your experience, which of the following do you believe may be contributing factors (circle all that apply)?

a) Misunderstanding on the part of defense counsel as to criteria for incapacity to proceed.

b) Misunderstanding on the part of prosecutors as to criteria for incapacity to proceed.

c) Use by psychology and psychiatry professionals of criteria that do not satisfy legal requirements. If you check this item, please indicate the major sources of confusion or disagreement about criteria that have occurred in your experience:

d) An attempt by defense counsel to delay trial in order to allow a "cooling off" period for witnesses and others involved in the case.

e) An attempt by defense counsel to build a case for diminished responsibility by entering psychological and psychiatric history into the trial record.

f) An attempt by the prosecutor to circumvent pretrial release.

g) An attempt by the prosecutor to build a case against diminished responsibility by entering psychological and psychiatric history into the trial record.

h) Other (please specify):_____

5. If a defendant is found to be "incapable of proceeding," current North Carolina law requires that an involuntary civil commitment hearing be held.

    a) Do you typically seek additional evaluative .... Yes ( ) 1
       information beyond the report submitted as part   No ( ) 2
       of the "competency" evaluation?

       If yes, where does this evaluation usually take place?

    b) Is the respondent usually present at the .... Yes ( ) 1
       involuntary commitment hearing?   No ( ) 2

    c) Do you believe that a prior determination of incapacity to proceed is sufficient grounds for involuntary commitment for:

       (1) defendants charged with violent or poten- .... Yes ( ) 1
           tially violent offenses (murder, voluntary   No ( ) 2
           manslaughter, rape, arson, armed robbery, etc.)

       (2) defendants charged with nonviolent felonies .... Yes ( ) 1
                                     No ( ) 2

       (3) defendants charged with misdemeanors .... Yes ( ) 1
                                     No ( ) 2

    d) Do you see any inconsistencies in holding an .... Yes ( ) 1
       involuntary commitment hearing for an individual No ( ) 2
       previously found to be incapable of assisting in his own defense?

       Please give a brief outline of your reasoning regardless of your answer.

Please circle one answer only to the remaining questions.

6. A psychiatric expert witness should be at least:

    a) a Ph.D. holder in clinical psychology.

    b) a medical doctor.

    c) a psychiatrist.

    d) a psychiatrist specializing in legal problems.

7. I prefer the following system of calling experts:

    a) Only the defense should be allowed to call them.

    b) Both defense and prosecution should be allowed to call them.

    c) Both attorneys should agree on which experts are called.

    d) Only the court should be allowed to call experts.

8. Which best describes the usual effect of psychiatric testimony on a jury?

    a) Jurors are so impressed that they conform their verdicts to the expert's opinion.

    b) Jurors listen carefully to the expert but base their verdicts on all factors in the case.

    c) Jurors ignore expert testimony because they don't understand it.

    d) Jurors treat psychiatric testimony like any other testimony.

9. Which best states the relationship between serious criminal activity and mental illness?

    a) Anyone who commits a serious crime is mentally ill.

    b) Most people who commit serious crimes are mentally ill.

    c) Most people who commit serious crimes are *not* mentally ill.

    d) There is no relationship between mental illness and serious crime.

10. The final determination of competency to stand trial should rest with:

    a) a jury of laymen.

    b) a group of medical experts.

    c) a judge.

    d) a combined group of medical and legal experts.

11. I think the following is the most sensible system regarding institutional commitment when the defendant is found incompetent to stand trial:

    a) Commitment should be automatic in every case.

    b) Commitment should be at the discretion of the person or groups rendering the verdict.

    c) A separate hearing before a jury should be held to determine the question of commitment.

    d) Medical experts should determine.

12. The following is the *most important* criterion to be considered in deciding whether the defendant is to be committed:

    a) He needs restraint because he is now dangerous to himself and others.

    b) He has been dangerous and needs to be deterred from becoming so again.

    c) Justice requires some form of penalty.

    d) He is mentally ill and in need of treatment.

13. A defendant who has been committed should be released from the hospital when:

    a) he has stayed for a predetermined period of time.

    b) in the judgment of the *court*, he is no longer dangerous.

    c) in the judgment of *doctors* at the hospital, he is no longer dangerous.

    d) in the judgment of doctors, he is cured.

14. Which position do you currently hold? ... Superior Court Judge ( )
    District Court Judge ( )

15. The remaining space is provided for any additional suggestions or comments you have regarding changes or potential problem areas. If additional space is needed, please use the back of this page.

APPENDIX J
Sample Motion

STATE OF NORTH CAROLINA	IN THE GENERAL COURT OF JUSTICE
COUNTY OF WAKE	DISTRICT COURT DIVISION
	76 CR 00000

STATE OF NORTH CAROLINA	)	
	)	
v.	)	AFFIDAVIT AND MOTION
	)	
J. M. Smith	)	

Robert Stills, being first duly sworn, deposes and says that I am an attorney at law and have been appointed to represent J. M. Smith, Docket No. 76 CR 00000.

I interviewed this Defendant in the county jail on August 1, 1976. In response to my questions concerning the circumstances leading to his arrest, this defendant responded by stating that it was predetermined that he be arrested so that he could stand as a martyr for his people. I then asked him his whereabouts at the time of the alleged offense, and he responded by saying that no mortal had a right to ask him that question. He refused to respond at all to further questioning. The information I attempted to obtain is critical to the defense since the absence of this information hampers my ability to confront witnesses against the defendant and to present an effective defense in his behalf. Therefore, I respectfully request a hearing to determine if this defendant is, pursuant to North Carolina General Statute Section 15A–1001, able to understand the nature and object of the proceedings and to assist in his own defense in a reasonable and rational manner.

LEGAL CITATIONS

Addington v. *Texas*. 99 S. Ct. 1804 (1979).
Allard v. *Helgemoe*. 527 F. 2d 1 (1st Cir., 1978).
Barker v. *Wingo*. 407 U.S. 514 (1972).
Baxstrom v. *Herold*. 383 U.S. 107 (1966).
Bishop v. *United States*. 350 U.S. 961 (1956).
Bolton v. *Harris*. 395 F. 2d 642 (1968).
Bowers v. *Battles*. 568 F. 2d 1 (1977).
Boykin v. *Alabama*. 395 U.S. 238 (1969).
Bruce v. *Estelle*. 536 F. 2d 1051 (1976).
Carroll v. *Beto*. 421 F. 2d 1056 (1970).
Carter v. *United States*. 252 F. 2d 608 (D.C. Cir., 1957).
Commonwealth v. *Price*. 421 Pa. 396, 218 A. 2d 758 (1966).
Covington v. *Harris*, 419 F. 2d 617 (D.C. Cir., 1969).
deKaplany v. *Enomoto*. 540 F. 2d 975 (9th Cir., 1976). *Cert*. denied, 429
   U.S. 1075 (1977).
Drope v. *Missouri*. 420 U.S. 162 (1975).
Durham v. *United States*. 214 F. 2d 862 (D.C. Cir., 1954).
Dusky v. *United States*. 362 U.S. 402 (1960).
Ex parte Kent. 490 S.W. 2d 649 (1973).
Feguer v. *United States*. 302 F. 2d 214 (1962).
General Statutes of North Carolina. Charlottesville, Va.: Michie, 1975.
Hansford v. *United States*. 124 U.S. App. D.C. 387, 365 F. 2d 920
   (1966).
Hayes v. *United States*. 305 F. 2d 540 (1962).
Higgins v. *McGrath*. 98 F. Supp. 670 (1951).
Holloway v. *United States*. 343 F. 2d 265 (D.C. Cir., 1964).
In re Causey. 363 So. 2d 472 (La. Sup. Ct., 1978).
Jackson v. *Indiana*. 406 U.S. 715 (1972).
Jenkins v. *United States*. 307 F. 2d 637 (1962).
Johnson v. *Zerbst*. 304 U.S. 458 (1938).
Lake v. *Cameron*. 364 F. 2d 657 (D.C. Cir., 1966).
Lessard v. *Schmidt*. 349 F. Supp. 1078 (1972).
Lyles v. *United States*. 254 F. 2d 725 (1957).
Marcey v. *Harris*. 400 F. 2d 772 (D.C. Cir., 1968).
Massachusetts v. *Lombardi*. 393 N.E. 2d 346 (1979).
Meador v. *United States*. 418 F. 2d 321 (9th Cir., 1969).
Mitchell v. *United States*. 316 F. 2d 354 (D.C. Cir., 1963).

Moore v. United States. 464 F. 2d 663 (9th Cir., 1972).
Noble v. Black. 539 F. 2d 586 (6th Cir., 1976).
Pate v. Robinson. 383 U.S. 375 (1966).
People ex rel. Myers v. Briggs. 46 Ill. 2d 281 (1970).
People v. Berling. 155 C.A. 2d 255 (1953).
People v. Dalfonso. 24 Ill. App. 3d 748 (1974).
People v. Greene. 203 Misc. 191, 116 N.Y.S. 2d 561 (Kings County Ct.,
    1952).
People v. Hays. 54 C.A. 3d 775 (1976).
People v. Lang. 26 Ill. App. 3d 648 (1975).
People v. Laudermilk. 67 C.A. 2d 272 (1967).
People v. Pennington. 426 P. 2d 942 (1967).
People v. Rogers. 309 P. 2d 949 (1957).
Pouncey v. United States. 349 F. 2d 699 (D.C. Cir., 1965).
Regina v. Roberts. 2 Q.B. 329 (1953).
Rollerson v. United States. 343 F. 2d 269 (D.C. Cir., 1964).
Rose v. United States. 513 F. 3d (8th Cir., 1975).
Schoeller v. Dunbar. 423 F. 2d 1183 (9th Cir., 1970).
Sieling v. Eyman. 478 F. 2d (9th Cir., 1973).
Smith v. Schlesinger. 513 F. 2d 462 (D.C. Cir., 1975).
State v. Freeman. 559 P. 2d 152 (1975).
State v. Hampton. 218 So. 2d 311 (1969).
State v. Murphy. 355 P. 2d 323 (1960).
State v. Maryott. Wash. App. 492 P. 2d 239 (1971).
State v. Plaisance. 210 So. 2d 323 (1968).
State v. Rand. 20 Ohio Misc. 98, 247 N.E. 2d 342 (1969).
Swisher v. United States. 237 F. Supp. 291 (1965).
United States ex rel. McGough v. Hewitt. 528 F. 2d 539 (1975).
United States v. Adams. 297 F. Supp. 596 (1969).
United States v. Bodey. 547 F. 2d 1383 (1977).
United States v. Brawner. 471 F. 2d 969 (1972).
United States v. Burke. 381 F. Supp. 334 (1974).
United States v. Cook. 332 F. 2d 935 (9th Cir., 1964).
United States v. David. 511 F. 2d 355 (1975).
United States v. Geelan. 520 F. 2d 585 (1975).
United States v. Gundelfinger. 98 F. Supp. 630 (W.D. Pa., 1951).
United States v. Horowitz. 360 F. Supp. 772 (1973).
United States v. Ives. 574 F. 2d 1002 (9th Cir., 1978).
United States v. Klein. 325 F. 2d 283 (1963).
United States v. Lancaster. 408 F. Supp. 225 (1976).
United States v. Makris. 535 F. 2d 699 (1976).
United States v. Nichelson. 550 F. 2d 502 (8th Cir., 1977).
United States v. Pardue. 354 F. Supp. 1377 (1973).
United States v. Sermon. 228 F. Supp. 972 (W.D. Mo., 1964).
United States v. Taylor. 437 F. 2d 371 (4th Cir., 1971).
United States v. Wilson. 391 F. 2d 460 (D.C. Cir., 1966).
Washington v. United States. 390 F. 2d 444 (1967).
Westbrook v. Arizona. 384 U.S. 150 (1965).
Whitehead v. Wainwright. 447 F. Supp. 898 (M.D. Fl., 1978).

Wieter v. *Settle*. 193 F. Supp. 318 (W.D. Mo., 1961).
Williams v. *United States*. 250 F. 2d 19 (D.C. Cir., 1957).
Wilson v. *United States*. 391 F. 2d 460 (1968).
Youtsey v. *United States*. 97 F. 937 (1899).

REFERENCES

Acheson, R. M. 1960. Observer error and variation in the interpretation of electrocardiograms in an epidemiological study of coronary heart disease. *British Journal of Preventive and Social Medicine*, 14, 99–122.

Alschuler, A. W. 1968. Prosecutor's role in plea bargaining. *University of Chicago Law Review*, 36, 50–112.

American Bar Association, Commission on the Mentally Disabled. 1978. Incompetence to stand trial on criminal charges. *Mental Disabilities Law Reporter*, 2, 636–50.

Anonymous. 1976. Cross-examination of psychiatric witnesses in civil commitment proceedings: A practice manual. *Mental Disabilities Law Reporter*, 1, 164–71.

Ausness, C. W. 1978. The identification of incompetent defendants: Separating those unfit for adversary combat from those that are fit. *Kentucky Law Journal*, 66, 666–706.

Balcanoff, E. J., and McGarry, A. L. 1969. Amicus curiae: The role of the psychiatrist in pretrial examinations. *American Journal of Psychiatry*, 126, 342–47.

Bazelon, D. L. 1974. Psychiatrists and the adversary process. *Scientific American*, 230, 18–23.

———. 1975. A jurist's view of psychiatry. *Journal of Psychiatry and Law*, 3, 175–90.

Beck, A. T., et al. 1962. Reliability of psychiatric diagnoses: 2. A study of consistency of clinical judgments and ratings. *American Journal of Psychiatry*, 119, 351–57.

Bendt, R. H., Balcanoff, E. J., and Tragellis, G. S. 1973. Incompetency to stand trial: Is psychiatry necessary? *American Journal of Psychiatry*, 130, 1288–89.

Bennett, D. E. 1968. Competency to stand trial: A call for reform. *Journal of Criminal Law, Criminology, and Police Science*, 59, 569–82.

Berry, F. D., Jr. 1973. Self-incrimination and the compulsory mental examination: A proposal. *Arizona Law Review*. 15, 919–50.

Blinder, M. 1974. Understanding psychiatric testimony. *Judicature*, 57, 308–11.

Bowers, K. 1973. Situationism in psychology: An analysis and critique. *Psychological Review*, 80, 307–36.

Brakel, S. J. 1974. Presumption, bias, and incompetency in the criminal process. *Wisconsin Law Review*, 1974, 1105–30.

Bromberg, W. 1969. Psychiatrists in court: The psychiatrist's view. *American Journal of Psychiatry*, 125, 1343–47.

Brooks, A. D. 1974. *Law, psychiatry and the mental health system*. Boston: Little, Brown.

Bukatman, B. A., Foy, J. L., and DeGrazia, E. 1971. What is competency to stand trial? *American Journal of Psychiatry*, 127, 1225–29.

Burt, R. A., and Morris, N. 1972. A proposal for the abolition of the incompetency plea. *University of Chicago Law Review*, 40, 66–95.

Campbell, D. T., and Fiske, D. W. 1959. Convergent and discriminant validation by the multitrait-multimethod matrix. *Psychological Bulletin*, 56, 81–105.

Caplan, N., and Nelson, S. D. 1973. On being useful: The nature and consequences of psychological research on social problems. *American Psychologist*, 28, 199–211.

Cattell, R. B. 1966. The scree test for the number of factors. *Multivariate Behavioral Research*, 1, 245–76.

Chernoff, P. A., and Schaffer, W. G. 1972. Defending the mentally ill: Ethical quicksand. *American Clinical Law Review*, 10, 505–31.

Ciccone, J. R., and Barry, D. J. 1976. Collaboration between psychiatry and the law: A study of 100 referrals to a court clinic. *American Academy of Psychiatry and the Law Bulletin*, 4, 275–80.

Cohen, J. 1968. Weighted kappa: Nominal scale agreement with provision for scale disagreement or partial credit. *Psychological Bulletin*, 70, 213–20.

Comment. 1967. Incompetency to stand trial. *Harvard Law Review*. 81, 454–73.

Cook, T. D., and Campbell, D. T. 1979. *Quasi-experimentation: Design & analysis issues for field settings*. Chicago: Rand-McNally.

Cooke, G. 1969. The court study unit: Patient characteristics and differences between patients judged competent and incompetent. *Journal of Clinical Psychology*, 25, 140–43.

Cooke, G., Johnston, N., and Pogany, E. 1973. Factors affecting referral to determine competency to stand trial. *American Journal of Psychiatry*, 130, 870–75.

Cooke, G., Pogany, E., and Johnston, N. G. 1974. A comparison of blacks and whites committed for evaluation of competency to stand trial on criminal charges. *Journal of Psychiatry and Law*, 2, 319–37.

Cooper, J. E., et al. 1972. *Psychiatric diagnosis in New York and London*. London: Oxford University Press.

Cronbach, L. J. 1964. *Essentials of psychological testing*. 2d ed. New York: Harper and Row.

Cronbach, L. J., and Meehl, P. E. 1955. Construct validity in psychological tests. *Psychological Bulletin*, 52, 281–302.

Cronbach, L. J., et al. 1972. *The dependability of behavioral measurements: Theory of generalizability for scores and profiles*. New York: Wiley.

Crowne, D. P., and Marlowe, D. 1964. *The approval motive: Studies in evaluative dependence*. New York: Wiley.

Department of Health, Education, and Welfare. 1974. Legal status of inpatient admissions to state and county mental hospitals—United States—1972. Statistical Note 105. DHEW Publication No. (ADM) 74–6.

Diamond, B. L., and Louisell, D. W. 1965. The psychiatrist as an expert witness: Some ruminations and speculations. *Michigan Law Review*, 63, 1335–54.

Eizenstat, S. E. 1968. Mental competency to stand trial. *Harvard Civil Rights–Civil Liberties Law Review*, 4, 379–413.

Endicott, J., and Spitzer, R. L. 1978. A diagnostic interview: The schedule for affective disorders and schizophrenia. *Archives of General Psychiatry*, 35, 837–44.

Engelberg, S. L. 1967. Pre-trial criminal commitment to mental institutions: The procedure in Massachusetts and suggested reforms. *Catholic University Law Review*, 17, 163–213.

Ennis, B. J. 1972. *Prisoners of psychiatry: Mental patients, psychiatrists and the law.* New York: Harcourt Brace Jovanovich.

Ennis, B. J., and Hansen, C. 1976. Memorandum of law: Competency to stand trial. *Journal of Psychiatry and Law*, 4, 491–514.

Ennis, B. J., and Litwack, T. R. 1974. Psychiatry and the presumption of expertise: Flipping coins in the courtroom. *California Law Review*, 62, 693–752.

Feighner, J. P., et al. 1972. Diagnostic criteria for use in psychiatric research. *Archives of General Psychiatry*, 26, 57–63.

Felson, B., et al. 1973. Observations on the results of multiple readings of chest films in coal miner's pneumoconiosis. *Radiology*, 109, 19–23.

Fenster, A. C., Litwack, T. R., and Symonds, M. 1975. The making of a forensic psychologist. *Professional Psychology*, 6, 457–67.

Finkelstein, M. 1975. A statistical analysis of guilty plea practices in the federal courts. *Harvard Law Review*, 89, 293–315.

Fitzgerald, J. F., Peszke, M. A., and Goodwin, R. C. 1978. Competency evaluations in Connecticut. *Hospital and Community Psychiatry*, 29, 450–53.

Fleiss, J. L., and Cohen, J. 1973. The equivalence of weighted kappa and the intraclass correlation coefficient as measures of reliability. *Education and Psychological Measurement*, 33, 613–19.

Fleiss, J. L., et al. 1972. Quantification of agreement in multiple psychiatric diagnosis. *Archives of General Psychiatry*, 26, 168–71.

Foote, C. 1960. A comment on pretrial commitment of criminal defendants. *University of Pennsylvania Law Review*, 108, 832–46.

Foucault, H. 1973. *Madness and civilization: A history of insanity in the age of reason.* New York: Vintage Books.

Gambino, R. 1978. The murderous mind: Insanity vs. the law. *Saturday Review*, 3 (18), 10–13.

Garfield, S. L. 1978. Research problems in clinical diagnosis. *Journal of Consulting and Clinical Psychology*, 46, 596–607.

Garland, L. H. 1960. The problem of observer error. *Bulletin of the New York Academy of Medicine*, 36, 570–84.

Geller, J. L., and Lister, E. D. 1978. The process of criminal commitment for pretrial psychiatric examination: An evaluation. *American Journal of Psychiatry*, 135, 53–60.

Gobert, J. J. 1973. Competency to stand trial: A pre- and post-Jackson analysis. *Tennessee Law Review*, 40, 659–88.

Gold, L. H. 1973. Discovery of mental illness and mental defect among offenders. *Journal of Forensic Sciences*, 18, 125–29.

Golding, S. L. 1975. Flies in the ointment: Methodological problems in the percentage of variance due to persons and situations. *Psychological Bulletin*, 82, 278–88.

———. 1977. Method variance, inadequate constructs, or things that go bump in the night? *Multivariate Behavioral Research*, 12, 89–98.

———. 1978. Invited testimony before the Special Joint Committee on Revision of the Mental Health Code, State of Illinois, Feb. 22.

Goldstein, A. 1967. *The insanity defense.* New Haven: Yale University Press.

Goldstein, R. L. 1973. The fitness factory. Part I: The psychiatrist's role in determining competency. *American Journal of Psychiatry*, 130, 1144–47.

Golten, R. J. 1972. Role of defense counsel in the criminal commitment process. *American Criminal Law Review*, 10, 385–430.

Goodstein, L. D., and Sandler, I. 1978. Using psychology to promote human welfare: A conceptual analysis of the role of community psychology. *American Psychologist*, 33, 882–92.

Group for the Advancement of Psychiatry. 1974. *Misuse of psychiatry in the courts: Competency to stand trial.* New York: Mental Health Materials Center.

Guttmacher, M. S. 1955. The psychiatrist as expert witness. *University of Chicago Law Review*, 22, 325–30.

Haddox, V. G., Gross, B. H., and Pollack, S. 1974. Mental competency to stand trial while under the influence of drugs. *Loyola of Los Angeles Law Review*, 7, 425–52.

Halpern, A. L. 1975. Use and misuse of psychiatry in competency examinations of criminal defendants. *Psychiatric Annals*, 5, 123–50.

Hardisty, J. H. 1973. Mental illness: A legal fiction. *Washington Law Review*, 48, 735–62.

Hart, H. L. A. 1968. *Punishment and responsibility.* New York: Oxford University Press.

Helzer, J. E., et al. 1977. Reliability of psychiatric diagnosis: II. The test/retest reliability of diagnostic classification. *Archives of General Psychiatry*, 34, 136–41.

Hess, J. H., Jr., and Thomas, H. E. 1963. Incompetency to stand trial: Procedures, results, and problems. *American Journal of Psychiatry*, 119, 713–20.

Hiday, V. A. 1977. Reformed commitment procedures: An empirical study in the courtroom. *Law and Society Review*, 11, 651–66.

Hoffman, B. 1977. Living with your rights off. In R. Bonnie (ed.), *Diagnosis and debate.* New York: Insight.

Janis, N. R. 1974. Incompetency commitment: The need for procedural safeguards and a proposed statutory scheme. *Catholic University Law Review*, 23, 720–43.

Joost, R. H., and McGarry, A. L. 1974. Massachusetts mental health code: Promise and performance. *American Bar Association Journal*, 60, 95–98.

Judicial Conference of the District of Columbia Circuit. 1968. Report of the Committee on Problems Connected with Mental Examination of the Accused in Criminal Cases Before Trial. In R. C. Allen, E. Z. Ferster, and J. G. Rubin (eds.), *Readings in law and psychiatry*. Baltimore: Johns Hopkins University.

Kaufman, H. 1972. Evaluating competency: Are constitutional deprivations necessary? *American Criminal Law Review*, 10, 465–504.

Kendell, R. E., et al. 1971. The diagnostic criteria of American and British psychiatrists. *Archives of General Psychiatry*, 25, 123–30.

Kipnis, K. 1976. Criminal justice and the negotiated plea. *Ethics*, 86, 93–106.

Koran, L. M. 1975a. The reliability of clinical methods, data, and judgments: Part I. *New England Journal of Medicine*, 293, 642–46.

———. 1975b. The reliability of clinical methods, data, and judgments: Part II. *New England Journal of Medicine*, 293, 695–701.

Koson, D., and Robey, A. 1973. Amnesia and competency to stand trial. *American Journal of Psychiatry*, 130, 588–92.

Kreitman, N. 1961. The reliability of psychiatric diagnosis. *Journal of Mental Science*, 107, 876–86.

Kuhn, J. 1970. *The structure of scientific revolutions*. Chicago: University of Chicago Press.

Kutner, L. 1962. The illusion of due process in commitment proceedings. *Northwestern Law Review*, 57, 383–99.

Laben, J. K., and Spencer, L. D. 1976. Decentralization of forensic services. *Community Mental Health Journal*, 12, 405–14.

Laben, J. K., et al. 1977. Reform from the inside: Mental health center evaluations of competency to stand trial. *Journal of Community Psychology*, 5, 52–62.

Laczko, A. L., James, J. F., and Alltop, L. B. 1970. A study of four hundred and thirty-five court-referred cases. *Journal of Forensic Sciences*, 15, 311–23.

Lakatos, I., and Musgrave, A. (eds.) 1972. *Criticism and the growth of knowledge*. Cambridge: Cambridge University Press.

Lanyon, R. I. 1970. Development and validation of a psychological screening inventory. *Journal of Consulting and Clinical Psychology Monograph*, 35, 1–24.

Law Reform Commission of Canada. 1976. *Mental disorder in the criminal process*. Ottawa: Information Canada.

Lewin, T. H. 1969. Incompetency to stand trial: Legal and ethical aspects of an abused doctrine. *Law and Social Order*, 2, 233–85.

Lipsitt, P. D., Lelos, D., and McGarry, A. L. 1971. Competency for trial: A screening instrument. *American Journal of Psychiatry*, 128, 105–9.

Livermore, J. M., and Meehl, P. E. 1967. The virtues of M'Naughten. *Minnesota Law Review*, 51, 789–856.

Livermore, J. M., Malmquist, C. P., and Meehl, P. E. 1968. On the justifications for civil commitment. *University of Pennsylvania Law Review*, 117, 75–96.

Loftus, E. F., and Palmer, J. C. 1974. Reconstruction of automobile destruction: An example of the interaction between language and memory. *Journal of Verbal Learning and Behavior*, 13, 585–89.

Loftus, G. R., and Loftus, E. F. 1976. *Human memory: The processing of information*, Hillsdale, N.J.: Erlbaum.

Lorr, M., and Vestre, N. D. 1969. The Psychotic Inpatient Profile: A nurse's observation scale. *Journal of Clinical Psychology*, 25, 137–40.

Luria, R., and McHugh, P. 1974. Reliability and clinical utility of the "Wing" Present State Examination. *Archives of General Psychiatry*, 30, 866–71.

McGarry, A. L. 1965. Competency for trial and due process via the state hospital. *American Journal of Psychiatry*, 122, 623–31.

———. 1969. Demonstration and research in competency for trial and mental illness: Review and preview. *Boston University Law Review*, 49, 46–61.

———. 1971. The fate of psychotic offenders returned for trial. *American Journal of Psychiatry*, 127, 1181–84.

McGarry, A. L., et al. 1973. *Competency to stand trial and mental illness*. Washington, D.C.: U.S. Government Printing Office.

McLemore, C., and Benjamin, L. 1979. What ever happened to interpersonal diagnosis? A psychosocial alternative to DSM-III. *American Psychologist*, 34, 17–34.

Maisel, R. 1970. Decision making in a commitment court. *Psychiatry*, 33, 352–61.

Mariotto, M. J., and Farrell, A. D. 1979. Comparability of the absolute level of ratings on the Inpatient Multidimensional Psychiatric Scale within a homogeneous group of raters. *Journal of Consulting and Clinical Psychology*, 47, 59–64.

Markush, R. E., Schaaf, W. E., and Seigel, D. G. 1967. The influence of the death certificate on the results of epidemiological studies. *Journal of the National Medical Association*, 59, 105–13.

Matarazzo, J. D. 1978. The interview: Its reliability and validity in psychiatric diagnosis. In B. Wolman (ed.), *Clinical diagnosis of mental disorders: A handbook*. Plenum: New York.

Mather, L. 1974. Methods of case disposition. *Law and Society Review*, 9, 189–99.

Maxson, L. S., and Neuringer, C. 1970. Evaluating legal competency. *Journal of Genetic Psychology*, 117, 267–73.

Meehl, P. E. 1954. *Clinical versus statistical prediction: A theoretical analysis and a review of the evidence*. Minneapolis: University of Minnesota Press.

———. 1960. The cognitive activity of the clinician. *American Psychologist*, 15, 19–27.

———. 1970a. Psychological determinism and human rationality: A psychologist's reactions to Professor Karl Popper's "Of clouds and clocks."

In M. Radner and S. Winokur (eds.), *Minnesota studies in the philosophy of science*, vol. 4: *Analyses of theories and methods of physics and psychology*. Minneapolis: University of Minnesota Press.

————. 1970b. Some methodological reflections on the difficulties of psychoanalytic research. In M. Radner and S. Winokur (eds.), *Minnesota studies in the philosophy of science*, vol. 4: *Analyses of theories and methods of physics and psychology*. Minneapolis: University of Minnesota Press.

————. 1970c. Nuisance variables and the ex post facto design. In M. Radner and S. Winokur (eds.), *Minnesota studies in the philosophy of science*, vol. 4: *Analyses of theories and methods of physics and psychology*. Minneapolis: University of Minnesota Press.

————. 1970d. Psychology and the criminal law. *University of Richmond Law Review*, 5, 1–30.

————. 1971. Law and the fireside inductions: Some reflections of a clinical psychologist. *Journal of Social Issues*, 27, 65–100.

————. 1973. Why I do not attend case conferences. In P. Meehl (ed.), *Psychodiagnosis*. Minneapolis: University of Minnesota Press.

————. 1978. Theoretical risks and tabular asterisks: Sir Karl, Sir Ronald and the slow progress of soft psychology. *Journal of Clinical and Consulting Psychology*, 46, 806–34.

Meehl, P. E., and Rosen, A. 1955. Antecedent probability and the efficiency of psychometric signs, patterns, or cutting scores. *Psychological Bulletin*, 52, 194–216.

Mischel, W. 1968. *Personality and assessment*. New York: Wiley.

————. 1973. Toward a social learning reconceptualization of personality. *Psychological Review*, 80, 252–83.

Modlin, H. C. 1976. Psychiatric diagnosis and the law. *Bulletin of the Menninger Clinic*, 40, 549–58.

Monahan, J. 1973. Abolish the insanity defense?—Not yet. *Rutgers Law Review*, 26, 719–40.

————. 1977. Empirical analyses of civil commitment: Critique and context. *Law and Society Review*, 11, 619–28.

Monahan, J., and Wexler, D. B. 1978. A definite maybe: Proof and probability in civil commitment. *Law and Human Behavior*, 2, 37–42.

Morris, G. H. 1975. *The insanity defense: A blueprint for legislative reform*. Lexington, Mass.: Heath.

Morris, H. (ed.) 1961. *Freedom and responsibility*. Stanford, Calif.: Stanford University Press.

New York City Bar Association, Special Committee on the Study of Commitment Procedures and the Laws Relating to Incompetents. 1968. *Mental illness, due process, and the criminal defendant*. New York: Fordham.

Newman, D. 1956. Pleading guilty for consideration: A study of bargain justice. *Journal of Criminal Law, Criminology, and Police Science*, 46, 780–90.

Norden, C., et al. 1970. Variation in interpretation of intravenous pylograms. *American Journal of Epidemiology*, 91, 155–60.

Note. 1974. Competence to plead guilty: A new standard. *Duke Law Journal*, 149, 149–74.

Note. 1961. Amnesia: A case study in the limits of particular justice. *Yale Law Journal*, 71, 109–36.

Oliver, J. W. 1965. Judicial hearings to determine mental competency to stand trial. *Federal Rules Decisions*, 39, 537–49.

Pacht, A. R., et al. 1973. The current status of the psychologist in the courtroom. *Professional Psychology*, 4, 409–13.

Pap, A. 1953. Reduction sentences and open concepts. *Methodos*, 5, 3–30.

Perlin, M. L. 1977. The legal status of the psychologist in the courtroom. *Journal of Psychiatry and the Law*, 5, 41–54.

Pfeiffer, E., Eisenstein, R. B., and Dabbs, E. G. 1967. Mental competency evaluation for the federal courts: I. Methods and results. *Journal of Nervous and Mental Disease*, 144, 320–28.

Piotrowski, K. W., Kosacco, D., and Guze, S. B. 1976. Psychiatric disorders and crime: A study of pretrial psychiatric examinations. *Diseases of the Nervous System*, 37, 309–11.

Pizzi, W. T. 1977. Competency to stand trial in federal courts: Conceptual and constitutional problems. *University of Chicago Law Review*, 45, 20–71.

Pollack, M. K. 1973. An end to incompetency to stand trial. *Santa Clara Lawyer*, 13, 560–78.

Pollack, S. 1973. Psychiatric consultation for the court. *Bulletin of the American Academy of Psychiatry and the Law*, 1, 267–81.

Popper, K. 1968. *The logic of scientific discovery*. New York: Harper Torchbooks.

Poythress, N. 1976. "Coping with psychiatric testimony in civil commitment proceedings: A handbook for guardian ad litem attorneys." Unpublished manuscript.

———. 1977. Mental health expert testimony: Current problems. *Journal of Psychiatry and Law*, 5, 201–27.

———. 1978. Psychiatric expertise in civil commitment: Training attorneys to cope with expert testimony. *Law and Human Behavior*, 2, 1–23.

———. 1979. A proposal for training in forensic psychology. *American Psychologist*, 34, 612–21.

Rabkin, J. G. 1979. Criminal behavior of discharged mental patients: A critical appraisal of the research. *Psychological Bulletin*, 86, 1–26.

Rappaport, J. 1977. *Community psychology: Values, research, and action*. New York: Holt, Rinehart and Winston.

Report of the Task Force on the Role of Psychology in the Criminal Justice System. 1978. (J. Monahan, Chair.) *American Psychologist*, 33, 1099–1113.

Robey, A. 1965. Criteria for competency to stand trial: A checklist for psychiatrists. *American Journal of Psychiatry*, 122, 616–23.

Robitscher, J. 1977. The uses and abuses of psychiatry. *Journal of Psychiatry and Law*, 5, 331–404.

———. 1978. The limits of psychiatric authority. *International Journal of Law and Psychiatry*, 1, 183–204.

Roesch, R. 1976. Predicting the effects of pretrial intervention programs on jail populations: A method for planning and decision-making. *Federal Probation*, 40, 32–36.

———. 1978a. A brief, immediate screening interview to determine competency to stand trial: A feasibility study. *Criminal Justice and Behavior*, 5, 241–48.

———. 1978b. Competency to stand trial and court outcome. *Criminal Justice Review*, 3, 45–56.

———. 1978c. Fitness to stand trial: Some comments on the Law Reform Commission's proposed procedures. *Canadian Journal of Criminology*, 20, 450–55.

———. 1979. Determining competency to stand trial: An examination of evaluation procedures in an institutional setting. *Journal of Consulting and Clinical Psychology*, 47, 542–50.

Roesch, R., and Golding, S. L. 1977. *A systems analysis of competency to stand trial procedures: Implications for forensic services in North Carolina.* Urbana: University of Illinois.

———. 1978. Legal and judicial interpretation of competency to stand trial statutes and procedures. *Criminology*, 16, 420–29.

———. 1979. Treatment and disposition of defendants found incompetent to stand trial: A review and a proposal. *International Journal of Law and Psychiatry*, 2, 349–70.

Rosen, G. 1969. *Madness in society: Chapters in the historical sociology of mental illness.* New York: Harper Torchbooks.

Rosen, P. L. 1972. *The Supreme Court and social science.* Urbana: University of Illinois Press.

Rosenberg, A. H. 1970. Competency for trial: A problem in interdisciplinary communication. *Judicature*, 53, 316–21.

Rosenberg, A. H., and McGarry, A. L. 1972. Competency for trial: The making of an expert. *American Journal of Psychiatry*, 128, 82–86.

Rosenhan, D. L. 1973. On being sane in insane places. *Science*, 179, 250–58.

Roth, R. T., Dayley, M. K., and Lerner, J. 1973. Into the abyss: Psychiatric reliability and emergency commitment statutes. *Santa Clara Lawyer*, 13, 400–446.

Rotter, J. B. 1966. Generalized expectancies for internal versus external control of reinforcement. *Psychological Monographs*, 80 (whole no. 609).

Ryan, W. 1971. *Blaming the victim.* New York: Random House.

Ryerson, T. H. 1975. Illinois fitness for trial: Processes, paradoxes, proposals. *Loyola University of Chicago Law Journal*, 6, 678–717.

Saks, M. J. 1978. Some psychological contributions to a legislative subcommittee on organ and tissue transplants. *American Psychologist*, 33, 680–90.

Sandifer, M. G., Pettus, C., and Quade, D. 1964. A study of psychiatric diagnosis. *Journal of Nervous and Mental Disease*, 139, 350–56.

Sandifer, M. G., et al. 1968. Psychiatric diagnosis: A comparative study in North Carolina, London and Glasgow. *British Journal of Psychiatry*, 114, 1–9.

Sarason, S. B. 1972. *The creation of settings and the future societies.* San Francisco: Jossey Bass.

Sawyer, J. 1966. Measurement and prediction: Clinical and statistical. *Psychological Bulletin*, 66, 178–200.

Schacht, T., and Nathan, P. E. 1977. But is it good for the psychologists? Appraisal and status of DSM-III. *American Psychologist*, 32, 1017–25.

Scheff, T. J. 1964. The societal reaction to deviance. Ascriptive elements in the psychiatric screening of mental patients in a midwestern state. *Social Problems*, 11, 401–13.

Scheidemandel, P. L., and Kanno, C. K. 1969. *The mentally ill offender.* Baltimore: Garamond-Pridemark.

Schmidt, H. O., and Fonda, C. P. 1956. The reliability of psychiatric diagnosis: A new look. *Journal of Abnormal and Social Psychology*, 52, 262–67.

Schreiber, J. 1978. Assessing competency to stand trial: A case study of technology diffusion in four states. *Bulletin of the American Academy of Science and the Law*, 6, 439–57.

Schroeder, M. A. 1974. Florida's incompetency to stand trial rule: Justice in a straightjacket. *University of Florida Law Review*, 27, 248–59.

Schulman, R. E. 1973. Determination of competency: Burial at the crossroad. In L. M. Irvine, Jr., and T. L. Brelje (eds.), *Law, psychiatry and the mentally disordered offender*, vol. 2. Springfield, Ill.: Thomas.

Seidman, E. 1978. Justice, values and social science: Unexamined premises. In R. J. Simon (ed.), *Research in law and sociology.* Greenwich, Conn.: JAI Press.

Shah, S. A. 1974. Some interactions of law and mental health in the handling of social deviance. *Catholic University Law Review*, 23, 674–719.

Silten, P. R., and Tullis, R. 1977. Mental competency in criminal proceedings. *Hastings Law Journal*, 28, 1053–74.

Silverman, H. 1969. Determinism, choice, responsibility and the psychologist's role as an expert witness. *American Psychologist*, 24, 5–9.

Sines, L. K. 1959. The relative contribution of four kinds of data to accuracy in personality assessment. *Journal of Consulting Psychology*, 23, 483–92.

Slovenko, R. 1971. Competency to stand trial: The reality behind the fiction. *Wake Forest Law Review*, 8, 1–29.

———. 1977. The developing law on competency to stand trial. *Journal of Psychiatry and Law*, 5, 165–200.

Smith, C. E. 1966. Psychiatric approaches to the mentally ill federal offender. *Federal Probation*, 30, 23–29.

Smith, J. T. 1976. The forensic psychologist as an expert witness in the District of Columbia. *Journal of Psychiatry and Law*, 4, 277–85.

Spitzer, R. 1976. More on pseudoscience and the case for psychiatric diagnosis. *Archives of General Psychiatry*, 33, 459–70.

Spitzer, R. L., and Endicott, J. 1975. Attempts to improve psychiatric diagnosis. In M. Rosenzweig and L. Porter (eds.), *Annual review of psychology*, vol. 26. Palo Alto, Calif.: Annual Reviews Inc.

Spitzer, R. L., Endicott, J., and Robins, E. 1975. Clinical criteria for psychiatric diagnosis and DSM-III. *American Journal of Psychiatry*, 132, 1187–92.

──────. 1978. *The Research Diagnostic Criteria*. Biometrics Research Division, New York State Psychiatric Institute.

Spitzer, R., and Fleiss, J. 1974. A re-analysis of the reliability of psychiatric diagnosis. *British Journal of Psychiatry*, 125, 341–47.

Spitzer, R., and Forman, J. 1979. DSM-III field trials: II. Initial experience with the multiaxial system. *American Journal of Psychiatry*, 136, 818–20.

Spitzer, R., Forman, J., and Nee, J. 1979. DSM-III field trials: I. Initial interrater diagnostic reliability. *American Journal of Psychiatry*, 136, 815–17.

Spitzer, R. L., et al. 1970. The Psychiatric Status Schedule: A technique of evaluating psychopathology and impairment in role functioning. *Archives of General Psychiatry*, 23, 41–55.

Steadman, H. J. 1979. *Beating a rap? Defendants found incompetent to stand trial*. Chicago: University of Chicago Press.

Steadman, H. J., and Braff, J. 1974. Effects of incompetency determinations on subsequent criminal processing: Implications for due process. *Catholic University Law Review*, 23, 754–68.

──────. 1975. Crimes of violence and incompetency diversion. *Journal of Criminal Law and Criminology*, 66, 73–78.

Steadman, H. J., and Cocozza, J. J. 1974. *Careers of the criminally insane: Excessive social control of deviance*. Lexington, Mass.: Lexington.

Steadman, H. J., Cocozza, J. J., and Melick, M. E. 1978. Explaining the increased arrest rate among mental patients: The changing clientele of state hospitals. *American Journal of Psychiatry*, 135, 816–20.

Stock, H. V., and Poythress, N. G. 1979. Psychologists' opinions on competency and sanity: How reliable? Paper read at the American Psychological Association Convention, New York.

Stone, A. A. 1976. *Mental health and law: A system in transition*. Washington, D.C.: U.S. Government Printing Office.

──────. 1978. Comment. *American Journal of Psychiatry*, 135, 61–63.

Sullivan, H. S. 1953. *psychiatric interview*. New York: W. W. Norton.

Suppe, F. (ed.). 1974. *The structure of scientific theories*. Urbana: University of Illinois Press.

Sussman, J., et al. 1975. *Assessment of pretrial competency examinations in the District of Columbia Superior Court*. Washington, D.C.: Criminal Courts Technical Assistance Project.

Szasz, T. S. 1963. *Law, liberty and psychiatry: An inquiry into the social uses of mental health practices*. New York: Macmillan.

Treffert, D. A. 1977. The practical limits of patients' rights. In R. Bonnie (ed.), *Diagnosis and debate*. New York: Insight.

Vann, C. R. 1965. Pretrial determination and judicial decision-making: An analysis of the use of psychiatric information in the administration of criminal justice. *University of Detroit Law Journal*, 43, 13–33.

Vann, C. R., and Morganroth, F. 1965. The psychiatrist as judge: A second look at the competence to stand trial. *University of Detroit Law Journal*, 43, 1–12.

Ward, C. H., et al. 1962. The psychiatric nomenclature: Reasons for diagnostic disagreement. *Archives of General Psychiatry*, 7, 198–205.

Watzlawick, P., Weakland, J., and Fisch, R. 1974. *Change: Principles of problem formation and problem resolution.* New York: Norton.

Wexler, D. B. 1976. *Criminal commitments and dangerous mental patients: Legal issues of confinement, treatment, and release.* Washington, D.C.: U.S. Government Printing Office.

Wexler, D. B., and Scoville, S. E. 1971. The administration of psychiatric justice: Theory and practice in Arizona. *Arizona Law Review*, 13, 1–259.

Wiggins, J. S. 1973. *Personality and prediction: Principles of personality assessment.* New York: Addison-Wesley.

Wing, J. K., Birley, J. L., and Cooper, J. E. 1967. Reliability of a procedure for measuring and classifying "Present Psychiatric State." *British Journal of Psychiatry*, 113, 499–515.

Wing, J. K., Cooper, J. E., and Sartorius, N. 1974. *The measurement and classification of psychiatric symptoms.* Cambridge: Cambridge University Press.

Winick, B. J. 1977. Psychotropic medication and competence to stand trial. *American Bar Association Research Journal*, 769–816.

Zilboorg, G., and Henry, G. W. 1941. *A history of medical psychology.* New York: Norton.

Ziskin, J. 1975. *Coping with psychiatric and psychological testimony.* Beverly Hills, Calif.: Law and Psychology Press.

———. 1977. *Coping with psychiatric and psychological testimony.* Pocket Supplement. Beverly Hills, Calif.: Law and Psychology Press.

NAME INDEX

SUBJECT INDEX